The Assessment of

Social Research

Second Edition

The Assessment of
Social
Research

Second Edition

Guidelines for Use of Research in Social Work and Social Science

Tony Tripodi
Phillip Fellin • Henry J. Meyer

The University of Michigan

F.E. PEACOCK PUBLISHERS, INC. ITASCA, ILLINOIS 60143

Contents

Introductory Statement to the Student and the Teacher:

For the Second Edition

The reading and use of scientific research is a continuing obligation for social workers and other professional persons. This book is written for consumers of the literature of empirical research in social work and the social sciences. The emphasis differs from that of most books on research methods that students are assigned. The reception of the first edition encourages us to believe that a book from the viewpoint of consumers of research is still useful.

You may find some concepts and terms from the vocabulary of social research that are unfamiliar if you have not previously studied research methods. For such readers we have included brief explanations as part of the relevant exposition of topics, and we have given specific references to sources in which you may find more extensive explanations. We have also identified technical terms and concepts in the index, so that you may readily return to locations in the book where they are explained or their meanings are made evident by the context. Most of the major concepts recur as the text develops and as examples of research are discussed. You can expect to gain a firmer sense of their meaning while proceeding through the book, but it will be helpful to keep at hand an elementary book on research methods, such as one of those mentioned in this introduction or in Chapter 1.

In the past decade there have appeared many new books that deal with the production and use of social research. The following references are exemplary of topics that have influenced research knowledge disseminated in schools of social work:

Babbie, E. R., *The Practice of Social Research,* 2nd ed. (Belmont, Calif.: Wadsworth, 1979).

Epstein, I., and T. Tripodi, *Research Techniques for Program Planning, Monitoring, and Evaluation* (New York: Columbia University Press, 1977).

Grinnell, R. J., Jr., ed., *Social Work Research and Evaluation* (Itasca, Ill.: F. E. Peacock, 1981).

Hardyck, C., and L. F. Petrinovitch, *Understanding Research in the Social Sciences* (Philadelphia: W. B. Saunders Co., 1975).

Jayaratne, S., and R. Levy, *Empirical Clinical Practice* (New York: Columbia University Press, 1979).

Mayer, R. R., and E. Greenwood, *The Design of Social Policy Research* (Englewood Cliffs, N.J.: Prentice-Hall, 1980).

Polansky, N. A., ed., *Social Work Research,* Rev. Ed. (Chicago: University of Chicago Press, 1975).

Reid, W. J., and A. D. Smith, *Research in Social Work* (New York: Columbia University Press, 1981).

Rossi, P., H. Freeman and S. Wright, *Evaluation: A Systematic Approach* (Beverly Hills, Calif.: Sage, 1979).

Tripodi, T., *Uses and Abuses of Social Research in Social Work* (New York: Columbia University Press, 1974).

Walizer, M. H., and P. L. Wienir, *Research Methods and Analysis: Searching for Relationships* (New York: Harper and Row, 1978).

In particular, there has emerged an increasing emphasis on the production and use of research geared to the evaluation of social programs and practices and to the development of social policy based on needs assessment, evaluation, and community research.

This book is focused on the consumption of research that informs social work policies and practices. The principles for classification, evaluation, and utilization of social research that were articulated in the first four chapters of the first edition continue to be useful today. Therefore, we chose to make only very minor revisions in the first four chapters and to add three new chapters that in our opinion reflect current and future developments in the use of research for social work. Chapter 5 introduces historical research as empirical research in terms broader than those that generally characterize the traditional history of social work and social welfare. Chapter 6 is aimed at specifying criteria for assessing evaluation studies, and Chapter 7 deals with social policy research.

Chapter 1

Consumption of Research: An Introduction

THE PURPOSE OF THIS BOOK

Research is the application of systematic procedures for the purposes of developing, modifying, and expanding knowledge that can be communicated and verified by independent investigators. When the knowledge obtained by research is about the observable world—that is, about phenomena that independent observers can apprehend—it is called *empirical research*. Because science (both natural and social) is more closely identified with empirical research than any other knowledge-seeking enterprise, empirical research is often referred to as scientific research but there is empirical research—as in history and law—that is identified with other routes to independently verifiable knowledge. This book is about empirical research that is relevant for social work. Such research is typically reported in the professional journals of social work and the social and behavioral sciences, and in monographs and books.

Characteristic of empirical research in the social sciences and social work is the use of a variety of available methods, such as sampling techniques, in order to obtain relatively unbiased observations of human behavior in different social situations. In addition to methods for producing standardized observations, the methodology of social research is concerned with logical alternatives for reaching degrees of certainty in conclusions that constitute additions to knowledge. Empirical research is thus characterized by *purpose* (to answer questions, to reduce ignorance) and *method* (standardized procedures of observation and logical procedures for reaching conclusions). A typical research study contains these interrelated aspects of the research process: problem formulation, research design, data collection, analysis of data, and the conclusions of the study (Selltiz *et al.*, 1959). Problem formulation and research design involve the articulation of the precise problem to be investigated and the specification of the logical approach to answer the questions posed for study. The sampling procedures are indicated, and methods of gathering data relevant to the research problem are considered. Data are collected and analyzed by quantitative and qualitative devices, and there is a consideration of the extent to which conclusions can be made regarding tentative answers to the major questions of the investigation.

Most books about empirical research, including those for social workers, are designed to help the reader learn how to conduct research. They are focused primarily on the *production* of research. This book, in contrast, is focused on *consumption* of research. Its aim is to increase the sophistication of the reader of research reported in the literature. The more one learns about doing research, the more sophisticated one is likely to become in reading research already done. Likewise, the more one becomes efficient in reading research, the more likely one is to understand how to do research. Nevertheless, there are different objectives and skills for the research producer and the research consumer. This book seeks to enhance the skills of research consumption.

In the years since World War II, along with the increased use of research in the development of technology in modern society, research has received increasing emphasis in the profession of social work. Social work educators have observed that trends include more research conducted by professionals within the field itself and a greater influence of the social sciences in both substantive and methodological contributions (Fanshel, 1962a, 1962b; MacDonald, 1960). In spite of this increasing production of knowledge through research, the typical social work practitioner has usually not been well trained either to produce or to consume empirical research. In undergraduate college or in the graduate schools of social work, social work students rarely achieve more than an elementary knowledge of research methods in courses that usually are about doing research. Yet educational objectives for instruction in research, according to the Council on Social Work Education (1971), are designed to help the social work student "utilize scientific and scholarly inquiry in advancing professional knowledge and improving standards of practice."

The critical evaluation of research reports and a consideration of the ways in which research findings can be utilized are skills that are regarded as increasingly necessary for social workers (Francel *et al.*, 1968). The importance of developing skills in assessing research studies is also reflected in the opinions of students in graduate schools of social work. A study concerned with the learning of research skills in five schools of social work concluded that students characterized the topic of reading and analyzing research reports as that portion of research teaching that was most useful for social work practice (Goldstein, 1967).

In keeping with the intent to facilitate learning how to consume empirical research reports, this book is written primarily for persons studying to become social workers. However, it is not a textbook on research methods, and it is not intended to replace existing texts, which explain and illustrate elementary principles of research. You will find this book more useful if you already have had some exposure to research concepts or if the book is used concurrently with standard research methods texts in a beginning course on research. Social work practitioners and social work educators who need to assess and codify knowledge from research for their own purposes are also among those for whom the book is intended. Our aim is to assist the research reader—whether a social worker, a psychologist, a sociologist, or someone in some other discipline—to read research more usefully, and perhaps even more pleasurably.

THE PLAN OF THIS BOOK

To become a proficient consumer of research, the research reader must learn how to assess published studies and must have practice in doing so. Assessment of research requires standards for judging how well a study has been done and how useful it can be. We refer therefore to *evaluation* and *utilization* as crucial features of assessment, and these, in turn, are facilitated by the *classification* of a study in terms of its purposes and research methods. The development of criteria for classifying, evaluating, and utilizing research that appears in the social work and social science literature is the prime objective of those who would learn to consume research. Following this introductory chapter, the next section of this book consists of chapters proposing criteria and guidelines for classifying, evaluating, and utilizing research. Then, we present three chapters on special topics in assessing research: historical research, evaluation research, and policy research. In each of these areas we provide additional criteria for assessment that are topical in the decade of the 1980s.

SHOULD A RESEARCH REPORT BE READ AT ALL?

As previously noted, our concern in this book is with the assessment of reported empirical research relevant to social work. The classification scheme and the guidelines we subsequently develop will not apply directly to articles that discuss research strategies and methods without presenting empirical data, or those that present portions of data from one or several research investigations to support theoretical propositions or practice principles, or to essay reviews of one or more research studies. Exclusion from consideration in this book does not imply that such literature is not valuable for the social worker. On the contrary, knowledge from these and other sources about a topic of relevance to the practitioner is most important. The more the research reader knows about a topic of interest, the more will be gained from reading research that bears on the topic.

The classification and assessment schemes that are developed are generally meant for use in reading research reports devoted to a single investigation. Such reports normally include information on the problem formulation, research design and data collection, and data analysis and conclusions of the research which are being reported. But should an article, or research report, of empirical research be read at all?

This may seem to be a trick question in a book devoted to assessing published research. Assessment begins, however, with a decision that an article or monograph deserves the time and energy its reading will require. You, the practitioner, are in a familiar dilemma: you must read the study to know if it is worth reading! You risk wasting time or overlooking something useful. The title of the research report may help decide whether to read it, but often the title will not tell anything about the quality of the research. Not all titles are reliable indicators of the content of a research report. The title *Girls at Vocational High* (Meyer *et al.*, 1965), does not reveal that this is a field experiment on casework and group counseling. "The 'Hang Loose' Ethic and the Spirit of Drug Use," (Suchman, 1968) is a title that may not imply that research is being reported. The titles, "Scapegoats, Group Workers, and Pre-emptive Intervention " (Shulman, 1967) and "Epilepsy and Social Adjustment" (Morgan, 1967) do not reveal that the latter reports a research study and the former does not. Fashions in titles for research reports vary, but readers soon become familiar with the practices of journals they find most pertinent to their interests. Even when titles—as they usually do—indicate a general subject-matter area, for example, drug use, illness, delinquency, and so on, the peripheral relevance of a research study to the practitioner may not be evident. Subtitles, abstracts, or headnotes preceding the article may be helpful, but often there will be no other way than a cursory first reading to decide whether or not to undertake more careful reading. Of course, a colleague who has read the study may offer helpful information.

Having a cursory first knowledge of a research report, what basis does the practitioner have for deciding whether it is worthwhile to go further? We may note a number of reasons that the practitioner may keep in mind to answer this question.

1. The practitioner may be currently, or persistently, faced with a particular problem in practice on which the research seems to bear. For example, he or she faces clients with excessive anxiety and the research appears to deal with effectiveness of different ways of treating the problem (as in Paul, 1966 and 1967). Or, the practitioner is an administrator of a large professional staff and the subject of the research is supervision (as in Scott, 1965). In short, the subject matter of the research may have direct relevance to an immediate problem of the reader's practice. Having a specific practice problem, like any other felt need, can be a stimulus for problem-solving research behavior. The practitioner with such a problem need not—indeed, should not—wait for the chance appearance of a pertinent research study but instead should examine the literature on the topic to see if studies have been made that will be useful. Articles reviewing the state of research on a particular question may be especially helpful in these circumstances. Also, there may be books that collect major research studies on a problem or area. Use should also be made of publication of abstracts, such as *Social Work Research and Abstracts, Psychological Abstracts,* and *Sociological Abstracts.*

2. The practitioner may choose to study the research even if it does not apparently bear on a current practice problem, because it seems likely to supply knowledge about a practice area where she or he might face problems or have questions. Such questions may be about client characteristics, social situations, or new approaches to practice or about other factors that affect the work. A counselor who works with persons with marital problems, for example, may find relevant an experiment with differential assignment of caseworkers to marriage partners (as in Pollak, 1963). Or, someone who works with groups of delinquents may want to know what was learned in a study of street corner gangs (as in Jansyn, 1966). In short, the subject matter of the research may be relevant to the reader's area of practice, if not to a specific current problem.

3. Practitioners may read a research report peripheral to their area of practice, or even entirely outside it, because they believe it to be important to social work as a profession and to them as professional social workers. They may want to "be informed," or "keep up with what is going on." (Some research studies become widely publicized, and knowing them is an unavoidable expectation of the professional social worker. Some of these "classics" will have been on reading lists when practitioners were in social work school, and they may want to get around to reading them at last!) Some studies that seem far from the practitioner's own area may be provocative and stimulating and, in an indirect fashion, offer useful knowledge. It is not the purpose of this book to promote knowledge for its own sake, but one answer to the question, "Why should I read a research study?" may be, simply, "Because it interests me." This is not the sort of usefulness for which we propose guidelines, but the double meaning of a title of an article by Abraham Flexner comes to mind: "The Usefulness of Useless Knowledge."

TYPES OF EMPIRICAL SOCIAL RESEARCH

Based on the objectives of the investigation and the use of different strategies and methods, empirical research studies can be classified into three broad groupings: experimental, quantitative-descriptive, and exploratory (Weinberger and Tripodi, 1968). Experimental studies have the general purpose of producing empirical generalizations, that is, verified hypotheses. Such studies attempt to establish cause-effect relationships by minimizing the influence of variables other than those specified in the hypothesis being tested through the use of such devices as random assignment of subjects to experimental and control groups. The field experiment conducted by Paul (1966) is an example of an experimental study. He was interested in assessing the relative efficacy of insight-oriented psychotherapy as compared to systematic desensitization with regard to the treatment of college undergraduates who had interpersonal performance anxiety ("stage fright"). Students who had shown evidence of anxiety and who were motivated for treatment were assigned randomly to three different treatment groups (desensitization, insight, attention-placebo therapies) and to an untreated control group. Five experienced psychotherapists worked individually with each student in each of the treatment groups for five interviews over a six-week period. Individuals were evaluated both prior to and subsequent to the experiment on anxiety scales, frequencies of symptoms related to anxiety, and on physiological indicators.

There are a variety of quantitative-descriptive studies which have a range of objectives from the production of facts to the determination of correlations among selected variables and the testing of hypotheses through approximations to rigorous experimental designs. An example of one variation of quantitative-descriptive studies is the cross-cultural study by Bacon, Child, and Barry (1963). They selected a sample of 48 societies for which there was sufficient ethnographic material available so that comparative ratings of types of crime and child-rearing practices could be made by independent judges. The researchers were interested in seeking correlates of crime as a function of different family structural and household arrangements in different societies.

Unlike experimental and quantitative-descriptive studies, exploratory studies have as their major purpose the articulation of concepts and the development of hypotheses. While a variety of research techniques (such as procedures for interviewing and participant observation) may be used, less concern is devoted to the systematic application of research procedures to describe accurate quantitative relations among variables. An example of an exploratory study is the study by Bonjean (1963), who attempted to refine the concept of community leadership. In a community in North Carolina he located influential persons by using a method which involves ranking of community leaders. He used sociometric devices to determine whether the leaders could be regarded as forming a group, and then differentiated three types of leaders. Using available documents, demographic information, and information from interviews, he developed a series of hypotheses pertaining to leadership type and the variables of social class, status, and power.

RESEARCH FOR SOCIAL WORK

All these strategies in social research can be used in research for social work, which is the use of systematic procedures in the seeking of knowledge relevant to the goals of social work practice (Greenwood, 1957). The goals of social work range from the development of social welfare programs and services in society to the enhancement of the social and psychological functioning of individuals, groups, and communities. Areas of practice within social work are designated typically as social casework, group work, community organization, and administration and policy development. Examples of selected areas of knowledge derived from research that can be construed as relevant for social work practitioners are as follows: the location of specific kinds of clientele who could use the services of social welfare programs; the relative efficacy of varying approaches in psychotherapy; the development of hypotheses for managing hyperaggressive children in residential treatment centers; the development of devices for determining the influential persons in a community; the accumulation of demographic information necessary for social planning; and the development of theories pertaining to the influence of different kinds of groups or organizations on individuals.

We have already noted that research has received increasing emphasis in social work. More funds have become available for research through public and private auspices, and the number of persons completing doctoral dissertations in schools of social work increased from twenty during the academic years 1949–52 to ninety-two during a comparable period of time in 1959–62 (Shyne, 1965). Another indication of the increasing production of research for social work is provided by a content analysis of selected social work periodicals (Weinberger and Tripodi, 1968). A systematic review of 1,894 articles from 1956 through 1965 indicated that the relative percentage of research articles increased from 13.8 percent in 1956-60 to 20.2 percent in the period from 1961 through 1965. It was concluded further that research studies concerned with producing empirical generalizations have increased, which is an indication that more sophisticated research techniques are being used in seeking knowledge for social work.

As a result of increasing research endeavors and a concern for systematizing knowledge for social work, articles that review research studies in specified areas of social work have appeared more frequently in the professional literature. Illustrative of this trend is the book *Five Fields of Social Service: Reviews of Research* (Maas, 1966), which attempts to review critically research in social work and related disciplines for the purpose of deriving knowledge that can be used for social work. Research studies applicable to the following areas of social work are reviewed: family services, public welfare, child welfare, neighborhood centers, and social planning. More recent books with this approach are: *Social Service Research: Reviews of Studies* (Maas, 1978) and *Research in The Social Services* (Maas, 1971).

The desire to synthesize and transmit knowledge from research which may increase the quality of social work practice is also apparent in the establishment in 1965 of the journal *Abstracts for Social Workers* (now *Social Work Research and Abstracts*) by the National Association of Social Workers. It contains abstracts of articles from more than 200 journals in social work and related disciplines. Its function is to summarize reports on all aspects of knowledge available in professional literature and related social science publications which may be used by social workers.

AVAILABLE GUIDELINES FOR ASSESSING EMPIRICAL RESEARCH

In spite of the availability of texts concerned with the methodology of research inquiry, there is very little in the professional literature that deals with systematic procedures for assessing research findings. Research texts such as *Research Methods in Social Relations* (Selltiz et al., 1959) and *Social Work Research* (Polansky, 1960) do not include the topic of evaluation of research; and the text by Goldstein (1963), *Research Standards and Methods for Social Workers,* contains only sixteen pages directly concerned with the evaluation and utilization of research. Although the monograph on *Guidelines for Evaluative Research* (Herzog, 1959) provides some useful criteria on what an administrator can expect from evaluative research studies, it is not concerned directly with the assessment of research. Furthermore, the few articles regarding the evaluation of research which appear in professional journals are typically brief and highly schematic (Anderson, 1954; Caplow, 1958; Goldstein, 1962; Knop, 1967).

Published guidelines for evaluating research are devoted primarily to research that has the purpose of producing empirical generalizations, and often seem to carry the implication that all research studies are to be evaluated solely from the perspective of absolute certainty. On the basis of our experiences in teaching research at several graduate schools of social work, we have observed that when some students learn to uncover the flaws of published research studies, they conclude immediately that no research is useful. This is particularly likely to occur when students apply criteria for evaluating experiments to exploratory studies, which have different purposes than those of verifying hypotheses. Thus, studies may be evaluated without taking account of their specific purposes and methods. This minimizes the possibility of differential assessment and appreciation of different sorts of usefulness from different types of studies. It also increases the likelihood that conclusions from different kinds of research studies will be regarded as equivalent.

Social scientists have been interested, particularly since the 1950s, in developing general guidelines for applying the findings of their disciplines to fields that work with practical social problems (Likert and Lippitt, 1953; Merton, Broom, and Cottrell, 1959; Gouldner, 1965; Lazarsfeld et al., 1967). During the same period, social work educators were concerned with the ways in which content from the social sciences could be used to expand the knowledge base of social work (Kahn, 1959; Bartlett et al., 1964). Moreover, in recent years efforts have been made to develop more systematic criteria for utilizing knowledge from the social sciences for social work. Significant publications in this regard are *Behavioral Science for Social Workers* (Thomas, 1967a), "Social Work and Social Welfare" (Meyer et al., 1967), and *Social Science Theory and Social Work Research* (Kogan, 1960a). However, these works do not deal typically with the evaluation of research *per se,* which we regard as prerequisite to the appropriate utilization of social science knowledge for social work.

In his study of 308 professional social workers in New York City, Rosenblatt (1968) concluded that professional social workers should use research findings to a greater extent than was evident. While approximately 30 percent of his respondents indicated they would read more research articles if they had the time to do so, only 9 percent of his respondents reported that they actually read research reports. A practitioner's published response to this study reinforced the idea that research findings should be used more often for practice (Franks, 1968), but the implication was that criteria for evaluating and utilizing the findings of research are not standardized and not readily available.

MAJOR ASSUMPTIONS AND SOURCES OF GUIDELINES
FOR ASSESSING EMPIRICAL RESEARCH

Since the essential reason for developing principles for classifying, evaluating, and utilizing research is to facilitate the use of research findings for social work, it is appropriate to delineate our major assumptions regarding knowledge. We endorse the position of Eaton (1958) who postulates that knowledge of a particular phenomenon is not absolute although it can be approximated by relative degrees of certainty through the scientific approach. In this context, then, social research can be regarded as the use of systematic procedures in an attempt to reduce uncertainty in the understanding of human behavior. In addition to the idea of relative degrees of certainty in approximating knowledge, we believe that it is important to consider forms of knowledge. In concurrence with Greenwood (1960) and Thomas (1967a), we view knowledge as being comprised of concepts, hypotheses, empirical generalizations, and theory.

Essentially, concepts are verbal symbols of ideas abstracted from experience, while hypotheses are predictive statements of relationship between two or more concepts. The following hypothesis specifies the relationship between the concepts of socioeconomic class and the receipt of psychotherapy for mental patients: mental patients of low socioeconomic status are less likely to receive psychotherapy than mental patients of middle socioeconomic status. Empirical generalizations are hypotheses that have withstood refutation in a number of research studies. Theory consists of an interlocking set of hypotheses that are logically related, and it seeks to explain the interrelations among empirical generalizations.

Different approaches in social research are dependent upon the form of knowledge sought, which ranges from the clarification of concepts to the testing of hypotheses derived from theory. In view of this, we believe that the potential utility of research could be enhanced if consumers of research would consider the form and the degree of relative certainty of the knowledge that is to be utilized from research studies.

The interrelated processes of classification, evaluation, and utilization can be viewed with respect to their relations to knowledge. In the assessment of research, one classifies the research by the types of information sought by the investigator and by the procedures that the researcher uses to seek knowledge. In addition, the research is evaluated with respect to the extent to which uncertainty is reduced in accordance with the purposes of the investigator. Finally, depending on the state of knowledge that is produced, the findings of research are applied to social work practice. Prior to application, however, there is the consideration of the specific aspects of social work practice to which the research findings may be applied.

We employ the criteria developed by Gouldner (1957) and Thomas (1964, 1967a) in our development of principles for utilizing research. These criteria involve considerations of *content relevance, knowledge power,* and *referent features. Content relevance* refers to subject matter and the levels of human arrangements to which the subject matter is applied. The levels range from individuals to organizations and societies. *Knowledge power* refers generally to the extent to which selected propositions are valid and relatively more predictive of social phenomena than other available hypotheses. *Referent features* include notions such as the degree to which variables are operationally accessible and can be manipulated easily by a practitioner. Thomas (1964) cites the example of "group size" as a variable which has a referent, number of persons in a group, which is accessible and can be manipulated in the context of group work. In addition, such notions as the cost and ethical suitability of manipulating variables are relevant to discussions pertaining to the utilization of knowledge.

With respect to the evaluation of research that seeks to verify hypotheses, we incorporate Campbell and Stanley's (1963) concepts of internal and external validity. *External validity* is concerned with the extent to which results can be generalized *beyond* the specific context in which the research is conducted, while *internal validity* refers to the degree of control of extraneous influences *within* the specific context of the research. These concepts are particularly relevant in the assessment of experiments and in approximations to experimental design because they serve to broaden the perspective of evaluators of research. Experiments ideally can maximize both internal and external validity with a resultant increase in the relative certainty of the research conclusions. However, due to constraints from the social situations in which research is conducted, the ideal is rarely achieved; consequently, much social research involves the use of survey methods with contrasting groups as alternatives to experimentation. The naive evaluator might assume that experiments are *ipso facto* more likely to lead to a greater degree of relative certainty, but this is not necessarily true. Using the notions of internal and external validity, one might conclude, for example, that a particular survey approach had a high degree of external validity, that is, generalizability, with a moderate degree of internal validity. On the contrary, an experiment may have a low degree of external validity with a high degree of internal validity. The point is that we do not assume that certain research designs and procedures *per se* are always superior to other research approaches. Such an assessment should be specific to the purposes of the research and to the manner in which the study is conducted. We further would subscribe to the viewpoint of Hirschi and Selvin (1967) who regard evaluation of research in terms of constructive criticism so that a reviewer of research should consider alternative approaches which could improve on the research investigation of a specific study.

Procedures for conducting exploratory studies are less systematic than those for conducting quantitative-descriptive and experimental studies, especially since the chief goals of exploratory studies are the refinement of concepts and the development of hypotheses. Consequently, criteria for assessing exploratory studies are more difficult to systematize. Illustrative of the need for more systematic procedures for exploratory research is the appearance of *The Discovery of Grounded Theory* by Glaser and Strauss (1967). These authors propose strategies for developing theories through comparative analyses of qualitative data, and they provide some useful ideas. For our objective of developing criteria for assessing exploratory research, the discussions by Riley (1963) on case studies, Katz (1953) on field studies, and Selltiz *et al.* (1959) on exploratory studies are also most provocative. Gouldner's article on "Explorations in Applied Social Science" (1965) is also instructive with reference to the potential utilization of results from exploratory studies, for he believes that the applied social scientist is more likely to use the concepts than the verified hypotheses of the social sciences.

In order to learn principles for assessing research studies, we assume that the discussion and articulation of general guidelines are not sufficient. We believe that the application of general criteria of assessment to specific research studies is necessary. It is also assumed that skills in assessment will develop through experience in actually assessing research studies. A further consideration for social workers in regard to developing skills in assessment is that social workers should evaluate research from the social sciences as well as research conducted under social work auspices. This is important since much substantive content of social work is derived from the social sciences.

Recognizing that social work students usually have limited experience in using concepts of research and statistics, we include throughout this book references to specific bibliographic sources in the context of discussions which presume familiarity with research concepts. For an overview of methodology in social research, we recommend several texts as general references. *Research Methods in Social Relations* (Selltiz *et al.,* 1959) provides a lucid description of the process of research and is geared appropriately to students who have had no previous preparation in research or statistics. Our scheme for classifying research studies is derived primarily from that text. *Social Work Research* (Polansky, 1960, 1975) includes discussions of various aspects involved in the production of research for social work, while *Guidelines for Evaluative Research* (Herzog, 1959) presents clearly key research concepts to be considered in research that attempts to evaluate the effectiveness of treatment programs for bringing about psychosocial changes in individuals. For students with a background in sociology either *Sociological Research: A Case Approach* (Riley, 1963) or *Methods in Social Research* (Goode and Hatt, 1952) is recommended. *Foundations of Behavioral Research* (Kerlinger, 1967) and *Research Methods in the Behavioral Sciences* (Festinger and Katz, 1953) are excellent in their coverage of research methods used in psychology and social psychology. An elementary text in statistics which includes illustrations appropriate to social work and sociology is *Social Statistics* (Blalock, 1960), while *Statistical Methods for the Behavioral Sciences* (Edwards, 1961) includes examples from psychological research, especially in regard to experimentation.

THE USE OF GUIDELINES FOR ASSESSMENT
OF EMPIRICAL RESEARCH

The next three chapters of this book develop criteria and suggest guidelines for the classification, evaluation, and utilization of empirical research by research readers. In order to develop and present these guidelines it is necessary to treat the subject matter of assessment as though it consisted of separate operations to be followed in sequence. However, this is not our intent, and as you use the guidelines, you will discover for yourself that all aspects of assessment must be related and considered together when an actual research study is read. One does not first classify, then evaluate, and finally utilize a research study. Being aware of these different aspects will alert you to questions that help reach a reasoned assessment of a study as a whole.

Likewise, the questions proposed as guidelines as you assess a study are not to be considered exhaustive, and they are not to be applied mechanically. Consuming research is an active and a creative process for the reader. As you gain experience by reading more research and assessing it, you will develop your own version of the guidelines and your own way of bringing them to bear as you adapt them to the particular character of a particular study. The guidelines we suggest are intended to stimulate you in this direction.

Chapter 2

Classification
of Research

DEVELOPMENT OF A CLASSIFICATION SYSTEM

The purpose of this chapter is to present a system for classifying empirical social research studies. Our primary objective is to provide a framework that can be used for locating different types of studies that the research reader wishes to evaluate and utilize. However, a classification system may have additional functions:

1. A device for teaching different types of research methods.
2. A scheme for systematizing research knowledge within a discipline in order to document trends over periods of time.
3. A system for differentiating the particular forms of knowledge sought in research investigations.

A typology of research studies should contain categories that are distinct from each other and to which research studies can be assigned uniquely. For example, a study assigned to the category of experimental research should be distinct from a study assigned to the category of exploratory research. Furthermore, it is assumed that research typologies should have reliable categories such that different persons should be able to read a research study and independently assign it to the same category. To facilitate understanding and use of a classification system, the following requisites are necessary: specification of the criteria used for classification; definitions of the categories in the system; presentations of examples for each category; and a demonstration of the reliability of the system.

In our review of the literature in the social sciences and in social work, we did not find a system for classifying research that satisfied the above requirements. Indeed, most of the typologies in textbooks on research had to be inferred, since they were not presented systematically so they could be used for classifying research. Nevertheless, we were guided by the literature in our quest for a classification scheme; and our classification system, in the final analysis, is essentially a reorganization of ideas derived from the works of previous authors.

Research classifications in sociology and psychology are based primarily on research methods, which include different logical approaches for the design of research investigations and the choice of a variety of techniques such as the construction of questionnaires and rating scales. The classifications range *from* a consideration of several methods for achieving a single purpose *to* a consideration of the use of one method for accomplishing a variety of purposes. For example, Campbell and Stanley (1963) discuss different types of research design that could be employed in the pursuit of empirical generalizations; and Hyman (1955) considers the use of survey procedures for testing hypotheses, for describing characteristics of a phenomenon, and for seeking quantitative relations among designated variables.

There are two general kinds of research classification schemes that have been articulated for social work. One kind of typology is based on substantive considerations, and the other is based primarily on the research methods linked to the level of knowledge at the researcher's disposal. Greenwood's (1957) typology is illustrative of the first approach. He identifies different substantive categories such as administrative information, social work philosophy, and practice theory, which includes principles of diagnosis and treatment. An illustration of the second approach is provided by Kahn (1960) who discusses several kinds of research studies in terms of the state of available knowledge about the research problem and the research methods that appear to be most appropriate for the solution of the problem. Using the distinctions posited by Selltiz *et al.* (1959), he specifies the following main categories of research: formulative exploratory, descriptive-diagnostic, and experimental. The categories of the classification system of Selltiz *et al.,* are: formulative or exploratory studies, descriptive studies, and studies testing causal hypotheses.

To develop the classification system used in this book, we first reviewed the literature in search of a comprehensive system that appeared to be reliable. Since we were unable to locate a system that had actually been used systematically for classifying research studies, we tried several typologies for a content analysis of research studies reported in social work periodicals (Weinberger and Tripodi, 1968). We used the typologies of Kahn (1960), Selltiz *et al.* (1959), Greenwood (1957), and Festinger and Katz (1953). It became clear that the categories were overlapping so that research studies could not be classified uniquely within any particular category. Further, it was observed that different labels were used by different research textbooks for classifying the same study. In view of these considerations, we arbitrarily selected the typologies posited by Kahn (1960) and by Selltiz *et al.* (1959) to be used as a general frame of reference. Then we revised and modified the categories as we tested the extent to which independent reviewers could read research studies and classify them in the same way. We followed this procedure in reviewing all of the articles in four social work journals from 1956 through 1965. Hence, the classification scheme evolved from the nature of the articles themselves and their distinctions from each other. A reliability test was made for the specific classification of research articles in the journal, *Social Casework,* for the years 1963 and 1964, and two independent reviewers agreed 98 percent of the time in their use of the general categories of research which were developed for our purposes: experimental, quantitative-descriptive, and exploratory studies (Weinberger and Tripodi, 1968).

Following the same procedure, the three authors of this book used the classification scheme for selecting and classifying research articles from sociology and psychology journals. Although no systematic reliability tests were conducted, it appeared that such a system could be used reliably in that the authors were able to agree in their classifications of studies selected for the first edition of this book and for the reader, *Exemplars of Social Research* (Fellin, Tripodi, and Meyer, 1969). The final procedure involved a comparison of the classification scheme with other typologies in order to revise it where necessary, so that it would be sufficiently comprehensive to be applicable to the ranges of empirical social research.

In subsequent sections of this chapter the classification system will be presented in detail. First, the basic criteria for conceptualizing distinctions within the system will be considered. Then definitions and examples within each of the three major categories—experimental, quantitative-descriptive, and exploratory studies—will be presented. Limitations of the typology and typical problems in using the system will be discussed, and guidelines for classifying research studies will be provided.

AN OVERVIEW OF THE CLASSIFICATION SYSTEM

This classification system is based on the conclusion that research studies should be categorized both in terms of the major purposes of research with respect to the seeking of knowledge and in terms of the various types of empirical methods employed to achieve such purposes. It will be recalled from Chapter 1 that forms of knowledge can be identified as concepts, hypotheses, empirical generalizations, and theories. It is to be emphasized that this typology is restricted to empirical research, which includes the use of systematic observations and standardized procedures that can be independently reproduced (Greenwood, 1957). Furthermore, reports of empirical research that can most usefully be subjected to the classification scheme are those that present a single investigation. Where more than one study is reported in the same article or book, each study can be separately classified. The typology is not applicable to nonempirical research, such as documentary or bibliographic studies. Likewise, the classification system is inapplicable to essay reviews of one or more research studies; it is not useful with articles that primarily attempt to develop practice implications or to support theoretical arguments, even though research findings may be cited; and it does not apply to methodological papers whose purpose is the development, exposition, or criticism of research strategies or issues.

As previously indicated, the classification distinguishes three major categories: experimental, quantitative-descriptive, and exploratory studies. These major categories are divided into eight subtypes.

Major Type: Experimental Research

The category of experimental studies is the category that can be most easily specified. Experimental studies have the primary objective of verifying research hypotheses in the quest for empirical generalizations. Although there is a variety of empirical methods and examples of experimentation in the literature, we chose to use the strict interpretation of experiments as delineated by Campbell and Stanley (1963, pp. 183-204). The distinguishing features of empirical methods used in experimentation include the experimental manipulation of one or more independent variables, the use of control groups, and the employment of randomization procedures to assure that the experimental and control groups can be regarded as equivalent. These features can be illustrated by a hypothetical research study, which has the purpose of testing the hypothesis that emotionally disturbed delinquents who receive tranquilizing drugs are less likely to engage in criminal activities than emotionally disturbed delinquents who do not receive tranquilizing drugs. In this hypothesis it is presumed that the receipt of tranquilizing drugs will reduce the frequency of engaging in criminal activities. The presumed causal variable is the *independent variable* of the hypothesis, while the presumed effect is the *dependent variable*. The research study uses several procedures. Emotionally disturbed delinquents are defined and identified. A group of delinquents is located by the use of sampling methods to obtain a representative sample of the population of emotionally disturbed delinquents (see Chein, 1959, for a discussion of sampling methods). There might be 200 delinquents identified for the study. These delinquents are then assigned randomly to either an experimental or a control group. Random assignment is a procedure based on probability theory, which assures that each delinquent has an equal chance of being assigned to either the experimental or the control group; it is that feature of experimentation which enhances the internal validity of the experiment by increasing the likelihood that experimental and control groups are initially equivalent with respect to potentially relevant variables. Those delinquents assigned to the experimental group receive tranquilizing drugs, while those assigned to the control group do not; hence, the independent variable of receiving tranquilizing drugs is manipulated by the experimenter. Measurements are made on the dependent variable of engaging in criminal activities over specified periods of time, and the relative frequencies for the experimental and control groups are compared.

SUBTYPES: FIELD AND LABORATORY EXPERIMENTS. Experimental studies are differentiated by the setting in which they take place, and subtypes can be identified as field experiments and laboratory experiments. *Field experiments* involve the manipulations of independent variables in a natural setting as in the example above. *Laboratory experiments* include the creation of artificial situations in which independent variables are manipulated by the experimenter. A typical laboratory experiment concerned with the effects of group influences on individual judgments might involve the use of volunteer subjects at a college who are randomly assigned to experimental and control groups which have been created for the first time in a relatively isolated situation. The experimental and control groups are structured so that individuals in each group participate in some common task. Members of both the experimental and control groups are asked to make judgments prior to and subsequent to their group participation. During the course of the experiment, the experimental group might receive contrived information from the experimenter that their initial judgments were discrepant from those of other members in the group, while the control group would not receive any information from the experimenter. The final judgments of members of the experimental group would be compared with the judgments of the control group members.

Laboratory experiments are frequently used in the testing of hypotheses related to various sociological and psychological theories. On the contrary, field experiments are frequently employed in studies that seek to evaluate the efficacy of various programs or techniques for helping people. In general, laboratory experiments are more likely than field experiments to have the purpose of seeking empirical generalizations for refining and modifying theories of behavior.

Major Type: Quantitative-Descriptive Research

The category of quantitative-descriptive studies is similar to that of experimental studies in that both seek quantitative descriptions among specified variables. Quantitative descriptions are obtained through the use of measuring devices to describe relationships among variables; hence, statistical concepts such as correlation, proportions, and so forth are employed. A hypothetical example of a quantitative description is that the percentage of lower-class families who participate in community activities is significantly smaller than the percentage of middle-class families who participate in community activities. With respect to the empirical methods employed, quantitative-descriptive studies differ from experimental studies in that they do not use randomization procedures in assigning subjects to experimental and control groups. In addition, they do not employ the experimental manipulation of independent variables.

Quantitative-descriptive studies cover the entire range of purposes in seeking forms of knowledge, and they include a variety of research designs and data-collection techniques. Accordingly, we have classified these studies into three subtypes, which form a hierarchy of research objectives within the major type: hypothesis-testing studies, studies describing characteristics of populations, and studies seeking to identify relations among variables.

SUBTYPE: HYPOTHESIS TESTING. Studies that have the purpose of testing hypotheses employ research methods that are essentially approximations to experimentation, and this subtype can be regarded as a transition from experimental to quantitative-descriptive studies. Campbell and Stanley (1963) refer to these approximations as "quasi-experiments," and they discuss a variety of research designs that researchers have used. For example, one approach for testing the hypothesis regarding the use of tranquilizing drugs by emotionally disturbed delinquents and their subsequent criminal activities might involve a selection of a group of emotionally disturbed delinquents who have received tranquilizing drugs and a comparison of that group with a contrasting group of emotionally disturbed delinquents who have not received tranquilizing drugs. Comparisons might be made with regard to the frequency of criminal activities in both groups. Unlike an experimental study, randomization procedures are not employed. Hence, the investigator would attempt to demonstrate by statistical methods that the experimental and control groups are similar with respect to potentially relevant variables which could influence the frequency of criminal activities observed.

SUBTYPE: POPULATION DESCRIPTION. Research that seeks to describe accurately some characteristics of designated populations are typically represented by survey studies, which are conducted at one or more periods of time. As a hypothetical example, a national sample may be obtained by probability sampling techniques, and the 2,000 or more persons in the sample may be asked their opinions concerning prospective candidates for president, their attitudes toward a program such as Medicare, and the like. These studies have the purpose of answering specific questions in regard to quantitative-descriptions of a designated population, and they strive to obtain samples which are representative of the population so that external validity, that is, generalizability, is maximized.

SUBTYPE: SEEKING VARIABLE RELATIONSHIPS. Studies that seek quantitative relations among variables explore the relations among a series of variables for a specific population. The investigator systematically collects information on a variety of variables, which are defined sufficiently so they can be measured (see Selltiz et al., 1959, pp. 144-98, for a discussion of measurement). For example, information on family income, age, ethnic group, and other variables may be obtained; the investigator then determines whether there are any significant correlations among these variables.

Major Type: Exploratory Research

The category of exploratory studies is distinguishable from the category of quantitative-descriptive studies in that the major purpose is to refine concepts and to articulate questions and hypotheses for subsequent investigation. A variety of data-collection procedures may be used, but less attention is devoted to the accurate description of quantitative relations among variables. Accordingly, representative sampling is of less importance than is the selection of a range of cases to stimulate ideas. In addition to quantitative data, researchers may use qualitative data in narrative form, which may be derived from their observations of a particular phenomenon.

Exploratory studies typically include a great deal of information for a single case or for a small number of cases. For example, detailed quantitative and qualitative information may be accumulated in a clinical study of one individual's response to psychotherapy over an extended period of time. This is different from many quantitative-descriptive studies, which may include brief information from a large number of respondents. We have classified exploratory studies into three subtypes.

SUBTYPE: EXPLORATORY-DESCRIPTIVE RESEARCH. The subtype of combined exploratory-descriptive studies is intended to serve as a transition between quantitative-descriptive and exploratory studies. The primary purpose of these studies is to refine and develop concepts and hypotheses. Both quantitative and qualitative descriptions of the phenomenon being studied are included in the research. For example, a study of the political system in a particular community may include quantitative descriptions of the voting patterns of community residents and unstandardized impressions of the ways in which political leaders attempt to influence the voters in the community.

SUBTYPE: RESEARCH USING SPECIFIC PROCEDURES. Studies that use specific data collection procedures to develop insights and ideas typically employ devices such as content analysis in an attempt to systematize qualitative material. Comparisons are made, and then hypotheses are developed. For example, it may be hypothesized from a review of case records in a particular agency that parents of retarded children are more likely to seek contacts with caseworkers than are parents of emotionally disturbed children.

SUBTYPE: EXPERIMENTAL MANIPULATION. Studies that experimentally manipulate independent variables to demonstrate ideas can be regarded as clinical studies or demonstrations of social action programs. Their essential purpose is to demonstrate the plausibility of using specified treatment methods or programs to accomplish some particular goal. These studies are distinguishable from experiments in that they do not use randomization procedures or experimental and control groups. They are different from quantitative-descriptive studies in that they typically involve the study of one case with little attention devoted to the problem of external validity. For example, an experimenter may be interested in using techniques of learning experiments to change the behavior of a patient. He uses the techniques on a single patient, and he observes systematically the changes in the patient's behavior over a period of time.

In summary, the classification system is based on a combination of the purposes of the research and the methods used to accomplish those purposes. Variations of purpose and method provide a basis for the distinguishing characteristics of the types and subtypes. In the sections that follow we present the major assumptions behind each research approach for seeking knowledge, more elaborate definitions of each category, and abstracts of research literature representative of each category. The purpose is to clarify the classification system more precisely.

EXPERIMENTAL STUDIES

Since the purpose of experimentation is to provide evidence that bears directly on the extent to which hypotheses may be refuted, it is instructive to consider some underlying ideas that contribute to the methodology of experimental studies. If the meaning of experimental studies is better understood, efforts toward classification of research will be facilitated.

As indicated in Chapter 1, a hypothesis is a statement that predicts the relationship between two or more variables. The formulation of the research hypothesis is of primary importance in experimentation. If a hypothesis is inadequately conceived, the research procedures of experimentation may not be applicable. Consequently, research educators have developed criteria for judging whether or not hypotheses are stated in a form that is amenable to research. Goode and Hatt (1952, pp. 68-71) have specified several guidelines for determining the potential researchability of hypotheses. These criteria are as follows:

1. The hypotheses must be conceptually clear.
2. Hypotheses should have empirical referents.
3. The hypotheses must be specific.
4. The hypotheses should be related to available techniques.
5. The hypotheses should be related to a body of theory.

Essentially, these criteria are derived from the assumptions of scientific method pertaining to the necessity of operationalizing concepts in such a way that they can be measured. It is believed that measurement will allow for systematic comparisons of observations and for reliable communication. The central notion pertains to the necessity for specifying the empirical referents of the concepts being investigated. Empirical referents refer to direct or indirect objects in the physical world that are potentially observable through the senses. For example, a variable such as education can be operationally defined by an indication of either the years of education completed in particular kinds of school systems or by the construction of tests of knowledge that reflect expected achievement for certain grade levels. Greenwood (1960, pp. 58-63) discusses in considerable detail the virtues and defects of operational definitions, and his discussion is recommended for an introduction to this subject.

Having specified the hypothesis to be investigated, the experimenter then faces the problem of designing his study so that evidence pertaining to the tentative acceptance of the hypothesis can be accumulated. Hypotheses for experimentation typically imply a cause-effect relationship between one or more independent variables and one or more dependent variables. For example, it might be predicted that the independent variable of group counseling will affect the dependent variable of anxiety.

Criteria of the verification of hypotheses that posit cause-effect relationships are essentially extensions of John Stuart Mill's *A System of Logic* (E. Nagel, 1950), which is a systematic theory regarding the nature of proof. Although such criteria have been discussed in many volumes on philosophy and research methods, we find the discussions by Selltiz *et al.* (1959, pp. 80-127) regarding the types of evidence for inferring a causal relationship between two variables sufficient for our purposes here. They summarize three major types of evidence that are necessary for testing hypotheses about causal relationships:

1. The assumed causal variable, the independent variable, should be associated with the dependent variable in the manner predicted by the hypothesis.

2. Changes in the dependent variable attributed to the independent variable should occur in time sequence so that the independent variable is prior.

3. Other variables, which might influence the dependent variable, should be ruled out as possible causes of observed changes in the dependent variable.

The third criterion above has been further specified by Campbell and Stanley (1963, pp. 175-76), who have delineated factors in the design of experiments which seek to provide evidence for the testing of hypotheses pertaining to human subjects. It will be recalled from our introductory chapter that Campbell and Stanley provide two key concepts for interpreting the validity of research studies concerned with causal inferences. These are the notions of internal validity and external validity.

Internal validity refers to the control of extraneous variables in the specific context of experimentation. Campbell and Stanley consider in detail the extraneous factors that are related to internal validity. They include such factors as the effects of testing and instrumentation, biases in the selection of different respondents for comparison groups, maturational and historical influences occurring while the experiment is in progress, variables that have influenced the subjects in the past, statistical artifacts, and the loss of subjects during the research. They also discuss factors that need to be controlled with respect to *external validity,* which refers to the generalizability of the results from the experiment to other populations in other settings. In particular, they provide a thoughtful discussion pertaining to the effects of experimenters *per se* on experimental subjects, as well as a consideration of the problems of bias in the selection of respondents for experimentation.

The design of experiments is built around the sources of evidence necessary for testing hypotheses. In addition to the consideration of ideal requirements for the design of research, experimenters must consider what is practically possible. Problems of manpower, financial auspices, ethics, and securing permission to conduct studies within different communities and organizations are types of constraints that typically render ideal experimental designs impractical. Thus, the research reader will observe in the literature numerous studies that depart from ideal experimental designs. These studies are more properly considered quantitative-descriptive studies that are approximations to experiments. Kerlinger (1967, pp. 275-408) and Kahn (1960, pp. 59-67), offer detailed discussions regarding experimental designs and approximations to experimentation.

In our classification system a research study must have several requisites before it can be classified as experimental. *There must be an explicit or implicit hypothesis that is being investigated.* An explicit hypothesis is one that is specified in the formulation of the problem for research. As alluded to earlier in the chapter, implicit hypotheses are those that are not articulated precisely in the formulation of the problem; however, they are implicit in the overall research study. In the evaluation of a tutorial program devised to increase the reading skills of students, for example, hypotheses might not be specifically stated, but the research design may involve the random assignment of students either to an experimental group for tutoring or to a control group, which does not receive tutoring. In addition, measurements of reading skills may be obtained from both groups before and after the experimental group receives tutoring. The implicit hypothesis is that tutoring will increase the reading skills of students. A second requisite for studies to be classified as experimental is that the *variables in the hypotheses of the study must be operationally defined so that measurement is possible.* This is necessary so that quantitative descriptions among variables can be ascertained in order to provide evidence for establishing an association between the independent and dependent variables. A third requisite is that *the independent variable must be manipulated by the experimenter.* This is done in experimental studies to assure that the independent variable (sometimes called the experimental variable) occurs prior in time to the dependent variable. The fourth requisite is that *one or more control groups must be employed* to provide a basis for contrasting the results obtained in the presence of the experimental variable to those results obtained in the absence of the experimental variable. The fifth requisite is that *randomization procedures must be employed in the assignment of subjects to experimental and control groups.* This is a minimum requirement for experiments; it provides some assurance of the equivalence between experimental and control groups, and it provides the basis for the use of tests of statistical inference in the interpretation of results. The student is referred to Edwards' text on *Experimental Design in Psychological Research* (1960, pp. 13-27) for a discussion of the importance of randomization in the execution and interpretation of experiments.

Based on the foregoing discussion, experimental studies may be defined in the following manner:

Experimental studies are empirical research investigations which have as their primary purpose the testing of hypotheses concerned with cause-effect relationships. All of these studies use experimental designs which include control groups, randomization procedures, and the manipulation of independent variables in order to control pertinent factors to as great a degree as possible. Relevant variables are specified so they can be described quantitatively. These studies may employ rigorous sampling techniques to increase the generalizability of the experimental findings.

Two subtypes of experimental studies noted earlier are (1) laboratory experiments, and (2) field experiments. Both types must satisfy the requirements of the definition for experimental studies. The chief distinction between laboratory and field experiments is the degree of control maintained by the experimenter in the setting in which the experiment is conducted. Since there is an artificially created environment by the experimenter in laboratory experiments, the possibility for the control of influential variables other than those postulated in the hypothesis is increased. The field experiment, which takes place in the natural environment, poses relatively more obstacles in experimental control. Field experiments may be used for testing hypotheses linked to theory and for testing hypotheses that are relatively more pertinent to practical situations, while laboratory experiments are used predominantly in testing theoretical propositions. Kerlinger (1967, pp. 379-87), French (1953, pp. 98-135), and Festinger (1953, pp. 136-72) contain detailed discussions regarding the conduct of laboratory and of field experiments. Definitions and examples of laboratory and field experiments are presented below.

Laboratory Experiments

Laboratory experiments are experimental studies in which the investigator creates an isolated situation in an artificial setting with hypothetically constructed variables. Relationships among variables are tested by the manipulation of one or more independent variables and by the control of the potential influence of variables which are extraneous to the hypothesis being tested.

"An Experimental Study of the Observational Process in Casework" by Roger Miller (1958) is an example of a *laboratory experiment*. The investigator began the formulation of his research problem by reviewing Reik's (1948) theoretical model of the observational process in interpersonal communication. In particular, he considered Reik's conceptualization of clinical observation in therapeutic interviews, which is based on the concept of the observer's active or passive attention. Active attention is regarded as the selection of specific kinds of information in the interview, and passive attention is conceived as "free-floating" in the sense that equal attention is presumably devoted to all perceived information. The concept of the direction of the observer's attention in therapeutic interviews is also discussed; the observer may direct his attention internally toward his own responses, or it may be directed externally toward the explicit content of communication. According to Miller (p. 98), Reik's theory suggests the following hypothesis: "The adequacy of the observer's conscious psychological comprehension is said to be positively related to the extent to which he uses free-floating attention and the extent to which his attention is directed internally."

In order to test the hypothesis, Miller designed an experiment. All subjects in the experiment were shown the same film of an actual interview to create a hypothetical situation in which each observer would view the client as a "common client" so that comparisons could be made with respect to attention and understanding. The independent variable of attention was assumed to be manipulated by the use of three experimental groups, which were given different kinds of information with respect to what they were to observe in the film. Members in the *process group* were told to write detailed reports on all they had observed to see how accurately they could perceive the client; members of the *diagnostic group* were told to be prepared to write a summary report of the most important information observed, rather than a detailed report; and members of the *empathic group* were told to develop impressions about the client in a natural manner as the interview in the film progressed. The process group was presumed to observe by active and external attention, which was predicted to lead to the lowest level of understanding. On the contrary, the empathic group was presumed to observe by "free-floating" and internal attention, which was predicted to lead to the highest level of understanding. It was further hypothesized that the diagnostic group would be intermediate in understanding in comparison to the other groups.

The dependent variable of psychological understanding was operationalized by the extent to which the rank orderings of descriptive statements made by the experimental subjects were similar to the rank orderings of descriptive statements made by a group of five "expert" clinicians. These descriptive statements were comprised of brief phrases, and the subjects were asked to order these statements in 11 groupings, which ranged from a group of most descriptive statements to a group of least descriptive statements.

Fifty-four casework students at a graduate school of social work were randomly assigned to the three experimental groups. Comparisons were made among all groups on a discrepancy score, which indicated the discrepancy of rankings in the experimental groups as compared to the panel of experts. As predicted, it was found that the greatest discrepancy occurred in the process group, while no differences were observed between the other two groups.

Field Experiments

Field experiments are experimental studies which involve the manipulation of one or more independent variables in a natural setting in order to determine causal relationships. These studies may attempt to control the influence of environmental constraints on the relationship between independent and dependent variables. They do not rely exclusively on natural conditions of the environment in that the independent variables are manipulated by the experimenter. Field experiments typically have less rigorous control features than laboratory experiments.

An example of a *field experiment* is "An Experiment in Prevention Through Social Work Intervention" by Meyer, Borgatta, and Jones (1967). The research was generated from a concern of Youth Consultation Service: "how to serve effectively the adolescent girl with types of problems that got her into difficulties at school and elsewhere" (p. 364). Youth Consultation Service (YCS) is a nonsectarian, voluntary social agency in New York City, which offers casework and group work services to adolescent girls between the ages of 12 and 25 with characteristic problems such as out-of-wedlock pregnancy, chronic truancy, and home management. Social workers in the agency believed that services were frequently offered too late in the lives of the adolescent girls for such services to be effective. In view of this, it was assumed that preventive services offered to girls at earlier ages might facilitate treatment, which would decrease the extent to which girls would be involved in serious difficulties in later stages of their lives.

The researchers devised an experiment in order to evaluate the effectiveness of a program of preventive services. The implicit hypothesis was that the provision of services by YCS to adolescent girls would result in improved school performance and social behavior. The research design first involved the selection of a group of adolescent girls who could be considered as having potential problems. A high school in New York City, referred to as Vocational High, agreed to cooperate in the research. The researchers reviewed each student's prior school records for four classes entering the high school in four successive years. The records were used to detect problems that each student might have had in school or at home, and approximately one-fourth of the students were identified as having potential problems. These students were randomly assigned either to an experimental group or to a control group. As a result of randomization, 189 girls were included in the experimental group, while 192 girls were included in the control group. To assure that the randomization procedures were effective, the experimental and control groups were compared on data obtained from the school records such as socioeconomic characteristics and family background and on a battery of attitude questionnaires and personality tests. The experimental and control groups were essentially equivalent with respect to those variables.

The girls in the experimental group were referred to YCS. In general, the reason for referral was explained to the girls as an opportunity to discuss problems which high school girls usually have. The girls were not required to participate in the experiment, and 3 percent of the 189 girls in the experimental group had no service contacts with a social worker at YCS. Girls in the experimental group participated in a median number of 16 casework interviews or group counseling sessions.

The investigators chose several criteria in an attempt to operationalize dependent variables relevant to the effectiveness of the treatment program. Dependent variables included data related to school performance, delinquent behavior, attitudes, personality changes, and friendship patterns. School performance criteria included truancy, suspensions, drop outs, academic grades, and the receipt of honors and awards. Delinquent behavior included the relative incidence of out-of-wedlock pregnancy and getting into trouble with the police. Two measures of personality, the Junior Personality Quiz and the Make A Sentence Test, were used to observe changes in behavior such as shyness, aloofness, and lack of confidence. The girls' attitudes toward help, general feelings about life, and future plans were estimated through a series of questions developed by the investigators.

Comparisons were made between members of the experimental group and members of the control group on the dependent variables included in the study. Although the girls in the experimental group were less likely to be truant than the girls in the control group, there were no significant differences observed on other criteria of school performance such as grades, completion of school, and so forth. The girls in the experimental group increased in self-control and orderly behavior to a greater extent than the girls in the control group. However, the researchers concluded that there were no significant differences between the experimental and the control groups on practically all other criteria that they considered indicative of success.

QUANTITATIVE-DESCRIPTIVE STUDIES

The category of quantitative-descriptive studies includes research investigations having various purposes with respect to seeking knowledge. These purposes fall into two general classes: (1) the testing of hypotheses, and (2) the description of quantitative relations among specified variables. Hypotheses subject to testing are *either* (1a) those that posit cause-effect relationships, *or* (1b) those hypotheses that simply state the existence of a measurable relationship among two or more variables. Hypotheses that posit cause-effect relationships have been discussed in the previous section on experimental studies. An example of the second type of hypothesis is as follows: There is a significant association between the variables of "slum conditions" and of "mental illness," that is, there is likely to be *either* a greater *or* a lesser incidence of mental illness for those persons who live in slums than for those persons who do not. The hypothesis merely states the existence of an association between the two variables. It does not predict the direction of the relationship; it does not state that living in the slums is the cause of mental illness, nor does it state that mental illness causes people to live in the slums.

The second general purpose—that of describing quantitative relations among specified variables—can be subdivided into two separate objectives. The first objective (2a) is that of measuring a series of specific variables in order to answer specific questions posed by the research study. One may survey a specified population concerning its social welfare needs, which might include questions regarding family composition and size, use of day care facilities, availability of day care facilities for different ethnic and religious groups of the population, and so forth. The purpose is to describe accurately the relationship among those variables presumed to be important. The second objective (2b) is to *search* for relationships among designated variables in order to articulate more precise hypotheses for subsequent investigation. For example, a researcher may be interested in identifying the social correlates of heart disease. The investigator may not know which variables are relevant for the research, and his approach may be to specify as many variables as possible for inclusion in the study. He selects a population of patients with heart disease and a corresponding population without heart disease. He then attempts to discern the correlation among all of the social variables, such as ethnic group and family income, with heart disease in order to locate significant clues for further research. Blalock's *Social Statistics* has an excellent discussion of correlation, association, and the strength of relationship between variables (1960, pp. 225-41, pp. 273-325).

As discussed previously in relation to experimentation, studies that seek to test hypotheses concerned with cause-effect relationships ideally attempt to provide evidence regarding the time order of independent and dependent variables, the association of independent and dependent variables, and the ruling out of other factors that could be responsible for the observed relationships between the independent and dependent variables. Since experimentation may not be feasible, alternatives to experimentation may be devised in quantitative-descriptive studies. The experimental features of randomization and the manipulation of independent variables are typically not included in quantitative-descriptive studies. In such studies it is assumed that the use of various alternative devices might approximate experimentation.

Approximations to experimentation may include such devices as matching or the use of an experimental group as its "own control." To obtain experimental and control groups, the researcher might select a group exposed to the independent variable, for example, a group of children enrolled in a preschool program. He then seeks a *contrast group* of similar children who are *not* enrolled in the program. He does this by specifying the characteristics of the experimental group such as proportions of males, average age, and so on, and by seeking to *match* the children in the contrast group with those in the experimental group with respect to characteristics presumed to be relevant for the study. Another alternative might be to use an experimental group as its *own control*. The members of the experimental group are compared to themselves with respect to their performance at two different time periods. For example, the independent variable might consist of a program to increase the verbal utterances of autistic children. Prior to the program the verbal utterances of the children are described and measured in order to establish a "base rate" of speech. The program is introduced, and the rate of speech is determined for the subjects in the research; their subsequent rate of speech is compared to their base rates of speech. These and other alternatives, which are described in detail by Campbell and Stanley (1963), have a lesser degree of internal validity than do experimental studies; the reason is that quantitative-descriptive studies have a lesser degree of control over potentially relevant variables. Nevertheless, quantitative-descriptive studies, particularly in the study of natural phenomena, may be the only approaches that are possible for the investigator.

All other quantitative-descriptive studies have the essential objective of accurately describing the associations among variables, but without regard to cause-effect relationships. These studies rely on basic assumptions that are concerned primarily with the establishment of associations among variables. These assumptions involve the concepts of measurement, reliability, validity, and the refinement of statistical associations in order to estimate the extent to which an association is spurious. An underlying assumption is that the variables are operationally defined so that they can be measured. As in experimental studies, the data used as indicators of the variables are assumed to be both reliable and valid. Reliability refers to the extent to which the measurements are free from error due to chance fluctuations and biases involved in the collection of data; it refers to consistency in measurement procedures and to the reproducibility of measurements. Validity is an indication of the extent to which the measurement corresponds with the concept being measured. For example, a valid measurement of intelligence might be an I.Q. test score that corresponds with one's concept of intelligence. For an extensive discussion of the concepts of reliability and validity, the student is referred to Selltiz *et al.* (1959, pp. 154-86).

Using statistical techniques of association, an investigator may observe that two or more variables are associated. However, it is possible that the association is *spurious*. Procedures for identifying spurious associations have been elaborated by survey methodologists such as Hyman (1955) and Hirschi and Selvin (1967), and these procedures have been employed in quantitative-descriptive studies. A spurious association is one that can be explained by another variable introduced into the statistical analysis of data. For example, a survey of a population in a designated community may uncover an association between church attendance and delinquency:

those who attend church show smaller proportions of adjudicated delinquency than those who do not attend church. For the same population, it
is noted that there is also a strong association between family income and
delinquency. The investigator may use family income as an approximation
to a statistical control in a more refined analysis of the data. He may divide
his population into two subgroups of lower income and of higher income
families. Then, he discerns the association between church attendance and
delinquency for each income subgroup. If he finds that there is no significant
association between church attendance and delinquency for each income
subgroup, he might infer that the association between church attendance
and delinquency for the total population studied is *spurious* because it is
explained by family income, which occurs prior in time to church attendance.

The primary research technique used in quantitative-descriptive studies
is that of survey methods, as described by Hyman (1955) and Moser
(1958). A particular population is selected, and a sampling plan is employed in order to obtain a representative sample or samples of that population at one or more periods of time. Data-collection procedures, typically
questionnaires or scheduled interviews, are constructed, and they contain
variables considered to be relevant for the investigation. Data are collected,
tabulated, and analyzed. The primary problem for the researcher is the
extent to which he can provide evidence concerning the description of
relations among attributes of the population being studied. In order to
achieve accuracy, the investigator attempts to reduce errors due to such
sources as sampling fluctuations and interviewer bias.

In our classification system a research study must have several requisites
before it can be classified as quantitative-descriptive. The first requisite is
that *the study must not be classifiable as an experimental study.* The
second requisite is that *the study must include variables which are amenable to measurement and, hence, quantitative descriptions.* There must be
provisions for the systematic collection of data for the purpose of accurately
describing relations among variables. Thirdly, *the study must have one of
the following purposes pertaining to the seeking of knowledge: the testing
of hypotheses or the accurate description of quantitative relations among
variables selected for inclusion in the research.*

We may define quantitative-descriptive studies in the following way:

Quantitative-descriptive studies are empirical research investigations which
have as their major purpose the delineation or assessment of characteristics
of phenomena or the isolation of key variables. These studies may use formal
methods as approximations to experimental design with features of statistical
reliability and control to provide evidence for the testing of hypotheses. All
of these studies use quantitative devices for systematically collecting data

from populations, programs, or samples of populations or programs. They employ personal interviews, mailed questionnaires, and/or other rigorous data-gathering devices and survey sampling procedures.

Three subtypes of quantitative-descriptive studies are identified according to the primary purpose of the investigation. As indicated earlier, these subtypes are: (1) hypothesis-testing studies, (2) population description studies, and (3) studies that search for variable relationships. All of these subtypes must satisfy the requirements for the definition of quantitative-descriptive studies. Hypothesis-testing studies include explicit hypotheses that guide the research inquiry. Typically, the hypotheses are derived from theory. In the testing of cause-effect relationships, formal methods such as the use of contrast groups and matching procedures may be used to approximate experimental design. Investigators may use purposive sampling procedures in seeking to "test" hypotheses concerned only with the association between independent and dependent variables. For example, one community may be selected purposively due to its reported high incidence of crime. The investigator may wish to demonstrate in that community that his hypothesis pertaining to different types of gangs for different types of criminal activity is plausible.

Studies that seek to describe accurately characteristics of populations are typically geared to answering specific questions posed by the investigators. These studies usually contain the use of survey procedures, and they have the purpose of describing simple facts about selected populations, organizations, or other collectivities. These studies often employ the same procedures as do research studies, which seek to discover quantitative relations among specified variables. The primary distinction is that of the researcher's purpose. In a study that seeks quantitative relations, the investigator attempts to discover correlations among the variables he includes in the survey. These correlations are then used to form the basis of hypotheses for future research investigations. Contrary to population description studies, the researcher is not likely to use such discovered relationships to serve as answers to specific questions that may have guided the research inquiry.

Definitions and examples for each of the three subtypes of quantitative-descriptive studies are presented below.

Hypothesis-Testing Studies

Hypothesis-testing studies are those quantitative-descriptive studies which contain in their design of research explicit hypotheses to be tested. The hypotheses are typically derived from theory, and they may be either statements of cause-effect relationships or statements of association between two or more variables without reference to a causal relationship.

"Group Levels of Aspiration in United Fund Campaigns" by Zander and Newcomb (1967) is an example of a *hypothesis-testing study*. The investigators began their study by considering the general relation of a subgroup in an organization with respect to the setting of goals for the organization by that particular subgroup. Since it was believed that the goals established for United Fund community campaigns are usually established by a committee or subgroup, Zander and Newcomb regarded financial canvassing in United Fund campaigns as an example of a situation in which a subgroup in an organization could be studied. In particular, they were interested in the relationship of repeated goals and repeated performances. They employed the concept of group aspiration level, which is the goal to which a group aspires, in considering the official goals established by the United Fund. Having articulated their assumptions about the nature of goal-setting, they then derived several interrelated hypotheses for study. One major hypothesis was that "committees with more failing campaigns, compared to those with more successful campaigns (a) fix their future goals at a greater distance above past levels of performance, and (b) change the levels of their goals a smaller amount from one year to the next" (p. 158).

They obtained the basic data for their study for the years 1961 through 1964 from directories and pamphlets published yearly by the United Community Funds and Councils of America. Included in those documents were items of information such as names of communities raising funds, goals of campaigns for each community, amounts of money raised, and monies raised in previous campaigns. The investigators selected 149 communities which were of similar size, with populations which ranged between 55,000 and 140,000 people.

A successful campaign was defined as one in which the amount of funds raised were greater than or equal to the goal set by a committee in a particular community, while a failure was defined as a campaign in which the amount of funds raised was less than the desired goal. The dependent variable of "fixing goals at a greater distance above past levels of performance" was operationally defined as the *discrepancy* between prior level of performance with respect to number of dollars collected per capita and the new goal. The dependent variable of "changing the level of goals" was determined by an index that reflected the direction and amount of shifting in goals for raising funds from one year to the next.

The investigators divided the 149 communities into five different types with respect to successes and failures in annual United Fund campaigns. These types ranged on a continuum from communities with four successes and no failures to communities with no successes and four failures. The number of communities in each type ranged from 27 to 37. The discrepancies between prior level of performance and new goals were examined for each of the five types. Those communities that were successful in fund raising showed a smaller discrepancy between prior performance and the setting of new goals than communities that were not successful. In addition to this analysis, the investigators examined the relationship between successful communities and the shifting of goals. Consistently successful communities tended to shift their goals upward, and consistently failing communities tended to maintain their goals. Thus, the investigators concluded that evidence from this study was in support of their hypothesis.

Population Description Studies

Population description studies are those quantitative-descriptive studies which have as their primary function the accurate description of quantitative characteristics of selected populations, organizations, or other collectivities. These studies frequently use survey procedures. They usually employ sampling methods to claim representatives, and they contain a large number of variables. Some of these studies are descriptive of characteristics of designated populations such as roles, functions, needs, attitudes, and opinions.

"Professional Functions and Opinions of Social Group Workers" by Main and MacDonald (1962) is an example of *a population description study*. The researchers were interested in describing job activities of social group workers and their opinions concerning job assignments and professional preparation for social group work. In particular, they wanted to describe the various functions of social group workers who were employed in agencies that provided direct services to groups. Main and MacDonald chose to restrict their population to 164 group workers who were members of the Group Work Section of the Chicago Area Chapter of the National Association of Social Workers in 1960.

An interview schedule was used in an attempt to obtain spontaneous responses from the group workers to questions regarding their job responsibilities. Graduate students in social work were used as interviewers, and approximately 92 percent of the group workers participated in the study. The investigators were careful to confine their findings to a description of group workers who were members of the particular organization being studied. Several of their major findings are summarized below.

The majority of respondents were 30 years of age or older, and most of the respondents had ten years or more experience in social work. Fifty-four percent of the group workers were women, and 96 of the 151 respondents had master's degrees in social work. Approximately two-thirds of the group workers were employed in agencies that provided direct services to groups such as settlements and neighborhood centers. More than one-half of the workers employed in such agencies identified themselves as supervisors. However, there were no distinctions among administrators, supervisors, and practitioners with respect to their reported job functions of direct service, staff development and supervision, and general administration. Essentially administrators were involved in direct services, and practitioners were engaged in administrative activities. Nevertheless, as noted by the researchers, the relative amount of time actually devoted to each job function was not included in the study.

Forty-three of the 151 respondents were not involved directly in the practice of group work; they were employed in such jobs as community organization, education, research, and social casework. The majority of respondents believed that, if there were a sufficient supply of funds and of trained group workers, group workers should be used primarily in direct service activities. In addition, approximately one-third of the respondents believed that recent graduates of schools of social work should have more training concerning direct services with groups. However, the majority of respondents aspired to be administrators rather than practitioners.

Variable Relationship Studies

Studies searching for variable relationships are those quantitative-descriptive studies which are concerned with the finding of variables pertinent to an issue or situation and/or the finding of the relevant relations among variables. Usually neither *a priori* hypotheses nor specific questions are formulated to guide the research. Survey procedures may be used, and a large number of potentially relevant variables are included in such studies. Often there is an interest in seeking variables with predictive value.

"The Decision by Unmarried Mothers to Keep or Surrender Their Babies" by Meyer, Jones, and Borgatta (1956) is an example of *a study searching for variable relationships*. The investigators were interested in studying the extent to which background characteristics of unmarried mothers served by a social casework agency were associated with the decisions to keep their babies or to surrender them for adoption. In addition to locating predictive variables, Meyer *et al.* were interested in extracting factors that could uniquely summarize and describe the interrelationships of variables related to background characteristics and agency contacts.

The researchers selected a social agency that provided services to unmarried mothers, and chose all active cases of unmarried mothers who made final dispositions regarding their babies during a six-month period of time in 1954. For their initial analyses, 100 cases were obtained. Background characteristics such as age, race, financial status, and family composition were derived from the case records. The authors indicated that 40 of the unmarried mothers gave up their babies for adoption and 60 kept their babies. Sixty-two percent of the 52 white girls surrendered their babies, while only 17 percent of the 48 Negro girls gave up their babies.

The investigators noted that the group of eight Negro girls who relinquished custody of their babies was too small to permit the statistical identification of background variables which were predictive of the unmarried mothers' decisions. Their analyses of background characteristics of the white girls revealed seven variables that were predictive: religion, education, marital status of putative father, age, employment status, financial status, and socioeconomic status. Combinations of these variables were tried out, and it was discovered that a white girl with two or more of the following characteristics was likely to surrender her baby: non-Catholic, attended college, putative father is single, and the mother is under age 18. Using these items, the researchers classified 83 percent of the cases accurately.

Meyer *et al.* applied the same predictive test to another sample of 175 closed cases for which decisions were recorded for the years 1952 and 1953 and for several new cases in 1954. They achieved 77 percent accuracy in predicting the decisions of white mothers. Simply predicting that all of the Negro mothers would keep their babies, the investigators classified 84 percent of the cases correctly.

Utilizing all of the 223 cases at their disposal, the investigators explored the interrelationships of 28 variables, of which 19 were used in a factor analysis. Factor analysis is a statistical technique that allows for the identification of a smaller number of factors which could account for the interrelationships of most of the variables used in the analysis. Five factors were extracted in the factor analysis, and it was believed that these factors constituted distinctions that were descriptive of the agency's caseload. Only two of the factors were related to the decision to surrender babies. These factors were identified as social class and casework ratings of the unmarried mother's appropriate handling of the social situation regarding her decision. The analysis also indicated that the factor of social class was that single factor that showed the strongest association with the decisions of unmarried mothers. Thus, the following hypothesis was suggested: "the higher the social class, the more likely the girl is to surrender the baby" (p. 108).

EXPLORATORY STUDIES

Exploratory studies have the major purpose of developing ideas and hypotheses. These studies are less definable than experimental and quantitative-descriptive studies, which include procedures to provide evidence for the association of variables and for the verification of hypotheses. Essentially, exploratory studies are based on the assumption that through the use of relatively systematic procedures relevant hypotheses pertaining to a particular phenomenon can be developed. In addition, it is assumed that measurement devices can be developed, and the feasibility of experimentation and approximations to experimentation can be assessed.

The logical strategy of exploratory studies consists of providing a framework that may facilitate the process of deriving pertinent questions in the investigation of a phenomenon. The process of discovery is not articulated sufficiently for a researcher to follow a prescribed set of rules; indeed, such a creative process does not necessarily follow orderly rules of logic. Nevertheless, research methodologists have described several guidelines for structuring investigations in such a way that the likelihood of discovery may be enhanced. These guidelines are usually applied to three general categories: *sources of information, types of data,* and *the use of data.* Sources of information include reviews of the published literature, "the experience survey" which involves the interviewing of those people who are closest to or are reputed to be knowledgeable about the particular area of inquiry (Selltiz *et al.,* 1963, pp. 53-59), and the location of available records (Webb, Campbell, Schwartz, and Sechrest, 1966, pp. 53-111).

Types of data included in exploratory studies may be both quantitative and qualitative. In addition to the use of quantitative data, much emphasis is also devoted to the methods of accumulating such qualitative data as narrative information from unstructured interviews and from the researcher's observations. In particular, the method of participant observation has been a primary tool for anthropologists and sociologists who have studied various types of communities and subcultures (*see* Riley, 1963, pp. 68-75, for a discussion of the advantages and limitations of participant observation). The investigator lives in the community, and he interviews and observes people in a variety of social situations. In such studies, a great volume of data may be collected over a period of time for very few behavior units. By unit we are referring to the intended target of inquiry, which may be individuals, groups, organizations, or communities.

Regarding the use of data in exploratory studies, guidelines have primarily involved the researcher's proper attitude and suggested procedures for categorizing and analyzing large amounts of quantitative and qualitative data. Katz (1953) indicates that in exploratory studies of a community the investigator should delimit his area of inquiry with respect to what he is to observe. This may be done through the investigator's previous hunches or theoretical notions. In addition, Katz notes that the researcher should be receptive to new information and be flexible in the use of his research procedures. He also suggests some relatively systematic procedures concerning the interviewing of community leaders and other key informants. The interviewer seeks out leaders who are presumed to view the community differently. Having interviewed one leader, he then seeks to make comparisons with another leader. He continues the process of comparing responses of a number of leaders until no more ideas are manifest. The notion is that the investigator seeks discrepancies and divergent opinions in order to stimulate his conceptualizing of the phenomenon.

A problem for researchers in exploratory studies is information overload. The investigator may not be able to assimilate large volumes of qualitative data; hence, he inevitably needs to resort to some device to categorize or code the data into manageable chunks of information. Content analysis (Berlson, 1954, pp. 488-522) provides a set of rules for casting narrative data into manageable categories amenable to quantitative descriptions. The assumption in such a procedure for exploratory studies is that the process of forming categories and of subsequently using them for quantitative descriptions will eventuate in researchable hypotheses. A more recent device is the "constant comparative method of qualitative analysis" of Glaser and Strauss (1967, pp. 101-15). They principally describe steps in a process that is assumed to lead to the development of theoretical ideas. Their chief idea is alerting the researcher to making a continuous comparison of similarities and differences among incidents that are assigned to a set of categories. For example, categories of various group behaviors might be tentatively designated by the researcher, and he might make comparisons of three-minute group discussions, which are regarded as incidents to be categorized. Each incident is compared with every other incident, and impressions of similarities and differences are noted. In addition, new categories are formed as necessary to classify the incidents. As many categories as possible are devised. Comparisons are made continuously among categories until there is theoretical saturation, that is, no new categories can be formed. The researcher then stops categorizing and writes down his ideas; from these impressions he derives hypotheses for further testing.

Another device for developing ideas is clinical studies or demonstration programs. For example, the investigator may identify a relatively new treatment technique, which he believes would be useful in practice, but he may be unclear about the consequences of such a technique. He may devise an exploratory study to determine the potentialities of his technique. In order to do this, he manipulates the independent variable in a field setting, and he observes the effects of the technique on the participants in the research. His purposes are to determine the feasibility of implementing the technique, to clarify the independent variable, and to locate possible dependent variables to be used in subsequent experimentation.

In essence, exploratory studies have the primary goal of developing, clarifying, and modifying concepts and ideas in order to provide researchable hypotheses for further study. This primary goal can be subdivided into three subordinate purposes:

> 1. The relatively detailed quantitative and qualitative description of a particular phenomenon.
> 2. The development of ideas through the systematic use of a specific data-collection procedure.

3. The systematic observation of the potential effects of an independent variable as it is manipulated for a small number of behavioral units in clinical and/or demonstration studies.

In our classification system a research study should have several requisites before it can be classified as exploratory. *It should not be classifiable as either an experimental or a quantitative-descriptive study.* However, there is one exception to this. *Searching for variable relationship studies* has the primary purpose of specifying hypotheses and locating associations among variables, which is a goal of exploration; such studies exclusively use quantitative procedures for describing quantitative relationships among variables. Nevertheless, many studies combine quantitative descriptions with qualitative descriptions in seeking to describe a phenomenon, and our subtype of *combined exploratory-descriptive studies* was created to include those studies. The subtype, therefore, includes aspects of both exploratory and quantitative-descriptive studies.

A second requisite for exploratory studies is that *relatively systematic procedures for obtaining empirical observations and/or for the analyses of data should be used.* However, the data may not be systematically analyzed in the form of quantitative descriptions. For example, Lewis' exploratory study of a poor family in Mexico City involved systematic tape-recorded interviews of each member in a Mexican family (1961); the descriptions, however, were in narrative form.

A third requisite for exploratory studies is that *the investigator should go beyond the qualitative and/or quantitative descriptions by attempting to conceptualize the interrelations among the phenomena observed.* This means that the investigator should attempt to construe his observations into some theoretical or hypothetical framework.

We offer the following definition of exploratory studies:

Exploratory studies are empirical research investigations which have as their purpose the formulation of a problem or questions, developing hypotheses, or increasing an investigator's familiarity with a phenomenon or setting for more precise future research. The intent to clarify or modify concepts may also be predominant. Relatively systematic procedures for obtaining empirical observations and/or for the analyses of data may be used. Both quantitative and qualitative descriptions of the phenomenon are often provided, and the investigator typically conceptualizes the interrelations among properties of the phenomenon being observed. A variety of data collection procedures may be employed in the relatively intensive study of a small number of behavior units. Methods which are employed include such procedures as interviewing, participant observation, and content analysis. Representative sampling procedures are typically not used. In some studies, there is a manipulation of an independent variable in order to locate its potential effects.

We have identified three subtypes of exploratory studies. These are (1) studies which combine features of exploration and description, (2) studies which use specific data-collection devices in searching for ideas, and (3) studies which involve the manipulation of independent variables in demonstrating the feasibility of practical techniques or programs. Combined exploratory-descriptive studies employ both quantitative and qualitative descriptions of a particular phenomenon. Studies that use specific data-collection procedures do not necessarily contain quantitative descriptions. They attempt to summarize qualitative data through abstractions in the form of categories in order to consider possible relationships for more accurate description in further research. The distinguishing feature of an exploratory study which manipulates independent variables is its experimental character. This type of study is different from experiments in that procedures to control for extraneous variables are usually not included. In addition, there may be only one unit for study as opposed to experiments, which must include many units for proper analyses.

Definitions and examples for each of the three subtypes of exploratory studies are presented below.

Combined Exploratory-Descriptive Studies

Combined exploratory-descriptive studies are those exploratory studies which seek to describe a particular phenomenon thoroughly. The concern may be with one behavioral unit, as in a case study, for which both empirical and theoretical analyses are made. The purpose of these studies is to develop ideas and theoretical generalizations. Descriptions are in both quantitative and qualitative form, and the accumulation of detailed information by such means as participant observation may be found. Sampling procedures are flexible, and little concern is usually given to systematic representativeness.

"Solidarity and Delinquency in a Street Corner Group" by Leon Jansyn, Jr. (1966) is an example of a *combined exploratory-descriptive study*. In his review of the literature on gang delinquency, Jansyn concluded that existing theories did not sufficiently explain the internal dynamics of gangs. Accordingly, he wished to "illuminate some of the ways in which variations in group activity are related to internal processes of the group and variations in group structure over time" (p. 600). His investigation involved the observation of one delinquent group for approximately two years. The group consisted predominantly of adolescent boys, and it was identified by community residents as the Dons. The Dons resided in a working-class neighborhood with a high rate of official delinquency.

The investigator used the method of participant observation to gather the data for his study. He lived in the Dons' neighborhood, and he associated with the group in his official capacity as a "detached worker." After he had associated with the group for three months, he began to record data systematically. The data consisted of attendance records for each member of the group and written daily accounts of the group's activities. Observations and attendance data were systematically recorded for approximately 150 days during a year, and the locations for observations were gathering places for the group members: a particular street corner, two restaurants, and a recreational agency.

Having defined attendance as the appearance of any member of the group during a daily three-hour period of observation, the investigator computed average attendance figures for the group members for a period of one year. In addition to attendance records for the entire group, which was comprised of 28 to 60 members during the year, Jansyn provided records for subtypes within the group. Based on his daily observations of group activity, he identified nine boys as core members; the remaining members were regarded as fringe members. A core member was defined as a group member who influenced other group members in their activities. Quantitative data on attendance indicated that core members attended meetings more often than the fringe members.

Jansyn observed that the group went through different phases of organization during the year. The two predominant activities of the group were fighting other gangs and club-type activities. Two identified leaders were influential with respect to each of these activities, and conflict emerged when there was dissension over the priority of delinquent or club activities. Conflict among the two leaders and their respective followers led to relative disorganization in the group. Concomitant with this reduction in group solidarity was an increased influence of lower-status members on the group. Jansyn noted that attendance records paralleled his observations of group organization; attendance was less when the group appeared to be relatively disorganized, and attendance increased as organization increased. After disorganization occurred, there was a change of meeting places and increased activity among the group members. The gang became involved in restructuring itself and in forming a closer network of interrelationships among the members, which resulted in increased group solidarity. As a result of the investigator's conceptual analysis of his data, he formulated a tentative hypothesis: "In corner groups, deterioration of group solidarity is followed by an increase of group activity and a revival of solidarity" (p. 601).

Studies Using Specific Data-Collection Procedures

Studies which use specific data-collection procedures for developing ideas are those exploratory studies which exclusively use one specific procedure for extracting generalizations. Such procedures may include content analysis and the critical incident technique. The purpose of these studies is to produce conceptual categories which can be operationalized for subsequent research; it is not to report accurate quantitative descriptions among variables.

"Some Concepts about Therapeutic Interventions with Hyperaggressive Children: Parts I and II" by Goodrich and Boomer (1958a and b) is an example of *an exploratory study which uses specific data-collection procedures for developing ideas.* The setting in which the research took place was at the Child Research Branch of the National Institute of Mental Health. Residential treatment of hyperaggressive children was the focus of interest for the investigators. A therapeutic program, which included 24 staff persons, was devised to treat chronically disturbed boys who were nine or ten years old. Staff persons were comprised of psychiatrists, teachers, social workers, and child-care workers.

The investigators assumed that long-term residential treatment by skilled staff members would produce behavioral changes in the disturbed children; yet they observed that there was no useful system of concepts that could be used for testing hypotheses relevant to residential treatment. They wished to derive concepts that could be useful for clinicians: principles of effective therapeutic intervention with hyperaggressive children. In order to develop such principles they decided to use Flanagan's critical incident technique (1954), which is a method devised to derive generalizations by inductively abstracting them from specific events.

The procedure involved the definition of a critical incident and the specification of a series of critical incidents by observers. Staff members of the residential treatment program were regarded as observers, and each staff member was interviewed periodically by the researchers over a time span of three months. In the interview each person was asked to describe "an actual incident involving a child and an adult (himself or another) in which the adult *did* something which the respondent felt was either good or bad for the child, in terms of the over-all goals of residential treatment" (p. 210). Thus, the critical incident was the respondent's recall of a specific attempt by an adult to deal with the child's behavior. The observers were asked to describe the behaviors of both the child and the adult for each critical incident. In addition, each respondent was asked to generalize a principle of intervention that he believed was illustrated by the critical incident. In this way, 240 critical incidents were collected from 130 interviews with the 24 staff members.

Having obtained the "critical incidents," the investigators then set out to classify them. They first discussed similarities and differences among the incidents; then they tentatively assigned sets of incidents with common themes to categories that they created. The incidents were sorted and reclassified into three levels of abstraction: specific behaviors of adults, concepts about therapeutic intervention, and concepts about "effective therapeutic intervention." Their final classification contained 31 principles of therapeutic intervention, which were grouped under four categories: *promoting personality change by helping child to learn to view his own behavior evaluatively, promoting ego growth, supporting existing ego controls, and managing one's own conduct as a staff person* (pp. 211, 212, 286, and 289). Two illustrative principles are as follows (p. 212):

> 1. Therapist welcomes and encourages instances of positive or affectionate relatedness.
> 2. Therapist fosters rapport with the child by responding to his manifest interests.

The investigators concluded their research by pointing out that they did not know whether the 31 principles they derived were actually effective. In essence, the "principles" formed a basis for the delineation of researchable hypotheses pertaining to therapeutic interventions with hyperaggressive children.

Experimental Manipulation Studies

Experimental manipulation studies are those exploratory studies which manipulate an independent variable in order to locate dependent variables which are potentially associated with the independent variable. Typically, one behavioral unit is studied in its natural environment. Often the purpose of these studies is to demonstrate the feasibility of a particular technique or program as a potential solution to practical problems. A variety of data-collection procedures may be employed, and observational techniques may be developed during the course of the research.

"Intensive Treatment of Psychotic Behaviour by Stimulus Satiation and Food Reinforcement" by T. Ayllon (1963) is an example of *an exploratory study which includes the manipulation of an independent variable.* The investigator was interested in demonstrating that behaviors of patients could be modified by using techniques derived from theories of learning. The study took place in a female ward in a mental hospital. The subject for research was a 47-year-old female patient who was diagnosed as a chronic schizophrenic. The patient stole food, hoarded towels in her room, and wore an excessive amount of clothing. Her behavior was regarded as undesirable, and attempts by the staff to change her behavior were unsuccessful.

The researcher attempted to demonstrate that the patient's behavior could be modified by the experimental control of relevant variables. To control the patient's stealing of food, the investigator employed several procedures. First, the extent of food stealing was determined by having the ward personnel observe and record the patient's behavior on the ward for one month. It was determined that the patient ate all of her regular meals and in addition stole food from other patients and from a food counter during two-thirds of her meals. She weighed over 250 pounds, and the medical staff indicated that her excessive weight was detrimental to her health. Attempts to persuade or coerce the patient to eat less food were unsuccessful. Ayllon employed a principle derived from learning theory: "the strength of a response may be weakened by the removal of positive reinforcement following the response" (p. 55). The response was considered to be food stealing, and the reinforcer was regarded as the patient's access to meals. Ayllon used a procedure that resulted in the withdrawal of a meal whenever the patient picked up unauthorized food or approached a dining room table different from her own. The patient was allowed only to eat alone at one dining room table. This procedure was applied systematically, and her food stealing was eliminated in two weeks. The patient's new response of not stealing food was virtually maintained for one year after the treatment, and her weight was reduced to 180 pounds.

Ayllon also used the withdrawal of food as a reinforcer to eliminate the patient's behavior of wearing excessive clothing. To change her behavior of hoarding towels, the researcher used "stimulus satiation," which involved giving the patient an overabundant supply of towels. After the patient accumulated 625 towels over approximately a three-month period of time, she began to discard the towels until she virtually had none. She reduced the number of towels she kept in her room from the 19 to 29 towels per week prior to the experimental manipulation to approximately two towels per week after the experimental manipulation.

Ayllon recorded data on the frequency of occurrence of the patient's behaviors, and he carefully maintained control over the patient's environment. The patient's undesirable behavior was reduced, and the researcher attempted to determine whether other pathological behavior patterns would develop. The patient was observed by staff members every 30 minutes during a 16-hour time span for each observation day. A selected number of observation days were specified for a period of one year. When the patient's environment was first manipulated, emotional responses of crying and shouting were observed. The researcher reported that these responses were quickly eliminated when the staff members ignored them. The observations were analyzed in gross behavioral categories which were developed for the study: violent, seclusive, socially accessible, and so on. The investigator concluded that the patient did not become less well adjusted on the ward and that the behavioral techniques that he employed were potentially useful.

SUMMARY OF CLASSIFICATION SYSTEM

In the preceding portions of this chapter we have presented our classification scheme for categorizing research studies. The categories for classification were defined and described in detail in an attempt to familiarize the student with each of the major categories and subtypes of research. In order to summarize the types and subtypes which have been defined, an outline of the classification system along with page references to definitions is presented below.

HOW TO USE THE CLASSIFICATION SYSTEM

A research study may have many objectives, and it may include a variety of methods to accomplish those objectives. Such a study may not be categorized easily by our classification system, or by any classification scheme, because it may be classifiable into more than one subtype of research. In fact, every research study may not be amenable to a unique classification within our system. For example, a survey of a particular population may include features of both population description and searching for variable relationships; a field experiment may also include a description of the characteristics of a specific population. In our review of the literature we devised two procedures in an attempt to overcome this basic problem. One procedure was to create a subtype—combined exploratory-descriptive studies—to accommodate the appearance of studies in the literature that included overlapping categories of exploration and description. A second device was to view a research investigation with respect to its major purpose, which is identified as that purpose to which more than 50 percent of the content of the published research is devoted. In the event that an investigation has two distinct but equal purposes, our solution would be to categorize the study into more than one subtype. However, in our use of the classification system we found that all of the studies we reviewed could be uniquely assigned to one of the subtypes.

A potential problem for users of the classification system is that if they see labels similar to the subtypes in a particular study, they might assume that such labels have the same meaning as intended in this chapter. In our own experience we have found that labels are used inconsistently by different investigators; thus, for classification purposes it is more efficient to ignore the labels presented in research studies. An investigator, for example, might say his study is experimental; but we would not classify the study on that statement alone. Essentially, we would determine whether or not the study had the requisites for an experimental study before classifying it as one.

Before using this classification scheme, the research reader should become thoroughly familiar with the typology by following these steps:

1. Read the chapter carefully. Pay particular attention to the definitions of the categories and subtypes.
2. Study the examples included in the chapter for each subtype.
3. Attempt to define each subtype in your own words; if necessary, elaborate the definitions to suit your own purposes for classification.

Having followed these steps, the research reader should be prepared to classify published research studies.

To facilitate efforts at classification, the following general guidelines are suggested for classifying any particular research study:

1. First read the article quickly in order to obtain an overview of the research study. Then read the study carefully, paying particular attention to the objectives of the study and the methods employed to accomplish such objectives. It is important to note that objectives may be included throughout the presentation of the study, as well as in sections devoted to problem formulation and to the conclusions of the research.
2. List the explicit and implicit objectives of the study, and arrange the objectives into a hierarchy of importance for the investigation. *Hierarchy of importance* refers to a rank ordering of objectives in terms of what was done in the research. If most of the study is devoted to describing a particular population, then that may be the most "important" objective.
3. List the specific research methods and procedures that were used in the study, and determine which procedures were used to accomplish each objective listed above.
4. Determine the major purpose(s) and the minor objectives of the study.
5. If the author classifies his study, ignore it. Look for the necessary ingredients for classification as discussed in this chapter.
6. In order to classify the study, begin with the most explicitly defined category, experimental studies. Determine whether or not the study can be classified as experimental. If the study is experimental, then decide whether it should be categorized as a field experiment or as a laboratory experiment.

7. If the study is not experimental, determine whether it can be categorized as a quantitative-descriptive study. If the study is quantitative-descriptive, decide to which one of the three subtypes the study could be assigned. The study would be categorized by that subtype which is most representative of the research.

8. If the study is not quantitative-descriptive, determine whether or not it can be regarded as an exploratory study. If the study is exploratory, decide on its appropriate subtype.

9. After the study is classified, review the specific classification to determine if it is in accordance with criteria outlined in this chapter.

10. Have another research reader classify the same study. If classifications are different, discuss the reasons for classification in an attempt to achieve consensus.

Chapter 3

Evaluation of Research: Principles and Guidelines

In this chapter we develop principles and guidelines for evaluating experimental, quantitative-descriptive, and exploratory research studies. The work in Chapter 2 on classification of research studies provides a foundation for the specification of evaluation guidelines for different levels of scientific inquiry. In the development of guidelines, we emphasize the fruitfulness of evaluating research studies in terms of the research methods employed and the form of knowledge sought. Accordingly, attention is directed to the procedures used in securing knowledge and to factors that influence the degree of relative certainty of the knowledge produced.

In developing guidelines, evaluation is defined as a systematic assessment of the methodological qualities of each aspect of an empirical research investigation, that is, problem formulation, research design and data collection, and data analysis and conclusions. Evaluation of research studies is to be distinguished from evaluative research, a term that usually refers to studies concerned with understanding the effects of a specific program or method of helping (French, 1953). Different types of evaluations of research studies can be found in the literature: essay reviews of single studies, journal articles that review a series of research studies concerned with the same substantive area, and monographic reviews of research. The first type is illustrated by MacDonald's (1966) essay review of the Meyer *et al.* study of *Girls at Vocational High*; the second type is illustrated by Tripodi and Miller's (1966) review of studies of clinical judgment; the third type is illustrated by Maas' (1966) monograph, *Five Fields of Social Service: Reviews of Research.*

While published evaluations of these types are invaluable to the student and the social practitioner who want to benefit from research, the actual evaluation of particular research studies constitutes an important activity for understanding given phenomena, for assimilating new knowledge into frameworks of previously obtained knowledge, and for utilizing research procedures and knowledge in further research. For the social practitioner, an additional purpose of evaluation is likely to be the utilization of knowledge for change purposes, that is, interpersonal change, organizational change, community change, and societal change.

For all these purposes, an important concern of the research reader is with ascertaining the degree to which an investigator has reduced uncertainty in regard to the phenomenon studied. Because of the difficulty of obtaining knowledge of all the variables operating in relation to a given phenomenon, it is never possible to accumulate sufficient evidence to attain absolute certainty, that is, truth. However, for hypothesis-testing studies, the relative degree of certainty of knowledge is estimated within the frameworks of internal and external validity and predictions are expressed in terms of probabilities. As Eaton (1958) notes in his excellent discussion, "Science, 'Art,' and Uncertainty in Social Work," hypotheses in science are accepted or rejected in terms of approximate certainty, and the concept of relative validity is utilized rather than the concept of absolute truth. As we have pointed out in Chapter 2, the experimental study is the principal approach for improving prediction through reduction of threats to validity. Quantitative-descriptive studies, which seek to test hypotheses, may also be assessed in terms of the relative certainty of the knowledge produced, for example, by examining ways such as randomization procedures in which an investigator attempts to increase validity of his results. In quantitative-descriptive studies designed to describe quantitative relations among variables, such as surveys describing facts about selected populations, the concepts of validity and reliability may be employed to assess the accuracy of the knowledge produced. For exploratory studies the focus of evaluation is also on the potential of such studies for reducing uncertainty. The major contribution to knowledge from exploratory studies is, however, in providing ideas and sharpening insights useful for developing hypotheses that can be investigated in future research studies. As a result, the modification, clarification, and development of concepts, hypotheses, and measurement procedures all serve as a foundation for improving the certainty of knowledge to be produced by further research endeavors.

By engaging in the differential assessment of different types of research studies, the research reader can increase the potential forms and content of knowledge considered useful for social work practice. Knowledge gained from exploratory studies will not be evaluated in terms of criteria appropriate only to studies that test hypotheses, and the unique contributions of such studies will become highlighted for the social practitioner. Increased recognition is thus given to the entire range of knowledge that can be produced through scientific inquiry, and to the range of methods that can be employed to clarify and measure concepts, develop hypotheses, produce descriptive findings, test hypotheses, produce empirical generalizations, and to develop and test theoretical frameworks and scientific theory.

GUIDELINES FOR EVALUATION: AN OVERVIEW

In our review of the literature we found no work that provides a set of guidelines focused on major aspects of the research process differentiated by both purposes and methods of research. We have undertaken the task of developing such guidelines, since our construction of a typology for classifying research indicates significant differences as well as similarities in the nature of experimental, quantitative-descriptive, and exploratory research studies. Differential assessment is necessary to achieve maximum utilization of research knowledge, particularly in the case of the social practitioner who must act on the basis of knowledge available at a given point in time.

The literature we reviewed is rich with materials directly and indirectly bearing on evaluation frameworks, and we have utilized a range of sources in the development of evaluation guidelines. Such sources include general frameworks for evaluation, such as one provided in *Social Casework* by Goldstein (1962), in which general criteria are presented as a guide for practitioners in evaluating research studies for the purpose of understanding and using research findings. Another example of a general framework comes from the work of Knop (1967) in *The American Sociologist*. Knop identifies key conceptual and procedural questions, which the student can use to evaluate sociological journal articles that present empirical research. These frameworks, as well as others by Caplow (1958), Anderson (1954), MacDonald (1959), Finestone (1959), and Fischer in Grinnell (1981), have in common an emphasis on the research process. The guidelines begin with the conceptualization and formulation of the problem of research, followed by the research design appropriate to the problem and the types of data collected and analyzed in accordance with the goals of the study. They conclude with an assessment of the conclusions and implications of the findings.

For the most part, general frameworks appear to be skeletal, to assume considerable knowledge of research terminology, and to assume a sequential nature of the research process from conceptualization to conclusion. These frameworks also assume that the research reader can adapt the general guidelines to specific studies. They are limited from our viewpoint because they tend to assume an ideal model of research and explicitly or implicitly deal with the evaluation only of research concerned with hypothesis testing (Knop, 1967). They imply a hierarchy of research from the prescientific phase to the scientific phase of experimentation (Lundberg, 1942). Accordingly, the tendency might be for the reader to attribute greater significance to an experimental study than to a survey study or an exploratory study, without assessing the strengths and weaknesses of each type of study in the context of its purposes. While general frameworks can be used to some extent for evaluating all types of research strategies, it is a major defect that they do not specifically deal with questions concerning the evaluation of exploratory studies or quantitative-descriptive studies other than those whose purpose is to test hypotheses. No recognition is given to the fact that standards vary according to research purposes and methods, and that compromises occur in most research endeavors. Nevertheless, these general evaluation frameworks have been useful to the development of our guidelines because they focus on the evaluation of a study as a whole piece of research, and they are presented in the form of questions for the evaluation of research studies.

In addition, by stressing phases of the research process, the frameworks are closely related to the materials presented in most standard research texts on methodology. Such texts provide a handy reference to the evaluator of research studies, as they typically cover a range of relevant information on such topics as: formulating the research problem, hypotheses, concepts, operational definitions, problems of measurement, sampling, observational methods, scaling, statistical inference, and inferring causal relations (Selltiz *et al.*, 1959).

We have drawn on these general frameworks and on selected research texts in formulating our major categories of questions for evaluation of research studies. The organization of our guidelines differs from more general frameworks in our reduction of categories of questions to three: Problem Formulation, Research Design and Data Collection, and Data Analysis and Conclusions. An understanding of the essential elements of the research process can be grasped within these three categories and a limited number of major areas facilitates evaluation. But these categories are applied differentially to the types of research distinguished by purpose and method.

The major differences between the three major research approaches are detailed in Chapter 2. The literature used to develop the classification system was helpful as well in the construction of questions for evaluation. From this source, a few selected books contained the most pertinent concepts and information regarding the designated research approaches. Thus, for the evaluation of experimental research studies we relied heavily on the work of Campbell and Stanley (1963), which is concerned with the basic concepts of external validity and internal validity and sources of variation, which should be controlled in experimentation (*see* Chapter 2). Ideally, experiments attempt to maximize both internal and external validity, but because of practical, ethical, or other constraints, such an ideal is usually not attainable. For example, in order to increase internal validity an investigator may restrict the range of the population to which he wishes to generalize, and consequently reduce external validity. On the other hand, in quasi-experimental designs, such as studies concerned with quantitative-descriptive hypothesis testing, the investigator may take means to insure representative sampling, with a broader population which increases external validity, perhaps at the expense of internal validity. He may use compromise, "after-the-fact," statistical manipulations in order to approximate control over other relevant variables thought to be responsible for the obtained relations between the independent and dependent variables. Campbell and Stanley review a number of factors that serve to jeopardize *internal validity*, such as history, maturation, and testing; and those affecting *external validity*, such as sample bias, interaction effects of testing, and reactive effects of experimental arrangements. These factors are used to view the validity of a number of experimental designs, and they provide a useful reference for the research reader in his evaluation of the findings produced through various experimental and quasi-experimental arrangements.

Another useful reference for the evaluator of experimental research is the work of Herzog (1959), *Some Guidelines for Evaluative Research.* Although Herzog's purpose is not to develop guidelines for research readers, her questions with regard to studies that attempt to evaluate change techniques in practice can be used as indirect guidelines for evaluating research studies of this type. By considering some "do's and don'ts" of research concerned with evaluating change, Herzog provides a good, general point of view for evaluating field experiments and quantitative-descriptive field studies. Her work is clearly written and particularly useful for individuals with limited sophistication in research, covering important research concepts such as reliability, validity, and sampling with particular reference to evaluative studies. Along these lines, the work of Suchman (1967) is also useful, as he considers strengths and weaknesses of various designs used in evaluative research. He rejects the notion that there is such a thing as one "correct" design for experimental research.

The works of Campbell and Stanley (1963), Herzog (1959), and Suchman (1967) are helpful in isolating areas of attention for evaluation of research studies devoted to hypothesis testing, particularly through experimental designs but also for quantitative-descriptive studies devoted to hypothesis testing. In regard to other studies designated as quantitative-descriptive, works such as those of Hirschi and Selvin (1967), Zetterberg (1954), and Blalock (1961) contribute to the development of evaluation guidelines. Hirschi and Selvin are concerned with making inferences from delinquency research based on survey data. Their work focuses mainly on the analysis phase of research studies, noting how investigators have presented and analyzed their data from a logical and statistical point of view. Hirschi and Selvin examine the findings of a number of studies in the delinquency area and discuss approximations to control through statistical manipulations of data and other problems of inference connected with quantitative-descriptive studies. In particular, they use schemes to try to uncover spurious relations and to refine or confirm relations among variables in cross-section studies in which variables are collected concurrently. Such considerations lead to significant questions to be asked by the evaluator in the attempt to find out what the research investigators are trying to do; to identify strengths and limitations of such procedures as sampling, measurement, and the manipulation of data; and to weigh the limitations in terms of the meaningfulness of the data and the probability that research will not be perfect. Of considerable merit is their view that critics of research must stress objectivity, vigilance, and sympathy in viewing the works of investigators in order to learn the most and benefit from the effort of evaluating research. The approach of Hirschi and Selvin is derivative from the tradition of the Columbia University Bureau of Applied Social Research. Other works in the same tradition are those of Lazarsfeld (1955), Kendall (1959), and Hyman (1955), which are also useful references for evaluating quantitative-descriptive studies.

For the third major category of research studies—that of exploratory studies—the work of Riley (1963) is especially useful. Riley is concerned with most types of research, but she makes exceptionally acute commentaries on descriptive case studies and field studies, which our classification would label exploratory. A range of studies is offered to provide examples for specific topics of research, such as measurement, use of available data, collection of data, and seeking relationships between variables. The studies that are reproduced are not discussed in terms of all aspects of the research process, but commentaries concentrate on a single topic for each study. While this approach contrasts with ours, in that we are interested in evaluating total studies, the work of Riley is instructive for the development of guideline questions. Particularly helpful are her considerations of the advantages and disadvantages of studies not having the objective of testing hypotheses, but rather of developing conceptual systems and elaborating observations—studies we would regard as exploratory studies. Thus, Riley examines Malinowski's (1926) study of *Crime and Custom in a Savage*

Society, and Whyte's (1943) *Street Corner Society,* both identified as case studies with exploratory objectives. These studies seek to locate and describe relevant variables and to suggest how they are related to each other. Concepts are not explicitly defined or measured in a systematic way, and the data are collected by means of participant observation. Riley notes that this approach has the advantage of providing a wide range of detail, with the opportunity to uncover latent patterns of behavior, and to view behaviors in a whole rather than in a fragmented way. On the other hand, limitations to this type of study are likely to come from the researcher's taking a role in the group under investigation, from the lack of reliability connected with the collection of descriptive data, and from limits to generalizing from the use of a single case. Significant for the development of our evaluation guidelines is the clear distinction between exploratory studies and other types of research based on systematic measurement. The use of actual studies to indicate the benefits of knowledge produced through exploratory studies, and the discussion of ways in which the methods utilized can be strengthened to reduce study limitations, are also contributions. In sum, Riley's perceptive treatment suggests that in evaluating exploratory studies we should be concerned with efforts to minimize bias in the collection of data, to benefit from previous work and literature related to the problem of investigation (Selltiz *et al.,* 1959), and to interpret findings within the context of the purpose and methods of the research.

GENERAL PERSPECTIVE ON EVALUATION

We have already noted our view that different standards should be used for different levels of scientific inquiry. In our general perspective, a central concept is the relative certainty of knowledge, and the confidence an evaluator of research can place in the generalizations derived from empirical research. Scientific knowledge is based on cumulative, replicative studies, and in the social sciences and social work, it is highly unlikely that any one study will resolve all pertinent questions about a single phenomenon. Based on the level and nature of knowledge that exists at any given time about a phenomenon, one research approach may be selected over another as the most appropriate method for investigating a research problem.

A number of general problems face the evaluator of studies presented in journal articles. In the first place, the article may not contain sufficient information and detail to allow for a meaningful evaluation. Several factors may influence the amount and kind of information available to the reader. In some cases, the author or the journal editor may exclude from the presentation certain kinds of information, such as key tables. In other cases, limits imposed by journals on the number of pages allowed per article may reduce the amount of information about research design necessary for evaluation. It is especially crucial for our evaluation system that sufficient information be presented to allow for classification of the research by purpose and method.

The information problem for evaluation concerns, in part, the type and extent of documentation given in a research report, that is, the degree to which the reader is provided with appropriate sources and references for further information. In research studies based on data collected by questionnaire or interview schedule, examples of questions may be offered by the author, but generally all data-collection instruments are not included. However, the author should indicate where the interested reader can obtain more detail about the instruments. Another example involves the documentation given to sampling procedures, with footnotes indicating where the reader can obtain full details. In all cases, sufficient information for understanding the major objectives of the study, the methods employed to reach the objectives, and the use of data in forming conclusions, should be included in the written report. The importance of accurate and adequate documentation comes from the emphasis in scientific inquiry on the accumulation of knowledge. The possibility of replication of research studies demands information or access to information necessary for such study. And the adequacy of a research report in this respect affects the adequacy of the report for evaluation by a research reader.

Not all research studies published in social work and social science journals will be clearly written. To the extent to which the written presentation is not systematic, clear, and internally consistent, it will be difficult for the reader to classify and evaluate the research study. For example, the purposes of the study are presented in a number of places throughout some articles, sometimes elaborating earlier statements and at other times contradicting them. The expectation of clarity in written materials does not imply that research terminology should be absent, but that it be used accurately, consistently, and clearly. The reader cannot expect to understand research studies without knowing the commonly accepted concepts pertaining to the research process as well as the terminology of the substantive area which the research investigates.

The classification and evaluation of research studies presumes a minimum level of sophistication in research methodology. In addition, the greater the degree of substantive knowledge of the area under investigation possessed by the research reader, the greater the potential for assessing the research study. In some substantive areas reviews of research are available, such as Levinger's (1960) review of findings concerning continuance in treatment. These reviews provide a foundation for the evaluator but usually must be updated. In other cases, the evaluator will need to provide his own review of the literature. The reader who is familiar with previous works in a particular substantive area is in a position to evaluate a study on its own merits from a methodological point of view and place it in the context of currently available knowledge. Familiarity with previous studies also allows the reader to assess the appropriateness of the methodology employed by the investigator. For example, a combined exploratory-descriptive study of success in nursing home placements may be the only research approach feasible in the light of existing knowledge in the field of aging.

Exercise in evaluating research studies is extremely beneficial for understanding research and as a foundation for the utilization of research based knowledge in social practice. We have noted the different ways in which research has been evaluated by authors such as Riley (1963), Hirschi and Selvin (1963), and Glaser and Strauss (1967). These works have been helpful in the development of evaluation guidelines and can be a useful procedure for learning.

FIRST STEPS IN EVALUATION

The evaluator should read a research study through once quickly in order to get a picture of the substantive area under investigation. With this reading the evaluator gains some overall understanding of the research methods employed. The reader then should proceed to read the article carefully with the goal of locating the major purpose or purposes of the research, and of ascertaining whether or not the report has sufficient information upon which to base an evaluation. Minimal information required for evaluation would include some background regarding the study, the articulation of relevant hypotheses and/or questions of the study, the presentation of the research design employed, discussion of the types of empirical data collected and methods of collection, and the presentation of data analysis and conclusions of the study. The work of Marks (1960) on *Research Reporting* can be used as a guide in regard to the content and form of materials included in the research report. Selltiz *et al.* (1959), also provide such a guide. In addition, the Publication Manual of the American Psychological Association (1967) is a useful reference to the types of information generally included within journal research articles.

If the reader determines that the research report provides sufficient information for classification and evaluation and appears to have sufficient relevancy to his purposes (i.e., for utilization of the knowledge in practice), then the reader should type the study into its major research classification. Detailed guidelines for this purpose were presented in Chapter 2. Following classification by major research approach, the study should be subtyped. For example, a study classified as quantitative-descriptive should be further classified according to its purpose of testing hypotheses, seeking of relations among variables, and so forth. Experimental studies should be subtyped as laboratory experiments or field experiments. An exploratory study should be carefully reviewed in order to ascertain if it is exploratory in nature only, or if it includes a mixture of purposes and differential use of methods.

Early in the reading of the research report the reader should be sensitive to alternative strategies that might have been pursued with regard to the topic being studied. It is useful for the reader to consider the relative advantages and disadvantages of alternative designs vis-à-vis the purposes of a study. A basic reference for comparing the general advantages and disadvantages of research designs is provided by Campbell and Stanley, who report on a number of experimental designs, as well as quasi-experiments which we classify as quantitative-descriptive studies. With respect to experimental studies, the works of French (1953) on field experiments and Festinger (1953) on laboratory experiments are useful for the reader. These references provide background for the reader and help sensitize him both to alternative research designs and to different techniques for sampling and for data collection.

Having completed these first steps in evaluation, the reader should follow the guidelines appropriate to the classification of the research study. In general the reader should assume the role of the researcher and attempt to follow the research process in its entirety. This procedure will assist the reader to achieve perspective regarding "ideal" and "possible" research designs. Thus the reader should consider the formulation of the problem, the specific research design and types of data collected, the presentation and analysis of data, and the conclusions and interpretations made about the study. Guidelines for the evaluation of experimental, quantitative-descriptive, and exploratory studies are now presented.

GUIDELINES FOR EVALUATION OF EXPERIMENTAL STUDIES

Problem Formulation: Experimental Studies

The problem formulation of an experimental research study should contain the researcher's statement of study purposes, the identification of the hypotheses for study, the rationale for the selection of study variables, conceptual and operational definitions of the variables, and the identification of the assumptions made by the investigators (Ripple in Polansky, 1960).

The formulation of a problem for study is likely to include a mixture of the researcher's ideas and ideas drawn from the substantive and methodological literature pertaining to the phenomenon under investigation. The researcher is expected to cite literature relevant to his investigation and to incorporate into his research the ideas and methods of other studies. The use of the literature is likely to appear in the author's explication of concepts, rationale for hypotheses, and statement of assumptions of the study.

The reader should list the major concepts discussed by the author and note the extent to which the author's use of the concepts is consistent with the definitions cited in references to the literature. For example, in their laboratory experiment on effects of close and punitive styles of supervision, Day and Hamblin (1964) formulate a study to test hypotheses involving the relationship of four supervisory styles to aggressive feelings and actions of subordinates. They define the concept of close supervision as "one end of a continuum that describes the degree to which a supervisor specifies the roles of the subordinates and checks up to see that they comply with the specifications" (Day and Hamblin, 1964, p. 500). A "general" style of supervision is defined as being somewhere in the middle area of this continuum, that is, moderate specification and checking on subordinates. Punitive and nonpunitive styles of supervision are also conceptualized in the problem formulation. The authors cite references to studies that have employed these concepts and also make use of this literature in identifying investigations that have shown support for a hypothesis that relates style of supervision to aggressive feelings and indirect aggression on the part of subordinates toward supervisors. In this example, the concepts of supervision and aggression constitute the major variables of the study, with supervision serving as the independent variable to be manipulated by the experimenters and aggression identified as the dependent variable. Assumptions necessary to test the supervision-aggression hypothesis are considered, and Day and Hamblin make use of the literature to discuss self-esteem as a mediating or *contingent* variable. (A contingent variable is any variable that could potentially qualify, modify, or explain any obtained relations between an independent and a dependent variable.) Rather than making the assumption that the variable of self-esteem is unrelated to the hypothesis being tested, the authors make different predictions for subordinates with high self-esteem and those with low esteem. In this way the authors include in their conceptual framework a variable suggested by the literature as relevant to the hypothesis being tested.

Occasionally the reader will find limited use of the literature in the formulation of a problem of study. In such cases the reader should attempt to discern whether or not the study could have been improved by the incorporation of known available knowledge about the study problem. The reader may have knowledge of other similar studies, which can be used to place the research being evaluated into a comparative context. Pollak's (1963) study, "Worker Assignment in Casework with Marriage Partners," is an example of an experimental study that appears to be related in a limited way to previous research and in which the study hypothesis was mainly generated from social work practice. The primary question from which a hypothesis was formulated concerned whether one or two workers should be assigned in cases in which both marital partners were involved in treatment. The number of workers assigned to marital problem cases was manipulated as the independent variable, with the hypothesis for study being that "Marriage partners whose relationships suffered from undue remoteness would benefit more from the experience of having one worker than from having two workers" (Pollak, 1963, p. 44). The dependent variable concerned the "benefit" derived by couples from treatment, conceptualized by Pollak in terms of family relationship improvement. The dimensions of improvement or deterioration of relationship were identified as communication and cooperation. However, the author cites no studies dealing with the substantive area of marital counseling or with the concepts of communication and cooperation.

The literature may be used not only in the formulation of a conceptual framework for an experimental study, but also in regard to relevant methodology. In the example of Pollak's study of casework with marital partners, the author makes use of judgments for the measurement of the concepts of communication and cooperation by drawing on the work of Hunt and his classic study of "movement." Pollak indicates how these concepts were operationalized for his study in a methodological appendix, which describes criteria for measuring communication. The reader should examine such materials as these to determine if sufficient methodological detail is included or available to allow for a replication of the study. In addition, the reader should assess whether or not the indices of the concepts appear to correspond with the conceptual definitions of the variables, and whether or not the author has included any evidence regarding the reliability and validity of the concepts being measured. In Pollak's study every case was subjected to three judgments, but the measurement of reliability was not reported. In regard to the identification of relevant contingent variables, Pollak took into account two major kinds of treatment needs thought to be related to the relationship between number of workers and improvement in treatment. These treatment needs are derived from practice in terms of members of a family requiring a unifying experience or a separating experience. The author was not willing to assume that the variable was of no consequence. Since he could not include families of both types in his experiment, he confined the families studied to a single type of treatment need. However, decisions about families to be included in the study were not reviewed, no reliability check was made, and the loss of eligible cases occurred. This suggests that while an author may take into account relevant factors that need to be controlled in the experiment, there may be limitations in the ways in which control is provided.

A field experiment, "Insight versus Desensitization in Psychotherapy" by Paul (1967), illustrates the extensive use of the literature pertaining to methodological issues in experimentation, particularly with reference to problems of follow-up assessment of effects of treatment. Paul is concerned

with selected methodological problems of follow-up studies of psychotherapy, such as the uncontrolled nature of client experiences during the post-
treatment period and "the practical difficulty of sample maintenance and
attrition" (Paul, 1967, p. 333). His work illustrates the use of extensive
references related to these problems, and his attempts to overcome the
major problems with a well-controlled outcome study. In short, the reader
focuses his attention on the way in which the researcher incorporates his
ideas and those of other investigators into a statement of the rationale for
the study, its purposes, explication of what is to be investigated, and major
substantive and methodological issues confronting the investigator (Ripple,
1955).

In evaluating experimental studies, the reader should identify and examine carefully the hypotheses proposed for study. A hypothesis may have
originated from one of several sources, such as a theoretical framework,
prior research, practice experience, systematic organization of facts, or
unsystematic observations and hunches. Understanding of the origin of a
study hypothesis provides a context for evaluating the appropriateness of
the specific design features and procedures employed in the experimental
study. If the author is testing more than one hypothesis, the reader should
ascertain whether or not the hypotheses are linked in any theoretical or
substantive way. As Thomas (1960) has pointed out, the hypothesis for
study in experiments may be implicit and can usually be made explicit by
the reader by identification of the variables being manipulated and the
dependent variables being measured in the experiment. For example, Thomas
and McLeod (1960) studied the influence of in-service training for ADC
workers on worker behavior and client change. The training of the workers
was manipulated as the independent variable, and the implicit hypothesis
involved the relationship of training to the provisions of effective service to
ADC recipients.

In all experimental studies, the reader should locate the independent and
dependent variables and determine whether or not the author is in a position to manipulate the independent variable. Contingent variables that may
link the independent and dependent variables should be identified, and the
reader should examine the way in which the author proposes to account for
such variables. The reader should determine if the study variables are
defined conceptually and the extent to which alternative definitions have
been considered from previous research and/or from theory. Since actual
testing of the hypothesis demands operational definitions of the concepts
(Blalock, 1960), the reader determines how the major concepts are operationalized by examining the actual measurements proposed for the variables. The reader should then consider the extent to which the conceptual
definitions correspond to the operational definitions, that is, the extent to
which evidence is provided in regard to the validity of the measures, such

as face validity or construct validity (Kogan, 1960b). The reader also considers any evidence stated in regard to the reliability of the measures of the independent and dependent variables.

Assumptions made in experimental studies must be identified, both in regard to the conceptual framework and to measurement. Assumptions are defined as propositions which have not been verified, but which are taken as given for the purposes of investigation. Since the investigator cannot study all variables, nor control for all variables, he frequently must make assumptions about relevant variables, based on previous research, on theory, or on the collective wisdom of colleagues.

Review of the researcher's formulation of the problem for study allows an initial judgment in regard to the appropriateness of the experimental design for the study. If the problem formulation suggests that the independent variable cannot be manipulated, for example, for practical, ethical, or other reasons, or if the concepts in the hypotheses do not have empirical referents or are inadequately conceived, then the reader is alerted to the fact that the study does not meet the requirements of an experimental study. The reader should be aware that some of the aspects we have included under problem formulation may not be presented in the initial problem statement of a study, but may be interspersed throughout the journal article. When the reader's review of the problem reveals that the requirements of an experimental study are met, the reader proceeds to an evaluation of the research design and data collection aspects of the study.

Research Design and Data Collection:
Experimental Studies

In classifying the study, the reader has determined that an experimental design is employed. The subtype classification of the study, that is, field experiment or laboratory experiment, should now be considered in terms of the relative advantages and disadvantages of these experimental approaches vis-à-vis the particular problem of study. While the field experiment takes place in the natural environment and presents obstacles to experimental control, this design may offer the greatest potential for testing hypotheses pertinent to practical situations. For example, the study by Paul (1966, 1967) referred to in Chapter 1 was concerned with assessing the outcome for individuals undergoing different types of psychotherapy. A field experiment was designed for the purpose of determining the overall comparative effects of the different treatments from pretreatment to two-year follow-up and to assess the stability of improvement during the post-treatment period. A laboratory experiment would have been impractical in relation to the problem under investigation, as the subjects could not be isolated under laboratory conditions during the period of time necessary for the experiment. The field experiment was selected in the light of previous efforts of an experimental nature, but with the additional effort of the author to approximate in the field the controls inherent in laboratory study. The work of Day and Hamblin (1964) on the effects of close and punitive styles of supervision utilized the laboratory experimental approach. While previous studies had been carried out through field experiments, the authors decided that the hypothesis involving relationships of supervisory styles to feelings and actions of subordinates could appropriately be carried out under laboratory conditions. The subjects could be engaged in the experimental tasks in an experimental room designed to "simulate" an industrial work station. In this case, testing the hypotheses did not demand that the independent variable be manipulated in the natural environment, for example, an industry setting, and the laboratory offered more rigorous control features than were possible with a field experiment. Thus, supervisors were trained to give uniform responses and to present uniform stimuli, and the tasks for the subjects were uniform. These conditions would have been difficult to achieve in the field setting. The Day and Hamblin study also illustrates ways in which the laboratory situation can be structured to approximate the natural setting; for example, words such as "supervisor," "work efficiency," and "production line" were used to convey the atmosphere of the industrial setting.

These studies by Paul and by Day and Hamblin illustrate the need to consider subtypes in relation to the problems for study, as they point to specific design features employed in experimental studies. In evaluating experimental studies, the reader should consider whether or not alternative design features could have improved the study, within the same constraints of cost, organizational factors, obstacles to control of variables, and the potential manipulation of the independent variable. The reader should focus on the extent to which an experimental study approximates maximal internal and external validity through the introduction of design features which promote validity.

In addition to considering the research experiment in terms of field and laboratory setting, the reader should examine the specific experimental design utilized in the study. Campbell and Stanley (1963) discuss three true experimental designs: the Pretest-Posttest control group design, the Solomon Four-Group Design, and the Posttest Only control group design. Each of these designs varies to some extent in the degree to which controls for internal and external validity are possible.

Several variables relevant to internal validity are history, maturation, testing, instrumentation, regression, selection, mortality, and interaction of selection and maturation. Campbell and Stanley (1963) and Sussman (1964) include discussion of these variables and the ways in which experimental designs attempt to control for them. For example, the effects of history are minimized when the time between observations is very short. Maturation, that is, growth of the individual in selected ways during the period of the experiment, can be handled by a control group in the design and by the randomization of subjects. Instrumentation involves the effects of the administration of instruments, the instruments themselves, and the way they operate to produce change. Several methods can be used to control for these effects, such as having the same researcher for both experimental and control groups, or using a "blind" approach where the observer does not know which respondents are in the control or in the experimental groups.

In regard to external validity, the reader should consider ways in which the authors have attempted to control such factors as reactive or interaction effects of testing. These factors are controlled in the Solomon Four-Group Design and the Posttest Only control group design. Other factors influencing external validity concern selection biases and interaction with the experimental variable. The reader should consider the author's definition of the population with which the study is concerned and the extent to which the author is able to generalize results to the population. Attention here is directed toward the external validity problem, which may be handled by various sampling techniques and the inclusion of evidence that a random sample is representative of the population.

One of the requisites for an experimental study is that randomization procedures be employed in the assignment of subjects to experimental and control groups. The reader should examine the process that the experimenter uses to assign subjects, objects, and so forth to study groups, and what evidence is presented to verify that his goals of assignment have been reached, for example, the extent to which equivalencies among groups are checked. The reader must also be alert in regard to the mortality, or loss of cases, which may occur during the experiment, and the extent to which such loss threatens the validity of the study.

Once the researcher has set up experimental and control groups, he must manipulate the independent variable, with such manipulation occurring prior in time to the anticipated changes in the dependent variable. The reader should identify the way in which the experimenter manipulated the independent variable. An example of variable manipulation is provided in the Day and Hamblin (1964) study, in which 24 groups were assigned systematically to four different experimental conditions of supervision: close supervision with high and low punitive styles; and general supervision, also with high and low punitive styles. In the case of the Paul (1967) study, different treatment modes were used with the experimental and control groups. The reader should consider the strength of the independent variable, for example, number of treatment sessions, length of time in treatment, and instructions used in styles of supervision, in order to assess alternatives to manipulation procedures. Particularly, the reader should be alert to weak independent variables and to ways in which they could have been strengthened (Thomas, 1960, p. 288), such as increasing the intensity and length of time over which the variable is manipulated. The independent variable must be potent enough to give a fair test of the hypothesis.

In regard to the manipulation of the independent variable, the reader should be alert to manipulation with respect to conditions of measurement. What is involved in the actual measurement process? Who does it? Is the researcher aware of which subjects are in the experimental and control groups? In essence, the reader attempts to locate potential sources of bias, which could have influenced the dependent variables during the course of the experiment. Having located potential sources of bias, the reader assesses the extent to which the experimenter has introduced checks or procedures to deal with these problems. The reader should evaluate the efforts made to control the effects of the measurement process, for example, the subjects' reactivity to manipulation of independent variables. This should be done in the context of the type of data collected by the experimenter, which should be identified by the reader and viewed in relation to the measurement process.

Ideal conditions are rarely possible in experimental studies due to lack of knowledge, lack of capacity to anticipate problems that occur once the research is undertaken, constraints of organizations, ethical considerations, voluntary nature of participation in experiments, and time available for the research. Any one or more of these items may be used by the researcher to justify compromises in ideal conditions for the experiment, and the reader must consider the impact of these constraints on the study, as well as possible alternative designs and procedures.

Data Analysis and Conclusions: Experimental Studies

At this point the reader is interested in the results of the experiment, which are presented through statistical analysis of the data collected, interpretation of the findings, and conclusions inferred from the findings. The first task of the reader is to ascertain the appropriateness of the use of statistical controls that have been used in the analysis of the data, in other words, the way relevant variables that could not be controlled in the experimental situation are introduced as control variables in the testing of a hypothesis. Secondly, the reader should attempt to determine whether there is contamination in the process of data collection which leads to nonindependent observations and built-in correlations. These factors are considered because they are relevant to the claims that the researcher makes in regard to support for his research hypotheses. The reader then considers whether or not the statistical tests are appropriate for the data, whether assumptions of the statistical model are tenable (Blalock, 1960). The reader considers the way in which the author deals with findings in relation to his hypotheses, determining whether or not they support the hypotheses, and any qualifications that must be made in relation to the nature of the support. For example, the hypothesis may not have the same amount of support when potentially contingent variables are introduced as controls. The reader should be alert to the way in which the researcher deals with "negative" findings, that is, those which do not support his hypothesis, to make sure they are not ignored or misinterpreted. In addition, the reader should note how the results are related to time factors, particularly in regard to whether the author has considered the persistence of effects over time. The reader should compare the data reported in tables to the claims made by the author in the text of the study report to determine the degree of consistency between these two locations of information. For example, the author may generalize beyond or without data, and the reader can check against this by examination of the data presented by the author.

As the reader views the author's conclusions, he should assess their internal consistency with respect to all phases of the research. The researcher should have achieved a test of his hypotheses, and the reader must distinguish between conclusions drawn from such a test and the implications of the findings. When the findings are not consistent, or straightforward, the reader must assess the plausibility of the inferences made by the researcher. In consideration of his findings and conclusions, the researcher may relate his study to other knowledge from the literature about the problem under investigation. He may also use his findings as a foundation for the development of new hypotheses regarding the study phenomenon, and for new ways of researching the problem.

At this point the reader should determine if the researcher has learned anything from the study that he didn't know previously. Does the study contribute to knowledge or ways of producing knowledge? More specifically, the reader asks to what extent the research has achieved the goals and purposes of the study stated in the problem formulation, and how the findings relate to previous research.

In following these guidelines for the evaluation of experimental research studies, the reader assesses a study in the context of its purposes and methods. Additional areas for evaluation may occur to the reader as he explores research methods texts and as he gains experience in evaluating research studies. While use of the guidelines will likely reveal limitations and gaps in studies being evaluated, the reader should concentrate on the contributions made by the study through the development of knowledge and ways of producing knowledge.

To assist the reader in evaluating experimental studies, evaluation guidelines are now stated in the form of key questions.

EVALUATION QUESTIONS: EXPERIMENTAL STUDIES

I. Problem Formulation

1. How does the author utilize the literature in conceptualizing the problem for study?
2. What major concepts are formulated for the study, and how well are they defined conceptually and operationally?
3. What hypotheses are proposed for test in the experiment? What is the rationale for the inclusion of concepts in the hypotheses, and the predictions made in the hypotheses?
4. What assumptions are made by the author in regard to the selection of variables for study?
5. What are the independent and dependent variables proposed within the hypotheses, how are they operationalized, and are they conceptually and operationally independent?
6. What potentially influential variables are recognized by the author, and how are they handled—through assumptions or controls?
7. What methodological issues are raised by the author which are believed to be relevant to the testing of the hypothesis, and how does the author propose to handle the issues?
8. Are there conditions that prevent the manipulation of the independent variable, or of measurement of the effects on the dependent variable?
9. To what extent is the experimental design appropriate for investigating the problem of the study?

II. Research Design and Data Collection

1. In what ways does the experimental design include provisions for maximizing the internal validity of the experiment?
2. What assumptions are made in the design?
3. What variables are not controlled, but considered relevant to the study?
4. What alternative experimental designs might have been employed?
5. What sampling procedures were employed in the study? How were assignments made to experimental and control groups?
6. How were the data collected? To what degree were the data reliable and valid?
7. To what extent does the experimental design maximize external validity?
8. Was the independent variable manipulated successfully, and to what extent were the effects of measurement controlled or handled?

III. Data Analysis and Conclusions

1. Do the data provide evidence for testing of the study hypotheses?
2. Are the statistical tests employed appropriate to the design of the study and the problem under investigation?

3. To what extent are the hypotheses supported by the data?

4. Are the author's claims for the findings consistent with the data?

5. What are the author's principal conclusions, and are they consistent with the findings?

6. What are the implications of the study as defined by the author?

7. To what extent did the researcher accomplish the purposes set forth for the study?

GUIDELINES FOR EVALUATION OF QUANTITATIVE-DESCRIPTIVE STUDIES

Problem Formulation: Quantitative-Descriptive Studies

Formulation of the problem for a quantitative-descriptive study will vary somewhat according to the subtype in which the study is classified. If the study is concerned with hypothesis testing, the reader should identify the study hypothesis and consider the origin of the hypothesis. The problem formulation of a quantitative-descriptive hypothesis-testing study is illustrated in Gamson's (1966) study of reputation and resources in community politics. Gamson was concerned with the role individuals with reputation for influence play in relation to the outcome of community issues. One of his hypotheses states that it takes more effort to change the status quo than to maintain it, and he discusses the "natural advantage" thought to obtain in community groups who would maintain a present arrangement as against groups who would change facilities or services. In his problem formulation Gamson takes into account prior studies from the literature that deal with community power, leadership, bases of social power, influence, and persuasion, as well as ways of identifying reputational leaders. As with the experimental study, the reader should review the author's use of the literature and practical experiences in the identification and formulation of problems in quantitative-descriptive studies.

For studies that seek to discover relationships among variables or to locate facts, the reader should identify the major questions that guide the research and attempt to understand why particular variables are selected for study. In a study by Ripple and Alexander (1956) of motivation, capacity, and opportunity as related to the use of casework services, the major question for research concerned how a client's ability to use help was related to his continuance with a social agency. This research focus led the investigators to develop a problem classification scheme, which permitted grouping clients with similar problems together. Their study formulation describes the rationale for the selection of variables, such as economic dislocation, intrafamilial conflict, and so forth, for inclusion in their problem classification scheme.

In all types of quantitative-descriptive studies, the reader should determine how well the variables for study are defined conceptually and whether the author has considered alternative definitions from previous research or theory. For example, in Ripple and Alexander's study, conceptual distinctions are made for situations characterized by external problems, and these distinctions are illustrated by case examples. The reader also determines how well the variables are defined operationally, that is, in terms of measurements of the variables, so that they can be identified with indicators for the concepts. This clarifies the meanings of the concepts used in formulating the problem and also allows for replication by independent investigators. The reader must also consider whether or not the author offers sufficient evidence in regard to the reliability and validity of the measures being used.

For quantitative-descriptive studies with the purpose of hypothesis testing, the reader should discern whether the author is trying to validate a hypothesis with implied cause-effect relations or to establish the existence of a relationship between selected variables. In regard to cause-effect relationships, the reader should identify the independent and dependent variables and consider evidence necessary to show support for a hypothesis. The reader should consider whether or not the author has conceptualized potentially contingent variables which may influence the relationship between the independent and dependent variables. To show cause-effect relations the independent variable must precede the dependent variable in time, and relevant "contingent" variables must be controlled.

In evaluating hypothesis-testing studies that include a series of hypotheses, the reader should determine what, if any, relationship exists among the hypotheses. They may be connected according to a theoretical scheme, according to a substantive area, or by some other accounting model. The reader should be alert to the possibility that a general hypothesis may be presented on an abstract level in the problem formulation, with hypotheses for testing presented elsewhere at a lower level of abstraction. The reader should ascertain the relationship among the hypotheses tested and the more general hypotheses which may have been introduced into the problem formulation statement. Hypotheses proposed for study should be considered in relation to the author's statement of the study problem to determine the degree of their correspondence.

Included in the researcher's formulation of the study problem should be a statement of major assumptions in regard to selection of variables, definitions of concepts, and measurement procedures. The reader should identify the explicit and implicit assumptions stated by the author. For example, Zander and Newcomb (1967) in their study of group levels of aspiration in United Fund campaigns explicitly state the assumption that when a community fails to achieve its goal in a United Fund campaign, the need of the community increases. The reader evaluates the reasonableness of such assumptions in terms of knowledge about the study problem and with respect to the purposes and methods of the research study. The reader then continues the evaluation by examining the research design and data collection aspects of the study.

Research Design and Data Collection:
Quantitative-Descriptive Studies

In classifying the study, the reader has identified the particular subtype of quantitative-descriptive study being evaluated. In this context, he considers specific features of the research design of the study. Major consideration is given to problems of internal and external validity. Threats to validity for experimental studies are also relevant to studies that approximate experimentation. The reader should review these problems, as previously discussed in the section of guidelines for evaluating experiments, and ascertain the extent to which the author has attempted to handle them in the quantitative-descriptive study. However, the reader should recognize that the researcher using quasi-experimental designs will not be in a position to overcome some of the validity problems to the extent that is possible with true experimental designs.

Since the author of a quantitative-descriptive study wishes to describe accurately relations among variables, provide accurate facts, and/or test hypotheses, rigorous sampling procedures are called for. The reader should determine the target population to which the author wishes to generalize and the units of analysis or behavior being studied, for example, welfare recipients in Michigan. The procedures for sample selection should be identified, and the reader should look for evidence that indicates the representativeness of the sample obtained by the researcher. The essential task of the reader is to assess the generalizability of the results of the research from the actual sample studied. He does this by identifying the sampling procedures, by considering the author's stated problems in sampling, and by considering alternative procedures which could have been employed in the study.

Procedures for the collection of data, the kinds of data collected, and the nature of the data collected are now evaluated by the reader. Important factors to be taken into account are the extent to which the data are nonbiased and systematic, and correspond to the major concepts of the study. In short, the researcher's efforts to establish the reliability and validity of the data collected should be evaluated. For example, Ripple and Alexander (1956) report on the agreement of research judges with caseworkers on 85 percent of the cases in which client problems are defined. Specific procedures for data collection should be identified, such as questionnaires, interview schedules, and participant observations. The reader should consider general problems connected with types of data collection, such as bias of the interviewer, wording and order of questions, effects of social desirability in responses, acquiescence response set, halo effects, and so forth. Matters such as these are discussed by Webb *et al.* (1966), and Campbell and Stanley (1963). The reader should seek to discover specific sources of bias, unreliability, and nonvalidity, and consider whether improvements in these areas could have been made, especially at minimal costs.

Data Analysis and Conclusions:
Quantitative-Descriptive Studies

With respect to the author's analysis of his findings, it is important in evaluating quantitative-descriptive studies to ascertain whether the author is using statistical inference or descriptive statistics (Blalock, 1960). In studies using statistical inference, the reader determines if the author has specified desired levels of significance in advance of his data analysis, so that the development of hypotheses can be distinguished from the testing of *a priori* hypotheses. Of particular importance in quantitative-descriptive studies is the analysis of data by the provision of statistical controls regarding contingent variables, in other words, cross tabulations of the findings under conditions of control variables. The reader should consider to what extent the findings are potentially spurious. Spurious relations are discussed in Chapter 2, with a spurious association identified as one that can be explained by another variable introduced into the statistical analysis of data (Blalock, 1961, p. 84).

Depending on the subtype of quantitative-descriptive study, the researcher's conclusions may be statements regarding the status of the stated hypothesis, descriptions of relationship between variables, or specification of variable characteristics. In each instance, these statements should be based on the data provided in the research. The reader should be alert to conclusions based on peripheral data, or inferences from the connection between the data and opinions, as they are likely to have the status of assumptions rather than hypotheses to be tested. For all studies the reader should distinguish between conclusions and implications and should determine if the author has been internally consistent in his use of concepts in the study. In addition, the reader should ascertain whether the author has answered the questions or tested the hypotheses he set out to examine in his study.

The researcher's presentation of data and conclusions should be characterized by impartial reporting, rather than an expression of his biases. This may be a particular problem when the findings are not straightforward and the interpretation of findings is a matter of inferences made by the researcher. Finally, the researcher should relate his findings to current knowledge about the phenomenon under investigation. In this way the reader can assess the contribution that the researcher makes to the understanding of the problem posed and the meaning of the study for the utilization of knowledge for practice, theory, and research.

To assist the reader in evaluating quantitative-descriptive studies, evaluation guidelines can be stated in the form of key questions.

EVALUATION QUESTIONS:
QUANTITATIVE-DESCRIPTIVE STUDIES

I. Problem Formulation

1. How does the author utilize the literature in conceptualizing the problem for study?

2. What major concepts are formulated for the study, and how well are they defined conceptually and operationally?

3. If the study has as its purpose the testing of hypotheses, what are the hypotheses, and what are the independent and dependent variables proposed by the author?

4. What assumptions are made by the author in regard to the selection of variables for study?

5. What potentially influential variables are recognized by the author, and how are they handled—through assumptions or controls?

6. To what extent is the quantitative-descriptive approach appropriate for investigating the problem for study?

II. Research Design and Data Collection

1. Could other alternative designs have been used more appropriately to carry out the purposes of the study?

2. If the study sought to test hypotheses, what efforts were made to approximate experimentation and to maximize internal and external validity?

3. What sampling procedures were employed in the study?

4. How were the data specifically collected, and how were potential sources of bias taken into account?

5. To what extent did the author attempt to increase the reliability and validity of the measurements in the study?

III. Data Analysis and Conclusions

1. Does the author use descriptive statistics or statistics for inference in his analysis of the data, and is the choice of statistics appropriate to the data and the assumptions of the study?

2. If hypotheses are tested in the study, are they supported by the data?

3. Were cross tabulations introduced in analyzing the data in order to take account of potentially influential variables?

4. What are the author's principal conclusions? Are they consistent with the data?

5. What are the implications of the findings as defined by the author? Are they logically related to the data and to the conclusions stated by the author?

6. To what extent did the researcher accomplish the purposes set forth for the study?

GUIDELINES FOR EVALUATION OF EXPLORATORY STUDIES

Problem Formulation: Exploratory Studies

The problem formulation of an exploratory study varies in terms of the particular subtype of exploratory research. For the combined exploratory-descriptive study, concentration is placed on the statement of the purposes of the study, the selection of variables to be studied, and some indication of the systematic procedures required to describe quantitatively the phenomenon under study. In studies that use specific data-collection procedures for developing ideas, the focus of the problem formulation will be both on the problem of study and on data procedures proposed for the development of conceptual categories. In experimental manipulation studies that have exploratory purposes, researchers state the problem for study in terms of the variable to be manipulated and the controls deemed necessary to ascertain the potential effects of the experimental variable on the presumed dependent variable.

For all the exploratory subtypes, the reader should be alert to the rationale given for conducting the exploratory study. Is the study being launched within some theoretical framework regarding the phenomenon under study? Is the investigator concerned with a practical problem for which he seeks to develop ideas, hypotheses, or measurements for further and more systematic study? In either case, the reader should identify the major variables dealt with by the investigator and consider the goals the researcher has in regard to these variables, such as conceptual modification, elaboration, and operational definitions. The reader should keep in mind that the requirements for conceptualization and operationalization of variables required for experimental and quantitative-descriptive studies do not hold for the exploratory study. However, since the exploratory study anticipates further research, efforts to quantify concepts and control relevant factors add to its value.

The reader notes the ways in which the relevant literature is employed in the researcher's problem formulation for exploratory studies. The reader is concerned with the extent to which relevant studies are cited, the ways in which the major concepts are defined, and the ways in which variables are measured. While the use of the literature is sometimes limited in exploratory studies, it is important that the reader identify whether or not the authors have searched the literature and the extent to which they follow up on the relevant aspects of the literature cited in the study. The reader should consider any leads that the researcher gains in regard to sources of data, types of data, and uses of data relevant to the problem under investigation. For example, in a study by Faunce and Clelland (1967), "Professionalization and Stratification Patterns in an Industrial Community," the authors extend a conceptual framework regarding community processes in order to take into account data from a number of community studies which deal with the division of labor within a community. They consider the implications of differences in patterns of division of labor for class, status, and power structures of the community. These concepts provide the framework for a community study utilizing a variety of sources of data.

The Faunce-Clelland study illustrates a combined exploratory-descriptive study, in which relatively systematic data-collection procedures are proposed in the problem formulation. The study includes the measurement of a number of concepts suggested by the literature as relevant to an examination of the impact of professionalization on community processes. The goal of the researchers was to draw from a number of sources of data to explain changes over time in one community. This was expected both to increase the researcher's familiarity with the nature of community change and to refine propositions for further study beyond the confines of a single community.

As long as the purpose of a study is exploratory, any one of a number of methods may be employed, and the data proposed for collection may be both qualitative and quantitative in nature. In a study by Ayllon (1963), "Intensive Treatment of Psychotic Behavior by Stimulus Satiation and Food Reinforcement," the patient's environment is manipulated in a mental hospital ward to demonstrate the effectiveness of behavioral modification treatment on the patient's behavior. The independent variables manipulated included towels and food, and the data collected were quantitative, for example, records of frequency of behaviors such as stealing food and the measurement of loss of weight. Selected laboratory principles regarding reinforcement were demonstrated in "successive experiments" with a single patient over time.

Our examples of exploratory studies thus far have been based on theoretical frameworks. Yet, in some cases the investigator has a concrete question in need of answer or a problem for which there has been limited theoretical development. As example, in their study of hyperaggressive children Goodrich and Boomer (1958) sought to explore the natural therapeutic situation by studying interactions between staff and patients. Their decision to proceed in this manner was based on a view that theoretical and technical issues were not sufficiently clear to undertake other study approaches, such as field or laboratory experiments. Goodrich and Boomer employed the critical incident technique with data gathered through interviews with staff members and developed a system of concepts dealing with therapeutic intervention. An exploratory study may be carried out with the purpose of formulating a problem for future research. In such cases, the investigator may focus on the requisites for problem formulation, such as identification of concepts, ideas, and facts that are relevant to the development of a problem statement as the foundation for further research.

By its very nature an exploratory study is likely to depend heavily on assumptions. The reader should identify the assumptions the researchers make in regard to their definitions of concepts, their proposed measurements, and the selection of variables to be investigated. In the Goodrich and Boomer (1958, p. 208) study referred to above, the authors made the assumption that treatment of children by skilled staff results in behavior changes in the children. They also assumed that "one important class of 'change agents' is the observable transactions between staff and children." Assumptions may also be introduced in the conclusions and implications of the findings.

Research Design and Data Collection:
Exploratory Studies

The problem formulation of the exploratory study provides a context for evaluating the specific design features proposed for the study. The reader should consider the advantages and disadvantages of the subtypes of exploratory studies for reaching exploratory goals in general, as well as in relation to the particular study under evaluation. In evaluating the exploratory study, the reader should examine the kinds and sources of the data obtained and the extent to which the variables selected by the researcher are consistent with the purposes of the study. For example, in the Faunce-Clelland (1967) community study, the authors do not rely entirely on census data but extend their sources to structured interviews with selected samples of occupational groups, as well as including loosely structured interviews with community leaders.

In regard to sampling design, the reader recognizes that the sampling plan need not be rigorous as required in other major types of research. However, the reader should determine if the sample selection is pertinent to the purpose of the study and should be aware of the relationship of sampling to the development of ideas for future research. Thus, the reader may find that sampling appears to be related more to groups or units of analysis that will support the author's previously held ideas, rather than to his development of new ideas. This is likely to occur in instances where the sample is purposive or highly selective. The study cited by Faunce and Clelland illustrates a range of sampling techniques, including selection of occupations for study, selection of samples of professionals, technicians, and hourly workers, and selection of community leaders. The first three samples were drawn randomly from lists of employees of a chemical processing firm, and only city residents were included. The latter group included 29 community leaders representative of major appointive and elective positions in the community. This study illustrates the inclusion of nonrigorous and rigorous (occupational samples) sampling, with the latter providing more empirical support for the author's idea than the former. In the combined exploratory-descriptive study, some rigorous sampling is required.

The reader should consider how alternative modes of sampling could have served to minimize potential bias in the study, although it is recognized that bias cannot entirely be eliminated in such a study. To illustrate, the Faunce and Clelland study presents data for which they recognize bias in responses, as their samples were not drawn from the whole community but only from selected occupational groups.

The reader should consider the kinds of data collected, both qualitative and quantitative, and the ways in which the data were collected, for example, participant observation, interviewing, questionnaire, or available records. The reader should consider any reliability and validity checks the researcher makes in relation to the kinds of data collected. The reader should keep in mind the limitations of the study in regard to checking these aspects of the data collected and consider ways in which reliability and validity could be introduced into the current or future studies of the phenomenon.

Data Analysis and Conclusions:
Exploratory Studies

The reader should first determine the extent to which the findings of the study are sufficient in terms of the purposes of the study. In the development of hypotheses, did the author already have hypotheses and seek evidence for their support, or did he develop hypotheses from the study? Are the findings sufficient to warrant future study based on a hypothesis developed from ideas of the study? The reader should consider the initial biases of the researcher, and the extent to which the presentation of the findings is related to such biases.

In studies that seek further understandings of concepts, the reader should determine if the concepts have been modified or clarified and to what extent they can be operationalized. When hypotheses are developed, the reader examines them in terms of their researchability. Are the independent and dependent variables identifiable, independent of each other, and amenable to operationalization?

The reader considers whether the researcher's conclusions and inferences are consistent with data in the study. If the author draws implications, it should be determined if the researcher distinguishes potential implications from conclusions. When authors introduce findings and discussions from the literature, the reader should be alert to the ways in which the researcher makes use of such literature in relation to his own findings.

The reader should not only examine the ways in which the authors use their data but the ways in which they could have made additional analyses within the purposes of the study. Since in some cases exploratory studies will also have purposes that are nonexploratory in nature, such as a description of accurate relations among variables, the reader should be concerned with the degree to which sufficient information is available to allow for replication.

Finally, the reader examines the extent to which the author goes beyond his data to conceptualize the phenomenon under study, to formulate hypotheses, and to clarify and extend the meaning of concepts, so as to contribute to current understanding and to future research endeavors. Thus, in Parnicky and Brown's (1964) study of institutionalized retardates, the authors indicate the possibility suggested by their study of developing an index of readiness for placement of patients into the community. This would enable testing of hypotheses developed in their exploratory study, such as "Success in community placement is facilitated as positive attitudes toward community living are relatively stronger than those toward residential living" (Parnicky and Brown, 1964, p. 83).

In the light of the foregoing considerations for evaluating exploratory studies, the following summary of guideline questions is presented to assist the reader.

EVALUATION QUESTIONS: EXPLORATORY STUDIES

I. Problem Formulation

1. What rationale is given by the authors for conducting the study? Is the study concerned with a theoretical or practical problem, or with both?

2. How does the author utilize the literature and previous experience in conceptualizing the problem for study?

3. What major concepts are formulated for the study, and how well are they defined conceptually and operationally?

4. What assumptions are made by the author in regard to the selection of variables for study?

5. What sources of data are considered by the authors, and what types of data are sought for the study?

6. To what extent is the exploratory approach appropriate for the investigation of the problem posed for study?

II. Research Design and Data Collection

1. Could other alternative designs have been used more appropriately to carry out the purposes of the study?

2. What sampling procedures were employed in the study? What alternative plans would have been appropriate?

3. What specific kinds of data were collected?

4. To what extent were potential biases minimized in the collection of data?

5. To what extent did the author attempt to increase the reliability and validity of the measurements in the study?

III. Data Analysis and Conclusions

1. What are the findings of the study? Are they derived from qualitative, quantitative, or both kinds of data?

2. If statistics are employed in the study, are they appropriate to the data analyzed, and to the purposes of the study?

3. What concepts, hypotheses, and ideas for future research are developed from the findings of the study?

4. Are concepts developed consistent with the findings, and to what extent are new concepts developed and old concepts modified or expanded?

5. Are the hypotheses developed researchable, that is, stated in testable form?

6. In what ways could the authors have used their available data for additional analyses and for development of other ideas consistent with their purposes?

7. Do the concepts and hypotheses developed in the study stem from the findings, from other literature, or from the initial biases of the authors?

8. To what extent have the authors achieved the purposes of the study?

Chapter 4

Utilization of Research: Principles and Guidelines

As a consumer of research, the social work practitioner is particularly interested in how to make use of the findings of a study in his own practice, or to get new ideas that he or others in the profession can translate into practice. The previous chapters have dealt with issues to which the sophisticated reader of research must be alert, so that he can usefully classify a study and evaluate how well it was carried out in reference to its objectives. The purpose of this chapter is to consider issues that bear on utilization of reported research. By "utilization" we mean the application of knowledge gained from the research to the professional objectives of the social worker or of the social work profession. Unlike questions about classification and evaluation, questions about utility for social work require the reader to consider *relevance* of the research to goals of social work practice. The context of the reader as a social worker as well as the qualities of the research itself are important for this chapter.

We will briefly review some of the literature dealing with frameworks for utilization of research in order to present a general perspective on utilization. Then, we will develop in some detail the guidelines for the reader to follow when considering utility of published research. Finally, we present special considerations for using the guidelines for each type of research study previously distinguished—experimental, quantitative-descriptive, and exploratory.

UTILIZATION FRAMEWORKS: AN OVERVIEW

There are many general discussions of the application of scientific knowledge to practical problems (Gouldner and Miller, 1965; Likert and Lippitt, 1953) and some discussions of issues presented when practitioners seek to use scientific knowledge (Bartlett *et al.*, 1964). There are, however, few explicit analyses of ways to judge the usefulness of research knowledge. A number of papers deal with utilization of knowledge in social work, and we draw on them in developing the perspective of this chapter.

In *Behavioral Science for Social Workers* Thomas (1967a) discusses the types of contributions behavioral science makes to social work, and he also considers the components of social work to which aspects of behavioral science may be applicable. In addition to a scientific stance, behavioral science contributes, Thomas notes, (a) conceptual tools, (b) substantive findings, and (c) methods of research. These components are all evident in the research process and hence constitute points of attention for the reader of research. *Conceptualization*—the mode of reasoning as distinguished from results of research or methods of doing research—contributes to clarification of concepts, their operationalization, and their use in hypotheses and theories. Thomas notes the need to conceptualize the "very process of utilizing behavioral science knowledge." He says:

> ... Both the increasing knowledge of behavioral science and its selective applicability to social work necessarily compel a conceptualization of what contributes to social work and what does not. ... Behavioral science knowledge must be selected for use, assimilated by educators and practitioners, amalgamated into the larger fabric of social work knowledge, introduced into educational and agency contexts, and subsequently evaluated and tested. This process, which begins with selection from the heartlands of the academic disciplines of behavioral science and terminates in the front lines of practice in the social work profession, is a complex intellectual, practical, and institutional transition in the engineering of behavior science knowledge ... (Thomas, 1967a, p. 7).

Substantive knowledge—including the insights and sharpened observations from exploratory studies as well as empirical generalizations aimed for by experimental studies—constitutes, of course, what research is all about. Reduced uncertainty about aspects of the world with which social workers must deal is the basis for taking the next steps in assessing in what ways the increased knowledge may be useful. A further contribution—*research methods*—is important not only because the methods of behavioral science research are applicable to most problems of social work knowledge, but also because research design and techniques of data gathering and analysis sometimes suggest procedures directly applicable to practice. For example, the experimental manipulation of the single case, systematically pursued, may increase both the deliberate provision of a service and its knowledge-producing consequences. Or, for another example, the technique of sociometric analysis can, and has, become an instrument by which to structure groups.

Just as such general features of behavior science can be differentiated, so Thomas suggests component features of social work as objects of analysis for which the contributions of behavior science are applicable. He lists the following points of attention when applying social science: (Thomas, 1967a, pp. 10-11)

1. the clientele of social welfare services
2. the social workers and related professionals
3. the programs of welfare
4. the services provided, including direct practice
5. the agencies and organizations through which services are offered and programs are implemented
6. the education and training of welfare workers
7. the research in social work
8. the knowledge of the profession of social work
9. the institution of social welfare

Such categories describe topics of interest in the literature of social work and social work research. Their listing calls attention to the need to identify what it is about social work we wish to apply knowledge to.

Thomas contributes further to a general framework for utilizing knowledge by proposing criteria for selecting useful knowledge from behavioral science (Thomas, 1964). Distinguishing the levels of social practice as concerned with the individual, the group, the organization, the community, and the society, he notes that scientific knowledge is useful to the extent that it has *content relevance* to the subject matter of social work. That subject matter is divided by Thomas into: normal behavior; abnormality and deviancy; growth, maturation, and change; and the helping process. In addition, knowledge is useful, Thomas says, to the extent that it has *power* (that is, represents valid empirical generalizations), and to the extent that the variables used have *referent features* (in other words, accessibility, manipulability, cost and ethical suitability) that link them meaningfully to the world of social work. The framework Thomas has sketched is a basis for our perspective on utilization in this chapter. Thomas has applied his analysis to points of potential contribution from social-psychological literature as it bears on the interpersonal helping relationship (in Lazarsfeld *et al.*, 1967, pp. 162-70). In this same paper, "Social Work and Social Welfare," there are further examples of application of knowledge from sociology to the organizational and the community level that also illustrate aspects of a framework for utilization (Meyer *et al.,* in Lazarsfeld, 1967). Among other pertinent sources, Kadushin (1964) presents a system that accepts three areas as objects to which knowledge is pointed: social policy and administration, growth and behavior, and social work methods (casework, group work, community organization); and he illustrates how this facilitates the orderly assessment of useful knowledge about one area of social work concern: homemaker services. He does not, however, develop specific criteria for selecting knowledge.

UTILIZATION: GENERAL PERSPECTIVE

We are interested in developing practical guidelines to help the social worker decide how useful a piece of research is. Therefore, we are less concerned with the ideal characteristics of useful research than with providing a perspective that encourages the research reader to maximize the potential usefulness of the research by judging what it may contribute as well as where its limits are. In general terms, we view different kinds of research as differentially useful, and we view usefulness as a judgment arising from the research reader's recognition of the broadest range of social work interests. Two questions frame the problem of utilization: "What knowledge does the research offer?" and "What activity of social work practice does it concern?"

With respect to the kinds of knowledge research may offer, we do not limit our interest to the empirical generalizations of tested validity for which science strives. These can be, of course, of the greatest importance and usefulness in some instances, but they may be less valuable for the practitioner in other instances than research intended to clarify concepts, establish or measure relationships between concepts, or develop hypotheses for subsequent research on some phenomenon. All the following kinds of knowledge have potential usefulness: (1) "Facts," that is, verified observations about some phenomenon identified by a concept. For example, the number of families in a community willing to accept a foster child may be a "fact" of considerable relevance to an agency that provides placements for children and to welfare planning bodies trying to assess the need for residential facilities. Like other research knowledge, a study that provides "facts" must be evaluated for its validity, as we have indicated in Chapter 3. (2) *Concepts* point us to the phenomena we call "facts." We have defined concepts as verbal symbols, or ideas, abstracted from experience (Chapter 1), and in this sense concepts themselves may be useful even before we have valid information about the phenomena to which they refer. They may sensitize the practitioner to variables that could affect his practice, for example, social class, as in studies of mental illness (Hollingshead and

Redlich, 1958), or role performance, as in studies of client continuance in treatment (Ripple, 1955). (3) *Hypotheses* that relate two or more concepts to one another and make predictions about the relationship may also be useful. For example, the hypothesis that role satisfaction of social workers will be related to the discrepancy between their ideal definition of what their role activities should be and their actual role performance gives us a way of approaching some problems of supervision of social workers and of agency structure and management (Billingsley, 1964). (4) When hypotheses have stood the test of empirical examination and acquired relatively high degrees of confidence that they represent what can be observed, we may view them as *empirical generalizations* within the context they describe. Such knowledge has great potential usefulness because it provides the most valid understanding available of phenomena of interest. We do not assume that such scientific knowledge is eternally "true" but only that it has relatively a higher degree of certainty than other knowledge.

Since different kinds of research offer different kinds of potentially useful knowledge, it is helpful for the research reader to identify the purpose of the research and the strategy it employs. Our classification of research as exploratory, quantitative-descriptive, and experimental facilitates this identification. In general, exploratory studies are more relevant to the generation, application, and modification of concepts and hypotheses and less relevant to the establishment of empirical generalizations. We should not ignore, however, the concepts and hypotheses in research that is quantitative-descriptive or experimental; such concepts and hypotheses may constitute useful knowledge with respect to some aspect of practice along with the specific findings themselves. The "facts" and established relationships of quantitative-descriptive studies allow other potential uses. Likewise, experimental research offers still other possible uses. We are unwilling to exclude any kind of scientific research from consideration for its usefulness because of the methods it uses or its purpose.

We also take a broad view of social work practice for which we seek useful knowledge in research studies. We believe that the same kind of knowledge—for example, a clear concept, or an empirical generalization—may find use across the range of social work practice interests. Therefore, the user of research should not narrow the definition of potential value by assuming that the research is applicable only to one practice method (such as community practice or casework), or to one field of social welfare (such as public assistance or mental health). Assessing the usefulness of research is a creative activity in which the user actively looks for the implications of the research in those areas of practice that can be informed with new knowledge. As Zetterberg points out, it is a fallacy to assume that the only useful research is that which studies the particular, concrete question the practitioner faces at a given moment.

Two examples may underline the point. An exploratory study that extends and clarifies the concept of community power structure (Bonjean, 1963), may be useful to the caseworker and group worker in understanding factors affecting availability of resources for clients; it may be useful to agency administrators seeking to introduce new services; it may be useful to social welfare planners who want to alter the balance of services in the community. The fact that the exploratory study might be made only in one community, that some of the observations are qualitative judgments, that historical events are noted as important in establishing the pattern actually found—all these may caution the user against expecting his own community to be accurately represented in the study. But insofar as the reader is made more perceptive about factors to be aware of in the practice situation, the research can be said to have usefulness.

A second example may be an experimental study (Poser, 1966) testing the efficacy of group therapy when it is provided for schizophrenic patients by professional and lay therapists. If the findings favor lay therapists and the research has a high degree of internal validity, this empirically tested generalization may be useful and suggestive to practitioners in various locations within social work. It may alert the caseworker or group worker to qualities in treatment efforts associated with characteristics other than their training; the agency administrator may have reason to ask whether the agency's effectiveness can be increased by adding lay staff members; the social work educator may look more carefully at what is trained in and trained out of social work students; and the welfare planner concerned with manpower will have an obvious interest in the research. The same practitioners should not, of course, ignore the limitations that reduce the applicability of the findings of their particular interests, for example, that this is only a single study, made with schizophrenic patients and not with their types of clients, that particular kinds of persons were used as lay therapists and so forth. The point is that practitioners with varied concerns can take something from the research that may be useful to them.

Although knowledge from a given piece of research may have relevance to all levels of social work practice, it may be more relevant to one level. Thus, the concept of community power is more salient to the community organizer than to the caseworker, and evidence of the effects of tokens as rewards for changing behavior of children is more salient to the caseworker or group worker. The practitioner's target of intervention and the tools of intervention will affect the use to be made of knowledge from a particular research study. But a piece of research cannot be assumed to be irrelevant or useless for any practice area just because it is more relevant to another area.

A perspective on utilization requires a brief statement of our view of the nature of social work. Social work includes a range of functions, and its practitioners work in a variety of jobs. Social work draws the knowledge it needs from many sources: academic disciplines of the social and behavioral sciences such as psychology, sociology, economics, and others; other helping professions such as medicine, psychiatry, law, public health, education, and others; accumulated experience and systematic study by social workers themselves of their clientele, programs, and processes of intervention to effect changes in keeping with a system of values. For our purposes, it is not necessary to delimit what social work is so much as to indicate the scope of its interest in knowledge derived from research under a wide range of auspices.

Knowledge considered relevant to social work is diverse. No single social worker could hope to master all of it, and hence specializations within social work focus on particular parts of the professional knowledge base and on particular modes of intervention and helping. Research from within social work and from social science disciplines is a basic source of knowledge. Our efforts in this book are to guide evaluation and utilization of research that appears in social work, psychology, and sociology journals. These are prime sources of knowledge for practitioners although we do not mean to exclude the research literature of the related professions and the other social sciences. We believe the same principles can be useful wherever scientific research is examined.

We particularly emphasize the view that competence of social workers must rest as much on sound knowledge from theory and research as on practice experience. This view is widely held, but few practitioners, as Rosenblatt (1968) reports in his study in New York, use knowledge from research or rate it as helpful. We believe this results partly from the fact that social work training has not included deliberate instruction in the use of research.

If the reader wishes to test the proposition that social science research and theory do, indeed, have pertinence to the practice of social workers in quite direct and concrete ways, he can examine as examples a publication of the Council on Social Work Education, *The Socio-Behavioral Approach and Applications to Social Work* (Thomas, 1967a). In that series of papers the reader can find illustrations of the direct application of some aspects of learning theory to inducing changes in clients, of the relevance of behavioral theory in administration, and of its implications in community practice as well as a consideration of the requisites in agency organization for its use. Thus a variety of uses of a research-based scientific theory are exemplified, with differential uses at different levels and for different fields.

We have noted earlier (Chapter 1) that social work journals are increasingly reporting research. There is an evident increase as well in the interest of social work in social science research. In recognition of this trend and in the conviction that social workers need to make increasing use of a broad range of research literature reported in journals and monographs, the general guidelines in keeping with our perspective on utilization are inclusive.

UTILIZATION: SOME GENERAL PROBLEMS
AND THE KEY QUESTIONS

The paradox for practitioners who would utilize research knowledge is that the more they already know about the subject of a study, the more useful it will be. This is only a reaffirmation of the observation that knowledge is cumulative for the learner and that the base from which one starts determines the level that can be attained. A social worker who has a good grasp of the substantive and methodological problems and the previous work done in an area on which research is reported will be able to assess it more fully, to recognize what it adds and where it falls short of other studies. Therefore, to a very real degree the utilization of research benefits from the reading of more and more research.

Prior familiarity with research methods and the substantive area of a piece of research provides for the reader first, a familiarity with methodological questions and a more ready skill in evaluating the research; second, a familiarity with what has previously been found through research on the subject, including the ways the concepts have been defined and operationalized, the results of various ways of formulating the problem, and the generalizations that are in the making on the subject or are awaiting more rigorous test; and third, a sense of the unanswered questions about the topic, which allows a given piece of research to be recognized as a replication of prior research or as a fresh attack on some aspect of the problem. Familiarity helps the more learned research reader decide how seriously to take the research report that is before him.

We do not mean to discourage the less informed reader by noting the advantages of prior knowledge. Such knowledge can be acquired by reading, and the social worker who spends the energy reading research articles regularly for a few months will soon locate research that fits the context of growing knowledge. Furthermore, a little practice at reading, evaluating, and utilizing research reports will show the practitioners that their training and experience generate questions on which published research often bears. Then the reading of research ceases to be casual, forced, and disconnected and begins to accumulate. This is the direction of sophistication in the knowledge base for practice.

There are a number of handicaps that social work practitioners may feel when they begin to use research. Unfamiliar vocabulary may require work to understand terms used in formulating problems and stating hypotheses and theoretical contexts. An abstract, rather than a concrete, statement of the problem may be another handicap, since much scientific research is put at theoretical levels in the attempt to see the general issue, whereas the practitioner often starts at the opposite pole, seeking the unique and concrete as the primary question. These two approaches are often not so far apart: the practitioner can readily recognize, for example, that a client's distress about her husband's "irresponsibility" may be visualized in the more abstract context of "role relationships" used as a concept in a research study. Such a conceptualization does not fully describe the concrete behaviors that the practitioner observes; it can seldom do so. This is why the prior knowledge and experience of the practitioner invariably form the context for assessment of what a research study will contribute to the handling of a problem. The question is whether, and in what ways, visualizing the general problem of role relationships contributes new and additional understandings that can be used in practice. In this sense research utilization is a creative endeavor, not passive absorption.

In our view the practitioner should approach a research report with an open sense of inquiry, just as the researcher should approach the problem studied. This does not call for the abandonment of the theoretical perspective brought from the practitioner's training or developed through experience. It calls only for accepting the research in its own terms so that it may be evaluated and utilized to expand the practitioner's knowledge for practice.

The practitioner should not expect, furthermore, that all research that is recognized as useful can be immediately put to use to improve work. The use of new knowledge is constrained by conditions other than its applicability. Among these conditions are the restrictions of agency or organizational setting in which the practitioner works, both in the formal or permissive sense and in the sense of providing the structural supports (resources, personnel arrangements, external linkages) to facilitate a change in practice (*see* Sarri and Vinter, 1967). Not all uses in practice of what is learned from research necessarily call for drastic changes in the practitioner's work. Indeed, some research will strengthen and confirm the basis of current practice; some will call practices into question or stimulate ideas for limited changes mostly within the control of the practitioner. Nevertheless, innovations in practice that use research knowledge require the practitioner to be aware of their implications in the operating situation.

Luxurious detachment, necessary to allow concentration and imaginative reading of the research, should not represent isolation. The objective is utilization, not merely understanding. The practitioner should guard against several temptations. One is the temptation to lose sight of the practice situation, as already mentioned. Another temptation is to confuse ideas stimulated by a piece of research with tested knowledge. Creative imagination is necessary to recognize implications of the research for use, but we warn against accepting with equal certainty all research, produced by any type of research strategy. Proper evaluation is an essential prerequisite to proper utilization. The dangers of these temptations will be progressively reduced as the social work practitioner becomes more skilled in reading research by reading more of it.

The guidelines that are presented in the following section are directed to the key questions that the research reader should ask about any research considered for utilization. These questions are applicable to all types of research we have classified as experimental, quantitative-descriptive, and exploratory. The key questions are:

1. Should the research report be read at all?
2. To what aspect of social work is the research relevant?
3. What knowledge content of the research may be useful?
4. How useful can the research knowledge be for practice?
5. What types of uses can be made of the research?

GENERAL GUIDELINES FOR UTILIZATION OF RESEARCH

1. Should the Research Report Be Read At All?

In Chapter 1 we considered this question in some detail. Its restatement here is only to remind the research utilizer that the question must be answered. The temptation to answer in the negative may be strong for the less experienced research reader, because the effort involved in reading research requires considerable concentration. Furthermore, the sense of relevancy is cultivated by recognizing the more general theoretical context, the more abstract level at which a problem becomes pertinent beyond its immediate empirical referents. Such a sense comes with experience in reading research. What may be a labored effort and a troublesome question about relevance of a research report becomes in time a matter of discriminating judgment. The lingering sense that an unread research report might be just what the practitioner needs, or in contrast that the effort to read an article was wasted, soon dissipates with more reading.

The decision to read a research report is affected by the judgment that it is relevant, and making this judgment involves all the other key questions that have been noted above.

2. To What Aspect of Social Work Is the Research Relevant?

The principal of "content relevance" of the research is the theme that runs through the answer to this question. We noted earlier the work of Thomas (1964, 1967a) on the subject of selecting applicable knowledge from behavioral science. We adapt his analysis for guidelines to help the reader place a research study within the activities and interests that make up social work.

Any scheme for representing the various aspects of social work will be incomplete, or excessively complex, and its categories will be imprecise and overlapping. Therefore, the scheme we propose should direct the research reader to sectors within which more refined discriminations should be made. The objective should be to locate the place in social work to which the research is relevant. As with other guidelines, only the leading questions are asked.

The framework of our scheme is indicated by the following questions:

> a. What objects of social work interest or activity does the research pertain to?
> b. Does the research pertain to current or potential objects of social work?
> c. From what value perspective are the objects of social work viewed?
> d. At what level are the objects of social work viewed?
> e. To what purposes of social work does the research pertain?

a. THE OBJECTS OF SOCIAL WORK INTEREST OR ACTIVITY.   The social work enterprise can be visualized as directed toward three interrelated classes of objects: *recipients,* the *process of serving,* and the *purveyance of services.* "Recipients" are not merely the individuals whom social workers try to help but may also be collectivities (for example, groups, organizations) and aggregates (such as children, the mentally ill). The "process of serving" as a social work activity includes what is often referred to as "the helping process," "treatment," or "therapy," but we use a more inclusive term to avoid clinical connotations only. The agencies, institutions, programs, and other social organizations, as well as the professional and nonprofessional personnel involved in providing social welfare services, make up the system of "purveyance of services."

A research study will rarely be applicable to only one of these objects of social work. Studies of recipients are often studies of clients, that is, of recipients of some helping process in some system of purveyance. For example, the decisions of unmarried mothers to keep their babies or place them for adoption may be studied in the caseload of an agency (as in Meyer *et al.,* 1956); the adjustment of young adults may be focused on their wartime residential nursery experiences (as in Maas, 1963). Sometimes, the research is fairly clear in its location. For example, a study of correlates of crime (as in Bacon *et al.,* 1963) or a study of stratification of a community (as in Faunce and Clelland, 1967)—both study recipients but in neither case *individuals* as recipients. A study by laboratory experiment of the observational process in casework is an example of research on the helping process (as in Miller, 1958). Using this scheme, the research reader can usually determine the *primary* object to which the research is directed, noting as well the other objects to which it is secondarily directed. Locating the content of a study by its applicability to an object of social work interest is different from deciding the purpose of the research so as to classify it as a type of research. The purpose and method may be exploratory, or quantitative-descriptive, or experimental when the object of social work studied is a category of recipients, a process of serving, or a system for purveyance of services. We shall see that classification by type of research is helpful at another stage of the utilization process, but not with respect to the objective of social work. All types of research are possible with reference to all objects of social work.

A study may sometimes be useful to the social worker even if it is not directed toward objects of social work we have identified. We do not include, for instance, the interest of social work in methods of research. Research to construct and validate diagnostic tests, for example, may be useful to social work researchers and to practitioners as well. A technique of research may itself be the object of interest. For example, the critical incident method (Flanagan, 1954) may be demonstrated in research whose object of study is quite apart from social work and yet it might find applicability in pertinent social work research (as in Goodrich and Boomer, 1958a and b) and in practice methods such as the life-space interview or crisis intervention.

Empirical research examines concrete objects, such as children, delinquents, youth courts, mental hospitals, casework interviewing, families of alcoholics, programs of job training, and so forth. The problems studied are viewed through specific concepts, hypotheses, and theories. The reader must always come back to the actual content of the research study after deciding what category of social work interest or activity it addresses. Within the categories we suggest—recipients, serving processes, and the system of providing services—the research reader should differentiate the particular aspect of social work to which the content of a study may be relevant.

b. CURRENT OR POTENTIAL OBJECTS OF SOCIAL WORK. The content of a research report may be relevant to *current* or *potential* objects of social work interest. Recipients, serving processes, and service systems may be recognized as within social work today or they may be recognized as potentially within the social work domain. How the distinction is made will depend on the reader's definition of the scope of social work and familiarity with current practice. In the reader's own area, at any rate, existing practice and emerging directions of practice are likely to be known.

Deciding whether research is *potentially relevant* in content is also a matter of judgment and imagination. In some instances, the subject matter is easily recognized as pertinent to social work even if it is primarily an object of other helping professions. Thus, studies of school children, mental hospital patients, residents of housing projects, race relations agencies, community planning commissions, and the like are readily recognized as potentially relevant to social work even if the research is not about anything social workers now do. Studies of helping methods that are new, even if not used by social workers, may have potential relevance. Content that may seem quite distant—for example, demographic studies, animal experiments, industrial relations research, and the like—may have potential relevance. Sensitivity to potential relevance will depend on breadth of perspective. Not all research content is potentially relevant, but the reader is alerted here not to confine his perspective too narrowly to existing social work activities and interests. Most practitioners will be aware that recipients, helping processes, and social services that were considered outside the interests of social work a few years ago are now prominent in professional attention.

c. THE VALUE PERSPECTIVE TOWARD THE OBJECTS OF SOCIAL WORK. The research reader can be helped to locate a study's relevance to social work by keeping in mind the continuum suggested by such terms as: *normality-abnormality, socially approved–socially deviant,* and *organized-disorganized.* The research reader does not need to make this sort of judgment about the objects that are studied. That is, the question is not whether the recipients (for example, families with female heads) are "normal" or "abnormal," or the purveyance of services (for example, a correctional institution or court system) is "functional" or "dysfunctional." His question is *whether the research has been conceived as a study of behavior or conditions that fall toward one or the other side of this continuum.*

The concern of social work with serving always implies values about the condition of some object of service. Therefore, a social worker will necessarily be alert to studies of problematic situations, such as the disturbed child, the family in stress or crisis, the inadequacy of welfare benefits, and the like. Implicit in such an interest is the assumption of "normal" or "healthy" states. Research on these states may be relevant because it supplies baselines for understanding "abnormality" and because it is assumed that some principles will be found to operate across the entire continuum from "normal" to "abnormal."

The research reader need not expect studies to fall at the extremes of the normal-abnormal continuum. Judgment of the use to be made of the research can be better, however, if the reader considers the extent to which the research views recipients as normal or abnormal, or looks at the serving process and service system from the viewpoint of its strengths or its weaknesses.

d. THE LEVEL ON WHICH THE OBJECTS OF SOCIAL WORK ARE VIEWED. The content relevance of research is also assessed by identifying the level of the social work interest or activity that is studied. By level, we mean to suggest broad distinctions that may be made in the targets of social work practice—from helping the individual to changing features of the social system—as well as distinctions in the methods of achieving these objectives—from the use of interpersonal interaction to social legislation (Meyer et al., 1967). Although they are interrelated, the levels mark distinctions that are generally recognized in social work and in the social sciences between the *individual,* the *group,* the *social organization,* the *community,* and the *society* (Thomas, 1964).

One need not struggle with the philosophical issues of emergent reality (that is, whether each successive level constitutes more than aggregations of lower levels) or the associated issue of reductionism (or whether each level can be understood in terms of the levels below it). We may simply accept the levels as familiar conceptualizations of the phenomena that social work and social science are concerned with.

The distinctions between individual, group, organization, community, and society are expressed in somewhat different ways when applied to different objects of social work. The vocabulary of social work reflects different levels of recipients when "clients" are defined as individuals, or groups, or agencies, or communities. When research is about actual or potential *recipients,* it will not often be difficult to locate the level on which the research is conceived. Sometimes the researcher may collect data at more than one level, and sometimes the analysis of data may shift from one to another level. For example, the data may be about social conditions in various census tracts (for example, family income, marital status of household heads, housing, and so on), which are correlated with rates of delinquency, or mental illness. It is the "ecological fallacy" to interpret such correlations of variables about geographical areas (community level) as applicable to the behavior of persons (individual level) (Robinson, 1950) except under special conditions (*see* Goodman, 1953). A study of members of families on welfare is different from a study of welfare families. Although the research may provide knowledge about several levels, its questions, concepts, and hypotheses will usually be formulated in terms of one level. The reader can often determine that level by asking what phenomena are sampled. Did the researcher, in fact, study individuals or groups or some other collectivity?

When the *process of serving* is the aspect of social work that is studied, the vocabulary of social work usually differentiates the various levels in forms of social work methods, that is, casework and group work (sometimes called "direct" methods), community organization and social welfare administration (sometimes called "indirect" methods). The following scheme may aid in identifying the level on which the process of serving is located:

RECIPIENT LEVEL	RELATED SOCIAL WORK METHOD	CHANGE OBJECTIVE OF SERVICE	TYPICAL MEANS OF INTERVENTION
Individual.........	Casework	Internal states of persons; relations between persons	Interpersonal influence (usually one-to-one)
Group..............	Group work	Internal states of persons; relations between persons	Interpersonal influence (usually in small groups)
Organization....	Administration	Structure and process of organizations, e.g., agencies, treatment institutions, etc.	Manipulation of organizational patterns and external relations
Community......	Community practice	Relations between groups and organizations	Intergroup and interorganizational manipulation by social action, planning, etc.
Society.............	Social welfare policy	Some aspect of the social welfare institution, e.g., programs of service	Policy proposals and development, legislation, reform movements, etc.

The overlap of levels, particularly contiguous ones, is evident. The levels are sufficiently distinguishable, however, to allow the research reader to locate the aspect of social work to which a study is primarily pointed. Using such a scheme, the reader may note the level of the serving process within the interests of social work whether or not it is explicitly identified by the researcher as concerned with one of the usual social work methods.

The idea of levels requires some adaptation when applied to the location of research on *purveyance of services*. Three kinds of distinctions may be useful:

1. Individuals, groups, and communities may be viewed as involved in some *field of practice* (mental health, child welfare, corrections) or some *problematic area* in which services are provided (race relations, job training and employment, income maintenance). Fields of practice and problematic areas can be classified in various ways. One way is to identify them as concerned with: (1) socialization (education, corrections, marital and family adjustment, child care, recreation), (2) physical and mental health (medical and psychiatric patients, public health and community mental health programs), (3) economic provision (income maintenance, housing, employment), (4) participation in citizen roles (racial discrimination, political influence on public decisions, the political process). Obviously these are not discrete categories; some services (for example, for the aged or for children) fall into

several or all categories. It is not necessary that a way of looking at social services be definitive; the changing social services make a definitive classification impossible. The research reader need only be alerted to the value of locating a study of purveyance of service in some such scheme in order to recognize the aspect of social work to which it may be applicable.

2. *The targets of various social services* may be conceived usefully for some purposes as recipients at the different levels, for example, individuals (the mentally ill), or groups (delinquent gangs), or organizations (correctional agencies), or community relations (between races, between agencies), or the societal level (income maintenance policies).

3. A useful distinction for locating research studies of the purveyance of services can be made between *professional* arrangements and *organizational* arrangements in their provision. Professional arrangements have to do with the numbers, sources, training levels, and deployment of manpower in social welfare. Research may be reported on all these aspects of providing services, and also on the characteristics of the social work profession itself (social work education, associations in the profession, and so forth). Studies of the use of nonprofessionals and clients as workers (indigenous workers) also come to mind. Organizational arrangements have to do with the complex of agencies (public and private; local, state, and national), their interrelations, their operations, and their changes. Studies of social welfare policies and their implementation through programs and agencies are also included. Both professional and organizational arrangements may be studied as they bear on all levels of recipients in various fields of practice or problematic areas.

e. THE SOCIAL WORK PURPOSE OF THE RESEARCH.   A final question to ask about the content relevance of a research study is its bearing on the different purposes of the social work enterprise. The reader may examine a study in terms of its social work purposes even if the research was produced with no awareness or interest in such purposes. The reader's intent is to assess utility for social work; the intent of the researcher is usually quite different.

Of the many attempts to summarize the mission, responsibilities, and domain of social work, the following is representative (Meyer, 1968, p. 495):

> The objectives of social work are to help individuals, families, communities, and groups of persons who are socially disadvantaged and to contribute to the creation of conditions that will enhance social functioning and prevent breakdown. These objectives commit the social work profession both to helping persons adapt socially in keeping with their capacities and the norms and values of the society, and to modifying or reforming features of the social system. The term "social worker" refers to a special group among those employed in rendering social welfare services or conducting programs of agencies and institutions that make up the social welfare system. The profes-

sional social worker is expected, because of his specialized training and experience, to bring a high degree of skill to the process of helping, and modifying the social conditions of, individuals, groups of persons, and communities. The special competence of the professional social worker is exercised in such tasks as providing material assistance for the needy and dependent; assisting those of whatever means who have difficulties in adjusting to their economic and social environment because of poverty, illness, deprivation, conflict, or personal, family, or social disorganization; and participating in the formulation of social welfare policies and preventive programs.

In view of such objectives, the reader may ask if knowledge from a research study contributes to his understanding of how to *alleviate* undesirable conditions, to *enhance* desirable conditions, or to *prevent* undesirable conditions from occurring. Knowledge from a research study may serve all three purposes or be more pertinent to one than another. All these purposes involve the exercise of some control over an aspect of the social world. When research is read, the practitioner can ask how the increased control that knowledge from the research may give will be useful for the treatment, facilitative, or preventive aspect of practice. Our emphasis here is on the ends to which knowledge may be put in social work practice.

3. What Knowledge Content of the Research May Be Useful?

The preceding section has dealt with aspects of social work that the research reader should think about when reading a research report. Equally important is the content of the research study itself. What kinds of knowledge can the reader get from the research? By "knowledge" we mean all that is cognitively contained in the study. Three kinds of knowledge may be distinguished: (1) empirical knowledge, (2) conceptual knowledge, and (3) methodological knowledge. Considerations of each of these kinds of content will help the reader assess the utility of the research.

Empirical research investigates some aspect of the observable world. What is investigated is the empirical referent of the research and what is reported about the empirical referent is the *empirical content* of the research. The study may be about mental retardates, or about race riots, or about groups of boys at a settlement house. It may be about what social workers do or about rates of mental illness or about families where marriage partners are in conflict. Some kind of behavior, some social condition, some set of events will be looked at through the concepts and methods of the research. Knowledge about that empirical content may have focal, or immediate, interest to the social worker whose own practice is concerned with the same empirical area. For example, a study of aftercare of institutionalized mental retardates has focal empirical relevance to a social worker whose caseload contains retardates, or one who works with families of retardates. A study of group work with street gangs of delinquents will have focal empirical relevance to social workers engaged in such practice. Often the research will not fall squarely in the empirical area of the reader's practice. Its empirical content may, nevertheless, be of adjunctive relevance. The phenomena of aftercare may be relevant to the practitioner whose clients include the mentally ill, delinquents, or persons whose chronic illness involves periodic institutionalization. Those who work with delinquents in community centers may gain useful knowledge from a study of delinquents in street gangs, and social workers working with groups of adolescents in any setting may learn more about the phenomena of group work from a study of group work in the streets. The reader should consider the classes of phenomena examined by the research and ask if these phenomena also are directly or adjunctively involved in his practice.

Empirical research studies also provide *conceptual knowledge*. The empirical phenomena are always viewed through concepts; concepts are often related to one another in hypotheses which may be explicitly or implicitly linked in theories; generalizations about the empirical phenomena may be established or suggested. The level of conceptual content that the reader can make use of from the study depends on the purpose and methods of the research (and hence its type) and also on the success with which the research achieves its purpose (and hence on an evaluation of it). Experimental research may allow the reader to consider applicability to practice of the empirical generalizations it demonstrates (with due regard to limitations of generalizability); it may allow the reader also to consider applicability of hypotheses tested and the concepts that have been used. The conceptual content of an exploratory study, on the other hand, will not include empirical generalizations; the knowledge it offers may be limited to hypotheses and concepts. All levels of knowledge may be useful to the reader, each in different ways providing a way to deal with problems in practice with increased awareness of the nature of the phenomena worked with and various ways of working. The reader should determine not only what level of knowledge the research provides, but also what level is most useful in relation to particular interests of his or her practice.

The research reader may gain useful *methodological knowledge* from a research study. We refer here not to knowledge about how to use methods to carry on research but to the possible uses of the research methods in social work practice. For instance, the test or questionnaire developed to collect data for a study of role conflict in marriage may be useful, or adaptable for use, in diagnosis of cases involving marital conflict. The method used to manipulate the independent variable in an experiment, for example, creation of group cohesion, may be adaptable to use in a practice situation where a similar manipulation is desired. Sometimes the research design of a study will suggest ways the practitioner can think of practice.

For example, research based on the comparison of continuing and discontinuing clients may suggest that looking at one's caseload in similar terms is useful. A method of identifying community leaders for study of community power may be useful for identifying community leaders for the board of an agency.

4. How Useful Can the Research Knowledge Be for Practice?

If the research reader finds that the content of a study has relevance to social work, the next question is how useful the knowledge it offers can be. We follow the analyses of Thomas (1964) and Meyer *et al.* (1967) and Gouldner (1956, 1957) to approach this question.

The usefulness of a research study will depend both on the *soundness,* or validity, of its contribution to the reader's knowledge and on the extent to which the knowledge is *engineerable,* or capable of being put into practice.

The *soundness* of the study is related, as we have indicated earlier, to the purpose of the research and the methods employed. Classification of the research (Chapter 2) and its evaluation (Chapter 3) help the reader to judge soundness and hence to determine how much confidence should be placed in the results. Soundness will be found not only in terms of generalizability of the findings (that is, what they can say beyond the particular study), but also in terms of what specific addition the study has made to the limited questions the research set out to answer. One should not expect, for instance, an exploratory study to produce empirical generalizations, but one may ask if the exploratory study has been well done and if its findings were derived on the basis of appropriate methods. In general the sounder a piece of research is found to be, the more useful it can be. It is tempting to dismiss less sound research as useless, but, as we have stressed throughout this book, the research should be evaluated for its contributions as well as its limitations. Judging its limitations and strengths is prerequisite to making judgments about other aspects of its utility for the practitioner.

When judging soundness, the research reader may find it helpful to think of the guidelines for evaluating research (presented in Chapter 3) as testing the *power* of the knowledge. Thomas points out three features of knowledge that affect its power in application: (1) Validity of the propositions, that is, the extent to which conclusions are corroborated by evidence. "If," Thomas notes, "the studies of a given domain are not well done, if the findings are inconsistent with what is otherwise known, or if there are precious few adequate investigations of a problem, empirically valid generalizations cannot be formulated and application would therefore be hazardous" (Thomas, 1964, p. 42); (2) predictive potency of the knowledge, that is, the extent to which the conclusions of research allow propositions to be stated that link with more inclusive and coherent theory, thus providing additional derivations to be made that are logical consequences of the theory; (3) potency of the variables, that is, the extent to which the independent variables of a research study account for the results. For a hypothetical example, if a study showed that both the degree of a client's anxiety and his ability to communicate verbally were related to continuance in treatment (Levinger, 1960), but the former variable (anxiety) was more weakly related, the latter variable (verbal communication) would be considered more potent. Variables that account for more of the variance in the dependent variable are likely to be more useful for the practitioner, if other things are equal.

The criteria of validity, predictive potency, and variable potency are most clearly applicable to judgments about studies seeking to establish empirical generalizations, such as hypothesis-testing studies. This does not imply that such research is always more useful than research producing limited results. Research in social work and the social sciences ideally strives toward production of knowledge with more power, but most of the research does not achieve this. Quantitative-descriptive and exploratory studies, like experimental research, reach toward the same objective, and results may be assessed as more promising if they lead to new studies with increasingly powerful variables. The criteria of validity, predictive potency, and variable potency can be used for different types of research to help the reader achieve a better basis for judging the soundness of the research.

Usefulness of research results will depend, as we have noted, on *engineerability* as well as on soundness. This quality in research knowledge has also been called its "referent features" (Thomas, 1964). Engineerability is concerned with three sorts of questions: (1) To what extent are the variables of the research available for control by the practitioner? (2) Will manipulation of the variables have much or little effect in achieving the practitioner's objectives? (3) Is the manipulation of the variables feasible? These are questions about the real world of the practitioner and must be asked in order to utilize the knowledge no matter how sound the research is. As Thomas notes: "With few exceptions, the empirical indicators, or referents, of the variables of potentially useful knowledge have simply been ignored in the applied behavioral sciences" (Meyer *et al.*, 1967, p. 167). Users, too, have tended to apply only the criteria of researchers (that is, criteria of soundness) without asking what other requirements the research knowledge must have if it is to be used in practice. We consider each question in turn.

(1) To determine if the research uses *variables available for control by the practitioner,* the research reader must determine to what extent the variables are identifiable, accessible, and manipulable. Variables are

identifiable to the extent that they have clearly specified referents that are observable in the empirical world. This usually means that the operational definitions of the concepts which the variables define are made explicit, clear, and capable of systematic observation. Concepts such as the "unconscious," "libido," and "id," for example, seem to have no discernible empirical referents, whatever sense of clinical insight they stimulate. Other concepts—for example "ego strength," "sympathetic support," "group cohesion," and the like—gain in identifiability as they become operationalized by researchers through specific tests, and the specification of concrete behaviors and conditions. Still other concepts have referents that are clearly established, such as group size, some indices of social class, and reinforcement of responses. *Accessible variables* are those that are, or can be, within the field of activity of the practitioner. For example, research might show that labeling a delinquent as such at school contributes to his delinquency, but the practitioner may not have access to the school teachers and peers who apply the label. This does not mean that the variable is necessarily of no use if, for example, it is linked by theory and other research to variables that connect it and the dependent variable of interest. To use the same example, if labeling is shown to be related to self-image and self-image to delinquent behavior, the practitioner may through his relationship with a client affect the delinquent's self-image and thus counter the effects of labeling. Without accessibility, a variable cannot be *manipulable*. That is, it may not be within the power of the practitioner to affect it. A variable with a high degree of manipulability, for example, is group size; another is the conduct of the caseworker in the interview with a client; another, an administrator's control over the budget of his agency. Like identifiability and accessibility, manipulability is usually a matter of degree since there are always limits to the practitioner's capacity and opportunity to effect changes. In general, the results of research are more useful if the variables of the research have high degrees of these attributes.

To find a research study useful, the reader need not conclude that the particular variables involved are duplicated in the particular practice situation. If the research shows, for example, that consistent and regular rewards to school children increase their studying, the practitioner can consider whether or not the class of variables involved (rewards) might be identifiable, accessible, and manipulable for purposes of the reader's practice and clients.

(2) The second question to be asked about research to assess its engineerability is the degree to which the variables that can be manipulated *have an effect on the condition or situation* the practitioner wants to affect. Even if the research reader is satisfied with the validity of a study and concludes that the variables it uses are manipulable, the relationships may be relative-

ly weak, and hence their use promises little effect. For example, although it is related to continuance, the referral source for a client to a family service agency may be less strongly related than the client's sense of making progress in the first interview with the caseworker. The research that provides evidence of stronger relationships is likely to be more useful. In any event the strength of the relationship needs to be considered when assessing utilization.

(3) Similarly, the *feasibility* for the practitioner of using the variables of the research should be assessed. Both the specific situation of the practitioner and the general situation of the profession must be taken into account. Among the factors affecting feasibility for manipulation of particular variables are the economic costs involved, the ethical suitability of the manipulations, and the organizational constraints imposed. An example of the first is seen in the difference between the cost of full field investigations of welfare applicants and the cost of having them file affidavits of need, with spot checks of accuracy. In general, on the principle of economy, the affidavit is to be preferred if research shows both practices equally satisfactory for getting information necessary for determining eligibility. Some variables that are manipulable may be prohibitively expensive on existing or realistically contemplated budgets as, for example, the reduction of class size to ten per teacher in slum schools, or the complete resettlement of an entire population. Conditions affecting costs change, however, and the research reader needs to consider possible sources of economic support so as to follow the lead of a promising variable. Utilization is also affected by the ethical suitability of manipulating the variables involved. Massive deprivation may be demonstrably effective in changing some attitudes, as studies of concentration camps have shown, but such deprivation would violate professional ethics as well as humanitarian values. Sometimes what is effective in a laboratory research study, for example, withholding information, is unethical in the practice situation. There are no fixed rules to decide such questions, but they must nevertheless be asked of the research when considering its utilization. The reader will have to weigh them against personal standards of professional conduct and the standards that the profession generally accepts, expressed sometimes in codes of ethics of social workers and sometimes in agency rules. The organizational constraints under which the social worker practices may extend beyond questions of costs and ethics to include limitations and possibilities of the particular agency, as in the example of supplying contraceptive devices when agency policy forbids it. Such constraints may subject the practitioner to conflicting commitments between professional and agency values and the user of research needs to be aware of such conflicts in judging the utility of the research.

5. What Types of Use Can Be Made of the Research?

The most obvious type of use for a research study is in *direct application.* It may be useful *indirectly,* even if not directly. If limited in both these ways, the research may still be useful because it *clarifies understanding, sharpens insights,* or *provokes new ways of thinking* about an aspect of social work.

Direct application is possible when the conditions previously discussed about the research—its relevance to social work, its soundness and feasibility—are favorable. Much research will not meet these criteria, but some will. It may be sufficiently established, for instance, that nonprofessional workers can be of service to clients of a neighborhood center and that this is a feasible addition to personnel. This type of research knowledge can be directly applied by an agency director in making a decision. Even in such a case the practitioner cannot apply the knowledge automatically but must weigh the actual situation in all aspects when making the decision. From the viewpoint of utilization, however, the research has maximum usability.

Indirect applicability of research results may be of several sorts, and the research reader should be alert to them. The study may provide knowledge of effective variables that are not manipulable (as previously illustrated) but which may lead to variables that are manipulable. It may allow the practitioner to take complementary action (Thomas, 1964, p. 46), such as the adaptation of treatment method to the circumstances of the client that are known to affect the desired outcome. Knowing, for example, that lower-class clients at psychiatric clinics discontinue more often than middle-class clients when the help offered depends on verbal interaction, the practitioner may deliberately apply that knowledge to change the style of service used. There are many adaptations of practice that research knowledge will suggest to the creative and imaginative practitioner. Research studies should be read with such possibilities in mind.

We repeat here our reminder that the methods used in a research study, as well as its results, may find direct or indirect applicability. What the researcher has done that produces a predicted effect in a dependent variable may possibly be done by the practitioner. This is most clearly the case when an experiment has been performed using different forms of treatment (Paul, 1967) or different kinds of personnel (Poser, 1966). The techniques used in a study to define community leadership may be adaptable by the practitioner to influence decisions in desired directions (Bonjean, 1963). A study of conditions that affect clinical judgment (Orcutt, 1964) may supply the social worker with further understanding of the diagnostic process being used, which in turn is related to choice of treatment techniques. Perhaps the best known example of research technique yielding a practice technique was the discovery of clinical uses for nondirective interviewing in the Western Electric studies in the 1920's (Roethlisberger and Dickson, 1939).

Finally, research that does not offer direct or indirect application may nevertheless be stimulating, clarifying, and provocative. Research reading is not the only source of these effects, to be sure. Many other kinds of literature and many experiences of living produce such stimulations, and they are not to be minimized for the practitioner. Our concern is that the reader be particularly alert to benefits to practice that may come from the ideas stimulated by the research read. Creative responsiveness is quite different from casual speculation, and ideas stimulated from reading research are not to be mistaken for conclusions based on the research. The research reader who has carefully assessed utilization of the research through all the steps of the guidelines is in a position to think creatively about issues of practice in the light of the research, and in this sense can make use of it for the stimulation of new ideas. One sign that this is a useful result of reading a research study is the recognition and formulation of new problems for research. The research reader has not finished the study of the research until he or she has thought about new or different research that will be more useful.

SUMMARY OF MAJOR QUESTIONS AS GENERAL GUIDELINES TO UTILIZATION OF EMPIRICAL RESEARCH STUDIES

For convenience of the reader, the major headings for the general guidelines discussed in the previous section of this chapter are reproduced below, as a set of related questions. When using this summary, remember that it is meant only to highlight the chief issues already discussed in more detail. The guidelines are not, we repeat, to be thought of as fixed and mechanical; they are supposed to suggest types of issues, orientations toward questions, and directions of analysis so that the research reader will develop personal guidelines and habits of critical and creative reading.

When looking over the summary of guidelines, remember too that there is no necessary sequence in which they are to be used. The research reader does not necessarily answer questions about relevance apart from questions about potential usefulness to practice. Judgments will be made on many or most of the features bearing on utilization simultaneously, just as they will with respect to evaluation of the research. The guidelines to utilization should stimulate differentiated and discriminative reading. In short, they should heighten sophistication of the social worker as a research reader.

GENERAL GUIDELINES TO UTILIZATION: SUMMARY OF MAJOR QUESTIONS

I. Should the research report be read at all?
    A. Does reader have a particular practice problem?

    B. Is the research likely to bear on reader's practice area?

    C. Is the research important for social work generally?

II. To what aspect of social work is the research relevant?

    A. What objects of social work interest and activity are addressed?

        1. Recipients?

        2. Process of service?

        3. Purveyance of service?

    B. Does the research pertain to current or potential objects of social work?

    C. From what value perspective are the objects of study viewed?

    D. On what levels does the research visualize the objects of interest?

        1. Recipients:

           a. Individual

           b. Group

           c. Organization

           d. Community

           e. Society

        2. Process of serving:

           a. Interpersonal intervention

           b. Manipulation of organizational patterns

           c. Interorganizational and intergroup manipulation

           d. Policy proposals and development

        3. Purveyance of service:

           a. Professional arrangements

           b. Organizational arrangements

    E. What social work purpose does the research serve?

        1. Treatment?

        2. Enhancement?

        3. Prevention?

III. What knowledge content of the research may be useful?

    A. Empirical knowledge?

    B. Conceptual knowledge?

    C. Methodological knowledge?

IV. How useful can the research be for practice?

    A. How sound is the research?

    B. How engineerable are the variables?

        1. How available are variables for control by practitioner?

        2. How much difference in the practice situation will it make if the variables are manipulated?

        3. How feasible is it to manipulate variables of the research in the practice situation?

           a. Economic feasibility?

           b. Ethical suitability?

           c. Organizational constraints?

V. What types of use can be made of the research?

    A. Direct application?

    B. Indirect or complementary application?
    C. General stimulation?

FIRST STEPS IN UTILIZATION

As you make the first quick examination of a research study or article, you can make tentative assessments about utilization. As the research becomes familiar, the general guidelines for utilization presented in this chapter should be brought more consciously to the forefront. After you have classified and evaluated the research, the utilization guidelines can be applied more specifically, with attention to the special considerations for experimental, quantitative-descriptive, and exploratory studies.

We would reemphasize the importance for the reader of considering what other knowledge is available that pertains to the area of inquiry of the research. An early step toward assessing the research for utilization should be a determination of the extent of ignorance and knowledgeability of the subject the reader has. It will usually be advantageous for the reader to check the summary of previous research often referred to in introductory sections of the report, including references to review articles and other means of gaining a secure sense of how the present research can be placed in the history of the problem. Prior work on application of knowledge about the subject to social work and related helping professions should be looked for. A broad and informed perspective will enhance assessment of the utilizability of the research.

If the reader is not thoroughly familiar with the general guidelines of this chapter, or with the literature cited in its earlier sections, it may be helpful to write summary answers to the major questions, leaving space on the work pages to fill in further details as the research becomes more familiar.

Follow the guidelines, or your own rendition of them, in some detail, particularly noting the special questions pertinent to the type of research.

UTILIZATION OF DIFFERENT TYPES OF STUDIES: SOME SPECIAL CONSIDERATIONS

Experimental Studies

Because they lead toward empirical generalizations, the findings of sound experimental studies may have much utility if the dependent variable has content relevance for the research reader and the independent variables are engineerable. The reader should judge these features of the research in the light of knowledge about other independent variables that may be related to the effects examined in the experiment. The conditions controlled in the experiment may be stronger in the situation the practitioner actually faces than the variables that are manipulated in the experiment. In laboratory experiments particularly, situations may be contrived in ways that do not have analogues in practice. For example, the extreme cases presented in an experiment on "anchoring effects" on clinical judgment (Orcutt, 1964) may not occur very often in actual practice. Nevertheless, such an experiment may sensitize the practitioner to the effects of "anchoring" and alert him to some of the determinants of diagnostic conclusions being used. The reader should judge how "unreal," that is, unlikely to be found outside the experiment, the experimental situation is and what features of it are approximated in the practice situation. Sometimes the conditions of an experiment can readily be created by the practitioner. For instance, candy or other rewards shown effective by experiments in changing behavior of children might easily be introduced into practice. Not infrequently, you will find opportunities in practice to approximate experimental situations. In some instances the experiment may be applied directly in practice, as when, for example, the independent variable is a form of group management (Lewin, Lippitt, and White, 1939). Subsequent field experiments may be necessary to establish empirical generalizations of the results of a series of laboratory experiments, but you can apply the implications to practice, keeping in mind that they are used only as hypotheses.

Field experiments face the risk of producing "negative" results, that is, results that fail to show that a practice technique, a program of service, or a special effort to help has succeeded. In fact, it is sometimes cynically said that the demonstration of successful treatment is inversely related to the rigor of the experiment testing it! A natural first reaction of a practitioner who reads the results of such an experiment is often defensive, as though the research was defective because it failed to substantiate the practitioner's hopes. Indeed, the research may be defective, and almost surely it will not be entirely satisfactory. The research reader should subject the research to severe criticism in order to judge its soundness and should also not fail to consider that the evidence may cast doubt on practice effectiveness, and hence stimulate thinking about alternative practice methods. Researchers often conclude reports of experiments that show disappointing effectiveness of practice with speculations about alternative approaches. These may be suggestive, but they should not be confused with the findings of the research, and the research reader should ask what implications negative findings have for practice. Negative results cannot "prove" anything conclusively, but they are very valuable for correcting illusions, for creating, as it were, realistic doubts. These, in turn, can be a stimulus for creative thinking about new practice approaches.

Field experiments directly pertaining to practice may provide the reader with more than knowledge bearing on effectiveness of practice. They often call attention to variables that need consideration in conceptualizing practice and building practice theory. For example, attention to the specific behavior of the helping person may result from recognition in a field experiment that "service" or "casework" is only vaguely conceived (Meyer *et al.*, 1965). Sometimes the actual arrangements made to conduct the field experiment are themselves applicable to practice, as when ways of reducing clerical tasks are developed to make more time available for training (Thomas and McLeod, 1960). When the vicissitudes of conducting the field experiment are described, the practitioner may often learn much about problems of resistance to change by social workers and agencies.

The types of side-products of experimental studies are numerous, and we have suggested only a few examples to encourage the reader to be sensitive to many more.

Quantitative-Descriptive Studies

Many quantitative-descriptive studies, such as those assessing community needs, produce directly applicable knowledge when they have content relevance. The reader should be careful in using findings from these studies not to generalize improperly to other populations (for example, other communities, other classes of clients, and so on), without taking into account differences that may affect the validity of the generalization. It is not necessary to read a survey study as though it could be applied only to the respondents, or even to the universe from which the respondents are drawn, provided the application is clearly recognized as uncertain and tentative and only as an approximation. It is better to err on the side of caution in making generalizations, but to be over-cautious is to deny the advantage of thinking of a population in the light of what is known about different populations.

Hypothesis-testing descriptive studies, and those showing the relationships between variables, can often provide a realistic sense of how a theory can be applied. They may reflect actual conditions and hence be more useful than experiments where controls are more rigorous. The reader may get information about multiple factors that bear on a relationship from analyses of descriptive data. When relationships between variables are translated into predictions, the contingent conditions may be more evident than in experimental studies. On the other hand, the less rigorous control of independent variables may weaken the relationships found and lead the reader to underestimate the validity of the theory.

Studies showing relationships of variables to some behavior of relevance to the practitioner do not, of course, establish cause-effect relationships. To show that lack of exercise or cigarette smoking is significantly correlated with heart attacks does not mean that these have been shown to "cause" heart attacks. To show that children who are poor readers come from homes where the parental educational level is low does not mean that the one causes the other. The research reader is alerted by such findings, however, to seek possible explanations (hypotheses and theories) for the relationships. This may lead to increased sensitivity to the meanings of the variables. For example, what is the meaning to the child of living with parents of low educational level? Is there some characteristic of persons who have little exercise that might be found to be causally related to heart attack? As a superficial example, the point may be illustrated by considering the findings that the religion of wives is related to the number of children they bear. Knowing the historical attitude of the Catholic church toward contraception, religion is readily translatable as an indicator of attitudes that in turn may be more meaningfully put into a theory of family planning. Refining the meaning of variables known to be related to one another is a useful step in thinking about the significance of knowledge from variable-relationship studies in terms of possible hypotheses that might illuminate aspects of practice.

One value of descriptive studies is that they may provide base lines for looking at trends and changes. Re-surveys are obviously useful for this purpose. Even without a second study, knowledge of the state of a population, a condition, or a service, if it is based on more than impressionistic information, provides the practitioner with a reference point for making judgments about what may have changed. Cross-sectional, one-shot surveys may also give information about changes when, for example, they provide breakdowns of the data in terms of time strata such as age of respondents, length of residence, or years of service in a given position. The assumptions made to conclude that change, rather than selective factors, may be responsible for differences need to be carefully examined. If the reader does so, reasonable judgments may be made about trends that may help in some practical decision.

Most quantitative-descriptive studies are based on samples and, as indicated in Chapter 3, the character of the sample is crucial for generalizing from the study. Another aspect of the sample that bears on utility of the results has to do with the relevance of the sample to some action or policy of interest to the practitioner. A study from a sample that permits generalization to a segment of the population, such as leaders or legislators or rioters, may lead to information especially relevant to the community organization worker or the planner of social policy. Of course, surveys that allow responses to be differentiated for several segments of a population have the added advantage of permitting comparisons to be made. Not all surveys present data in this form.

Exploratory Studies

By their nature, exploratory studies do not produce findings of generalizability. Therefore, the principal use of these studies is to enhance sensitivity to problems, to help clarify concepts, and to stimulate differential thinking about phenomena of interest. This order of usefulness is worthy of attention, and indeed, it may be said that most of the use made of social science research in social work has been of this sort. Concepts that have been elaborated or specified by exploratory research have often been applied to phenomena the practitioner deals with. For example, the concepts of role, culture, bureaucracy, and others have been found useful for thinking about client behavior and agency organization. Often concepts rather than findings have been used from quantitative-descriptive and experimental studies.

Concepts and hypotheses can be more useful if they are precisely defined. The reader should note how studies operationalize concepts and whether or not there are parallels in practice that allow similar operationalizations. Can the concept be referred to particular behaviors or measures? Sometimes pinning down a concept to its operational meaning will call attention to the need for other concepts to describe a phenomenon sufficiently.

When exploratory studies examine a given research technique—for example, the use of the critical incident—you should ask yourself what potential use such a technique has in practice. You should think beyond the technique itself and try to imagine other ways of observing, measuring, or manipulating variables that might be adapted for practice purposes.

It is particularly useful to ask of exploratory studies what potential lines of practice are suggested by the research. This question is directed to the stimulation of practice questions rather than research questions. The latter, too, may be usefully considered by the reader because research questions may lead to fresh ideas for practice. What are the unanswered questions about practice that emerge in the light of the research? What research might lead into these questions, and how can the practice implications be put to test? Like the conduct of research, the utilization of research ends, as it begins, with a question.

Chapter 5

Assessing Historical Research

Since the first edition of this book was published in 1969, research in areas pertinent to social work by social historians has become increasingly visible. Studies of the origins, operating experiences, and consequences—often unintended—of social programs, such as juvenile courts, are reviewed in the popular press. In academic locations, visibility is reflected by attention in college and university courses to historical studies, some assembled in anthologies such as *The American Family in Social-Historical Perspective* (Gordon, 1973). Topics that have attracted special attention, such as social gerontology and women's studies, make evident their roots in historical studies of issues that are of concern today. Illustrative titles are *Old Age in the New Land* (Achenbaum, 1978) and *Women, Work and Family* (Tilly and Scott, 1978). Social work shows its own renewed attention to the history of social service institutions and policies, as in Leiby's *A History of Social Welfare and Social Work in the United States* (1978), and in the characteristics of its practice in earlier periods, as in "Social Casework Practice during the 'Psychiatric Deluge' " (Field, 1980). A book about research methods and how social workers can use research (Grinnell, 1981) contains a chapter (by Stuart) on "Historical Research," a topic seldom treated as part of the regular content of research courses for social workers.

It is appropriate and timely, in light of this development, to include in this book a discussion of how historical research might usefully be assessed. The student or practitioner of social work will find the guidelines presented in Chapters 2 to 4 useful in general as an orientation to the kinds of questions to ask of historical research. This chapter will use the frame of reference of classification, evaluation, and utilization with modifications required to fit the nature of reports of historical research appearing in the literature.

Historical research is viewed as empirical research in the meaning that this book adopts in Chapter 1. The objective of research by historians to which we address our attention is to obtain knowledge about the observable world, about phenomena that independent researchers following the same or other appropriate methods can identify and communicate about. Since historical research deals with events and behaviors that occurred in the past, it is deprived of opportunity to make new, direct observations that bear on the topic of interest. Even memories of past events—with their own inherent limitations as observations of events and behaviors—last only the lifetime of informants. This does not mean that new information about a problem cannot be obtained. New sources and records, new ways of organizing the information in documents and reports, and new ways of synthesizing and analyzing available observations are possible. Whether the research leads to quantified data or documentary and nonquantified observations, we may consider it empirical research when its *purpose* is to answer questions and reduce ignorance and it uses a *method* involving reported and systematic procedures to acquire information and expose logical processes to reach conclusions. Historical research as empirical research in the sense here indicated is squarely within the purview of this book which is to facilitate effective reading of empirical research by social workers and other consumers of research.

ISSUES OF RESEARCH METHODOLOGY FOR HISTORIANS

Recent decades have seen a lively debate among historians over their concepts of research methods (see Barzun, 1974; Beringer, 1978; *Journal of Interdisciplinary History,* 1981). The tone of the debate is suggested by putting a question often directly stated but sometimes implicit: "To what extent should history adopt the mode and where possible the research methods of social science?" This is not a new debate. The Social Science Research Council published a bulletin in 1954 on *The Social Sciences in Historical Study.*

The issue has been posed as a contrast between the humanist and the social science modes in the view of methodology used in historical research. A useful summary of the polar positions, stated as ideal types, has been presented by Landes and Tilly (1971). The historian with a social science approach seeks to contribute to understanding a general problem that transcends time and place and that reflects uniformities of human behavior. The assumption is that statements can be made that test alternative views (for example, about the relationship of women's work and family life) in successive refinements toward a generalization applicable in the present as in the past. With a humanist approach, the historian assumes that the complexity of human life is a reality that must be presented as unique to time and place. Therefore, generalizations can be abstracted only by impairing the integrity of reality through oversimplification. These polar positions lead on the social science side to emphasis on methodological rigor, acceptance of (and sometimes preference for) quantitative evidence, and analytical-descriptive styles of presentation. On the humanist side, the art of bringing the complex reality to light is emphasized. Illustrative, biographical, anecdotal materials are valued for their intrinsic worth; and quantitative evidence is looked on as usually deceptive by implying certainty when it is selective and as incapable of revealing the complex actuality. From this perspective, the presentation of the historian's research is a literary work. Of course, the extremes of these positions are rarely defended by historians, but their studies often reflect a tendency toward one or the other perspective.

It is social-scientific history that has our attention in this chapter. This is not to imply that the more humanistic history is of no interest to social workers and cannot contribute to their deeper appreciation of social behavior and enrich their view of human life. The canons of appreciation for such works extend, in our opinion, to aesthetic judgments beyond those to which empirical social science claims pertinence. But because social-scientific historians address problems that social sciences deal with and social workers find relevant, the special features of this sort of research deserve attention by the sophisticated reader.

THE RANGE OF SOCIAL HISTORY

The premise of the historian and, indeed, of the idea of history itself is that everything has a past and understanding the present properly is enhanced (or, in the extreme, made possible) by understanding the past. This truism, as Landes and Tilly (1971) note, often leads social scientists to accept a view of the past based on limited evidence or authority more dubious than most historians find acceptable. Social workers and other practitioners also see the past through selective and received wisdom. There is no logical limit, therefore, to the range of contemporary interests in society and behavior that does not call for historical research. Statements about the past continuously need refinement and correction. In this respect the observations of the past and conclusions based on them are always tentative.

Like statements of social science, they are subject to further research, to replication, and to reformulation.

In this perspective, the range of social history is inclusive and what is pertinent must be determined by the social worker from criteria of interest and relevance. What leads to reading empirical research studies of social and behavioral sciences leads likewise to the choice of relevant historical studies. In narrowest view, the social worker may limit interest to the immediate task or field of concern in practice, therefore taking the history of social work and social welfare institutions as most relevant. In broader view, historical research in any of the aspects of social life and behavior that bear on current practice responsibilities and on knowledge about the context of client behavior may be considered relevant. Although the boundaries are not sharp, such considerations allow the reader to select research within a range that will become more clearly defined with experience in reading historical research.

Paul Stuart (1981) offers a general view of the range for "social work historians" in his chapter on historical research (p. 316).

> Most social work historians have attempted to explain the development of the social work profession and of the major social welfare institutions within which social workers practice. Some have emphasized heroes and heroines, particularly early social workers who were influential in the development of the profession. Others have traced the development of such "modern" institutions as social insurance or federal aid to the states for social services, or have concentrated on such enduring forms of social provision as public assistance or residential treatment.

Subjects implied by the idea of "social work history" appear in journals and books abstracted by *Social Work Research and Abstracts. Social Service Review* has been through the years the professional journal most attentive to social work history. Among other journals that have included articles on social work history, especially in the 1970s and 1980s, the *Journal of Social History* is notable.

A selection of titles from journals gives a sense of the range of interests: "Reformers and Charity: The Abolition of Public Outdoor Relief in New York City, 1870–1899" (Kaplan, 1978); "Black Charity in Progressive Era Chicago" (Jackson, 1978); "Intellectual Origins of Community Organizing: 1920–1939" (Austin and Betten, 1977); "Family and Foster Care: Philadelphia in the Late 19th Century" (Clement, 1979); "Police Social Workers: A History" (Roberts, 1976); "And Heal the Sick: The Hospital and the Patient in 19th Century America" (Rosenberg, 1977); "The Rank and File Movement in Private Social Work" (Haynes, 1975); "Social Casework Practice during the 'Psychiatric Deluge' " (Field, 1980).

The research appearing in articles such as these is often closer to the tradition of interpretative history than to social-scientific history. Such work deserves attention for what it may contribute to thinking about present-day problems and social service institutions. Many of the articles on social work history are written by social workers, but some report the research of social historians. Work of the latter often comes to the attention of social workers as books. Examples are: *The Professional Altruist: The Emergence of Social Work as a Career* (Lubove, 1965), *The Discovery of the Asylum: Social Order and Disorder in the New Republic* (D. Rothman, 1971), *Conscience and Convenience: The Asylum and Its Alternatives in Progressive America* (D. Rothman, 1980), *The Child Savers: The Invention of Delinquency* (Platt, 1969).

At its margins, social work history fades into the larger arena of social history, as some of these titles imply. Social-scientific historical research in this larger arena may be of even more pertinence to social workers. The history of the family, of childhood and youth, of old age, of community change, of schools and hospitals, and many other areas offers meaningful knowledge for understanding problems and making decisions required of social workers. The following examples may suggest the range of topics that are attracting the interest of social historians.

The family has been a prominent object of attention. Often considered the beginning of modern interest by social historians in the family is the contribution of Philippe Aries, *Centuries of Childhood: A Social History of Family Life* (1962). Subsequently, many studies have focused on various aspects of family life. There has been deliberate concern to base interpretations on findings from documents and records reflecting the general population as a corrective to an earlier tendency to rely on sources of information that led to interpretations of family life from the limited perspective of educated or elite social levels. Other works of broad scope that have been influential include *Household and Family in Past Time* (Laslett, 1972), *The Making of the Modern Family* (Shorter, 1975), and *The Family, Sex, and Marriage in England, 1500–1800* (Stone, 1977).

Other research points to specific issues. This is illustrated by a collection of articles from the *Journal of Interdisciplinary History* drawn together in a book (Rabb and Rotberg, 1973). Some titles are: "Illegitimacy, Sexual Revolution, and Social Change in Modern Europe" (Shorter, 1973), "Age at Menarche in Europe Since the Eighteenth Century" (Laslett, 1973), "Demographic Change and the Life Cycle of American Families" (Wells, 1973), "Adolescence and Youth in Nineteenth-Century America" (Kett, 1973), and "Patterns of Work and Family Organization: Buffalo's Italians" (McLaughlin, 1973).

Interest in the history of the family intersects with interest in race relations, a topic of particular importance. Sociological studies of black families often accepted a portrait of the Negro family from slavery to recent times as matriarchal and disorganized. This image entered analyses of social problems of blacks and debates about social policies. Careful and detailed research on the black family has brought a major revision of view. Of special note is Gutman's *The Black Family in Slavery and Freedom, 1750–1925* (Gutman, 1975). This has stimulated an important line of research utilizing census manuscripts, directories, and other sources treated so that quantitative analysis can bear on earlier generalizations derived from more limited documentary sources.

Adolescence and youth have been another focus. John R. Gillis' *Youth and History: Tradition and Change in European Age Relations, 1770– Present* (Gillis, 1974) is a good example. Illegitimacy, sexual behavior, and fertility provide other examples of family-related topics that have received the attention of social historical research. Some are broad in scope, as *Bastardy and Its Comparative History: Studies in the History of Illegitimacy and Marital Nonconformism in Britain, France, Germany, Sweden, North America, Jamaica and Japan* (Laslett, Oosterveen, and Smith, 1980). Others, more limited, are illustrated by "Premarital Pregnancy in America, 1640–1971: An Overview and Interpretation" (Smith and Hindus, 1975), "London's Sodomites: Homosexual Behavior and Western Culture in the 18th Century" (Trumbach, 1977); and *Wanton Wenches and Wayward Wives: Peasants and Illicit Sex in Early Seventeenth Century England* (Quaife, 1979).

Emergence of the concept of "the aged" and its changing meanings is another area of attention, illustrated by Achenbaum, 1978, mentioned at the beginning of this chapter, and by *Growing Old in America* (Fischer, 1977) which offers an interpretation somewhat different from the former.

Other research by social historians appears in areas that social workers have long considered as important as those noted above: the history of community and features of urban life, immigration and the immigrant experience, institutions for mental and physical health, education, the industrial work experience, juvenile and adult corrections, and other topics. Examples of research on some of these topics can be illustrated by titles of some of the chapters of *Social History and Social Policy* (Rothman and Wheeler, 1981): "Inward Vision and Outward Glance: The Shaping of the American Hospital, 1880–1914" (Rosenberg, 1981), "Education and Inequality: A Historical Perspective" (Katz, 1981), "The Diary of an Institution: The Fate of Progressive Reform at the Norfolk Penitentiary" (D. Rothman, 1981), "The Morass: An Essay on the Public Employee Pension Problem" (Fogelson, 1981), "Urban Pasts and Urban Policies" (Mandelbaum, 1981), "Women's Clinics or Doctors' Offices: The Sheppard-Towner Act and the Promotion of Preventive Health Care" (S. Rothman,

1981), and "History and the Formation of Social Policy Toward Children: A Case Study" (Demos, 1981).

The examples offered in this section are intended to suggest the range of historical research appearing mostly since 1970 that can bear on the domain of responsibility of social work. The citations are by no means a systematic guide to the literature of these many topics, but they may serve to introduce the reader to starting points from which to pursue interests further. What has been cited varies widely in specificity, in the sources and nature of data used, and in the sorts of knowledge that can be drawn from the research. Most of what has been cited shares a common concern to use historical research to examine a problem of social behavior in temporal depth and not merely to present history as descriptive of earlier time periods. The very richness of information and variety of its sources invites a thoughtful assessment as a means of heightening appreciation of the knowledge produced and how it may be used in the interests of social work practice.

GUIDELINES FOR ASSESSMENT OF HISTORICAL RESEARCH: A PRELIMINARY NOTE

The research into social history for which we propose guidelines is, as indicated earlier, that which approaches the social-scientific mode in its purpose and methods. We will therefore pay attention to methodological issues and conceptual perspectives while minimizing features of historical studies that may be enriching to the liberal arts background of the social worker. Just as general reading of novels, poetry, drama, and the like makes contributions to the sensitivities and insights of the reader, so also will reading studies in social history enhance the capacities of the social worker. There is no way in which the personal qualities of the practicing social worker can be entirely excluded from practice, whether face-to-face with a client or in interactions with the systems of service, program, and policy. The function of empirical research for the practitioner, including historical research, is to increase the extent to which decisions of practice may be based on firmer knowledge, but it is not thereby to diminish the humane qualities that enter professional actions. We consider the scientific and humane components of social work practice complementary rather than contradictory. The reader of historical research should seek to absorb as humanistic enrichment the illustrative anecdotes, quoted remarks, photographs, drawings, and the like that usually appear in even the most rigorous reports of social-scientific history.

With this perspective the suggestions that follow are intended as guidelines toward assessment of social-scientific historical research.

CLASSIFICATION OF HISTORICAL RESEARCH

It is useful to begin assessment of historical research, as of other empirical research, by looking at the major purposes of the research and the methods employed. In this way you can locate the study within broad classes of research, so that subsequent evaluation and considerations of usefulness may be more appropriate. The general emphasis throughout this book is on assessing research for what it purports to do and how well it is done rather than against some ideal standard applied to all research. The classification scheme proposed in Chapter 2 was devised primarily for consideration of social science research. With more caution because it is a less familiar body of research for social practitioners, we suggest some broad classes of historical research.

The distinction noted earlier in this chapter between social-scientific historical research and humanistic research is a starting place. To which type of history should the research be assigned? We may follow Landes and Tilly (1971) in characterizing social-scientific history. They describe three salient concerns (pp. 71–73):

> 1. Social-scientific history seeks to produce *collective history,* or "history directly linking the recorded experiences of large numbers of persons or social units to patterns of behavior or change." Even when a study focuses on a person or one group, the effort is to see the subject in wider terms that can bear on more general knowledge. Landes and Tilly illustrate by noting that the history of epidemics can be effectively written from the accumulated records of individual victims rather than from general impressions of observers or illustrations by scattered cases.
>
> 2. Social-scientific history tries to understand the behavior described in terms of *concepts* and *theories.* Thus, the reader will be able to find in the research report an explicit or implicit statement of assumptions, concepts, and hypotheses that have guided the selection of empirical information and the analytical use that is made of it. Although the concepts and theories are usually drawn from the social sciences, the conclusions and generalizations are, as Landes and Tilly note, "characteristically historical in their emphasis on the time dimension and the relationship of phenomena to context."
>
> 3. Social-scientific history seeks to compare systematically the phenomena or processes of interest in different settings in order to provide a more general test for the theories used. It therefore has a *comparative orientation* even if the information for such comparisons is limited.

The first criterion—that the history is collective—expresses a trend noted among recent social historians to be concerned with fundamental social realities of social structure and human experiences within it. This differentiates much of social-scientific history from historical research whose traditional concern has been with the reconstruction of particular events, ordinarily in the spheres of war, politics, and diplomacy (Rosenberg, 1975, p. 3). Thus, a preliminary identification of social-scientific historical research often may be made by the reader by noting what population or institutional area of society is of central interest. Social workers will be attracted to books and articles about groups, problems, and institutions most salient to their own concerns.

If the research is classified as social-scientific history, the reader may ask whether it is primarily intended (*a*) to offer a factual description of a phenomenon, or (*b*) to examine the generality of some theory or hypothesis about that phenomenon in the place and time studied.

An example of the former is Laslett's study of "Age at Menarche in Europe since the Eighteenth Century" (Laslett, 1973). He examines information derived from a document listing Christian Orthodox residents of Belgrade (in present-day Yugoslavia) in 1733–1734 to see if data about female sexual maturation as inferred are consistent with the reputed decline in age at menarche reported for Western Europe based on nineteenth-century records. Another example is Greven's "Family Structure in Seventeenth-Century Andover, Massachusetts" (Greven, 1973). Town records and genealogies for the period between 1651 and 1699 are used to describe demographic composition of families and aspects of inheritance and other relations between families. The conclusion is that, contrary to the common view, the family in this colonial town is best described not as a patrilineal extended kinship household nor a nuclear independent family but as a "modified extended family." A third example is the research of Field, "Social Casework Practice during the 'Psychiatric Deluge' " (Field, 1980). She used case records and other documents of a social agency in Illinois to show that what has been widely accepted in social work history as dominance of psychodynamic orientation during the 1930s and 1940s is partially true in the literature produced by caseworkers but largely absent from practice as reflected in the records examined.

These examples illustrate also what has been called the *demythifying function* of social-scientific history (Landes and Tilly, 1971, p. 72). This is the modification of conceptions of earlier social life that have become the received and conventional image used by contemporary social analysts and social scientists.

An example of social-scientific historical research presented to test a hypothesis or a general theory (subtype *b*) is a study "Women's Work and the Family in Nineteenth-Century Europe" (Scott and Tilly, 1975). These historians muster a wide range of facts about work and attitudes of working-class women in various locations to contest the theory that changes in women's participation in the labor market derived from changes in values accompanying industrialization. Their research leads to a model of social change "that posits a continuity of traditional values and behavior in changing circumstances" (p. 152). The study of youth and history, cited earlier, is another example (Gillis, 1974). Gillis uses in-depth studies of records and other documents of Oxford and Göttingen to examine the emergence of the status of "youth" and changes in its meaning through time. He seeks to show how these are related to demographic and economic changes mediated through parental expectations, economic opportunities, conditions of education, and leisure. He finds the specifics of behavior from which the more general interpretation is drawn by focus on the interface between the expectations of the young, with some independence in their own traditions, and those of their elders.

The scholarly conventions of historians differ from those of social scientists and social work researchers. The statement of problem or hypothesis and discussion of research methodology appear less often at the opening of the report of the research. In longer monographs it is often necessary to read the preface and look at the appendix to decide whether it is more sensible to view the study from a social-scientific or a humanistic perspective. When used in the research, quantitative data may be less evident as a clue to aid classification. Nonquantitative data are almost always also used. Some knowledge of methods of historiography and familiarity with historical writing will help the reader learn through experience to detect the researcher's purpose and method in such materials. It is sensible to be tentative in making the classification decisions we have suggested. Studies that are not obviously intended to describe or to consider theoretical questions may deal with topics that are pertinent to social work or to special interests of the reader.

In particular, historical research not readily classified otherwise may sometimes be considered as *explorative*. The purpose of the research may seem best described as seeking to generate theories and hypotheses and to make tentative generalizations. The commitment to a social-scientific approach may be evident, but the researcher may seek to look at the data that can be assembled and see what explanations of the phenomena are suggested. David J. Rothman describes such a process in the introduction to *Conscience and Convenience: The Asylum and Its Alternatives in Progressive America* (Rothman, 1980):

> When I began this book, I not only intended to complete the story that I traced in *The Discovery of the Asylum* (that is, to take the account from the 1870's and 1880's down to 1940), but I believed I would be examining the rise of alternatives to incarceration. The *Asylum* volume had analyzed the origins of institutions. This book would analyze their decline. My initial orientation reflected my awareness in the early 1970's of the declining rate of incarceration not only in mental hospitals but in prisons and training schools. I also had the notion that probation, parole, juvenile courts, and

outpatient clinics were frankly efforts at community placement, that they were the forerunners, in spirit and in practice, of the present-day commitment to deinstitutionalization, as though Progressives had a fundamental quarrel with the principle of incarceration. In fact, my starting assumptions were far too simple. The Progressives were anti-institutional in a very special way. Their quarrel was not so much with the institution per se, as with uniformity and rigidity. They were not so much struggling to return the offender to the community (although that theme does appear in one form or another) as attempting to individualize treatment.... (pp. 11–12)

In summary, with respect to classifying historical research as a first step toward evaluating how well the tasks of the researcher were achieved, the following guidelines may serve:

1. By initial scanning of the report, paying particular attention to statements that indicate purpose and methodological orientation toward sources of data, decide whether it is useful to view the research as social-scientific or to accept it as primarily humanistic in type. If the latter, you may wish in any event to read the report for its intrinsic interest, applying critical reservations as appropriate. If the former, you may find the next steps useful.

2. Considered as social-scientific historical research, the report can be carefully read, taking note whether the chief purpose is to describe a phenomenon or to examine how data bear on a general theory or more limited hypotheses about the topic.

3. If the research is organized around the examination of hypotheses and theories, consider whether the researcher primarily (*a*) tests the theories or hypotheses, or (*b*) seeks to generate further hypotheses that are offered as starting places for further research.

EVALUATION OF HISTORICAL RESEARCH

In this book we have used the term evaluation of research to mean the systematic assessment of methodology in each component of an empirical research investigation: (1) *formulation* of the problem for study and plan for obtaining information bearing on the problem (*research design*), (2) the source and character of *data* obtained, and (3) the mode of examination or *analysis* of the data, presentation of findings and *conclusions* about the problem. Producing historical research can be viewed as involving these steps, which form the basis for the following guidelines for the reader when evaluating historical research.

As a foreword, we remind the reader that these steps represent logical components of the research process and not necessarily a fixed sequence in the production of research reports. How the steps are carried out in a piece of historical research will often have to be inferred rather than found explicitly expressed. Nevertheless, it sharpens the appreciation of the quality of the research to apply questions about each component to a study. Making a judgment about the quality of the research allows the reader to decide how much value to attribute to what has been learned from the research, an important element when making further judgments about the usefulness of the knowledge gained.

When evaluating the quality of the reported research with respect to *formulation* of the problem for study, a central question is: How well specified are the main and secondary problems, and how well identified are the phenomena intended for examination? If the researcher has not stated the purpose or purposes, can they be reasonably inferred from the way the subject is presented? If the point of the historical study is excessively diffuse, its value as an empirical addition to knowledge is likely to be limited. How has the researcher used the literature of previous research on the subject in conceiving this study and formulating its purpose? Are the concepts used in formulating the subject made explicit and clear? Are concepts defined by indicating the operations that the researcher followed when using them? For example, Shorter (1973), interested in the "sexual revolution" in nineteenth-century Europe, looks for changes in premarital sexuality, which he examines from the evidence of illegitimate births, derived primarily from parish records in different countries. Using the concept of patterns of family organization to examine the theory that employment opportunities in the industrial city increased the power of women within the family and encouraged the decline of "traditional" male dominance, McLaughlin (1973) uses marital and occupational composition of families as determined from manuscript censuses (of Buffalo in 1905) and contemporaneous documents to determine employment of girls and women from which to infer "family organization." Field (1980) looks for contemporary language of the literature of psychodynamic casework in the records of agency cases during the 1930s and 1940s as the operational definition of psychiatric orientation in case process. These examples may suggest a variety of ways in which problems are formulated for historical research and concepts defined to bear on the formulation. The key question for the reader is: How clearly can the researcher's problem be visualized, and how well do the concepts express the questions at issue when examining the phenomena studied?

Merging with this aspect of the research is the second component: examination of sources of information and character of data presented. Because historians must use documents and other remains from the past, they face problems of selection. How adequately do the sources offer information that is representative of the phenomenon of interest? They may use artifacts (for example, tools, household items, and the like) or interviews with persons present or knowledgeable about an earlier time, but they are usually dependent on documentary and archival sources. How skillfully and appropriately they use these sources is difficult to assess unless the reader is trained in such research and familiar with the literature on the topic and period involved. Fortunately, appearance of the research report in acknowledged scholarly journals can provide some confidence. Book reviewers through whom the historical study comes to attention may offer some testimony to the propriety of sources used, distinguishing, for example, between scholarly and fictionalized history. More important is internal evidence in the research report, indicated by the manner in which the sources are revealed and cited.

Since the data on a historical problem can never be complete, the most important basis for judging the evidence is the way the researcher identifies and appraises the sources. Is there serious, open recognition of limitations of the information obtained? The traditions of historical research call for thorough and critical citation. Academic history is notable from copious footnotes. Social-scientific historical research adds explicit attention to representativeness of sources for quantitative data, to limitations of place, to consistency of reported information, and to the social context of observations. At the least, a research report that does not clearly reveal the sources of its factual materials, how representative they are, and the assumptions involved in drawing conclusions from them should be read in that light and with those reservations. Knowing how the historian proceeded in the research, the reader can, with awareness of his own level of familiarity and ignorance of the subject, decide how much confidence to put in the interpretations and conclusions drawn from the research.

For example, in what he calls "The Argument" as introduction to *The Making of the Modern Family,* Shorter (1975) discusses the evidence used to show how the traditional European family changed into the modern family through changes of "sentiments." How to demonstrate the "chronicle of sentiments" is the methodological issue. He notes that "the structures that encase a family's life are . . . fairly visible: the number of people in the household; their relationships with one another; their births, deaths, and marriages." But, because varied patterns of emotional relationships are possible within any structure, the family historian must, he says, "trace the tale of sentiments." The three classes of data considered are information from local medical doctors, from minor bureaucrats, and from antiquarian scholars, all mainly in France and parts of Germany and Scandinavia. Consistency of his findings between these locations and with reports of other scholars and with inferences from statistical series in many places are noted to test the representativeness of his own observations. Shorter's book is a broad analysis rather than a detailed presentation of findings. Hence the details of sources and data are limited, but he provides the reader with a good sense of the character of his evidence, its values, and its limitations.

Gutman's massive study (1975) *The Black Family in Slavery and Free-*

dom, 1750–1925 has an abundance of data assembled from detailed examination of plantation documents, manuscript census schedules, and voluminous records, which supply a richness of descriptive material and personal portraiture to deepen the meaning of the quantitative measures of relationships between members of the black families described. Achenbaum (1978) describes in a technical note how he used a form of content analysis to study conceptions of the elderly reflected in popular and scientific periodicals, books for and about the aged, statutes, public records, and other documents. He considers in another note problems of using the federal census, especially underenumeration. Dawley (1976), in *Class and Community: The Industrial Revolution in Lynn,* details the steps by which he used and extended the information from census manuscripts of 1860 and 1870 by tracing names through directories and compilations from newspapers and from union records of trade union activity and a strike of shoemakers in 1860. His further note on sources and bibliography list the large number of manuscript, periodical, and documentary materials examined. Quaife (1979) based his study of illicit sex in early seventeenth-century England on depositions presented between 1601 and 1660 to courts in Somerset, Bath, and Wells. Rejecting the claim that this is writing social history as though the conduct of the working classes today could be based on current criminal records, he points out the extensive reach of secular and ecclesiastical courts into almost every aspect of life in the very small world of rural parishes. In some cases almost the whole village is involved in giving evidence.

In each of the examples the objective is to give the reader, in abbreviated form, the same basis for accepting or doubting the trustworthiness of the research that the researcher has. The reader can thereby gauge the level of confidence to be placed in evaluation of the research.

The use of earlier social science research as source documents about conditions, events, and relationships that are subject of historical research merits additional comment. The reader should note whether the researcher has evaluated the quality of these earlier social science reports. Although this involves essentially the application of general rules of evaluating documentary sources to a special type of document, the kinds of assessment set forth in this book may be additionally helpful. Contemporary empirical research becomes the documentary archive for future historical research. For example, the Kinsey Report portrays sexual behavior as reported in the 1940s and in a later century will tell of the behavior of mid-twentieth-century Americans. The limitations of Kinsey's research (for example, interviewing and sampling problems) will persist, and in addition the categories of observation and context in which the studies were read in their own time will require explication.

The third component in evaluating historical research—presentation of factual material, *analysis,* and drawing of *conclusions*—merges into the first two components. Here evaluation is concerned with how well the data bear on problems formulated as the purpose of the research. The essential question is whether the information offered bears appropriately and logically on the argument the researcher makes about the subject. If the reader knows what the researcher proposes to study and can make a judgment about how appropriate and reliable the information obtained is, the research report can be examined for objectivity and caution in analysis and reaching conclusions. Have all the data been used rather than selective parts? Have alternative interpretations been considered? Are the conclusions clearly stated and reasonably qualified in recognition of limitations of the evidence? Questions such as these lead to a critical but open stance that the reader should take as the research is evaluated.

As previously noted, historical research by necessity and tradition depends on documentary materials that offer verbal observations: diaries, letters, personal and official records, and so forth. Even when quantitative or other systematic analysis carries the main weight, historical research usually includes such materials as part of the evidence. The variety of materials increases appreciation as well as understanding and is a special virtue of historical research. When evaluating a study, the reader should ask whether such materials are used as supplements and enrichments of data that can be more rigorously examined. In other words, has the most reliable and valid material available been used as the basis for the conclusions or has the researcher by selection among the kinds of data tended, perhaps unwittingly, to support some favored conclusion? The reader should be alert to how the researcher has allowed the data to answer the questions asked in the study.

Shorter (1975) is dealing with this issue when he discusses the problem of getting information about intimate family relationships representative of all levels of the population in earlier centuries. He notes the problem of representativeness when using available documents for the less literate population. "Let us assume," he writes, "that we clutch in our hands a rare working-class autobiography, or a collection of love letters of popular origin. How are we to know whether their tales of masturbation or handholding are typical? . . . This is the old fallacy of confusing illustrations with verification. Representing a general point with an example is not at all the same as establishing the generalization's validity." (p. 10)

Shorter may also supply a final word to the reader when evaluating a report of historical research. We propose that as part of the process the reader react to the literary quality of the report. Ask not only how clear and coherent and precise in meaning it is and how cogent the argument. Ask also if the report conveys what the historian appreciates about the subject, how the meaning of his interpretation comes to life. How well will the viewpoint and conclusions be remembered when the "facts" are forgotten? This is not to value literary style over the more austere style of academic social science writing. It is to invite the reader to ask how effective a piece of writing is in clinching not only the logic and proof for a conclusion but the import of the conclusions. Taken by itself, the following paragraph of Shorter (p. 8) may be only amusing and clever. He is introducing the element of his argument about change from the traditional to the modern family that holds that parental social controls over children have greatly diminished. "We have lost interest in the family lineage," he says, and "thus let fall the ties which bind one generation to the next."

> ... Adolescents now soon realize that they are not links in a familial chain stretching across the ages. Who they are and what they become is independent (at least so they believe) of who their parents are. And they themselves are responsible for what their children become only to the point of seeing that they march into the future with straight teeth. The chain of generations serves no larger moral purpose for adolescents, and therewith the moral authority of parents over their growing children collapses.... If the argument of this book is right, that is the crisis of the postmodern family.

This is argument, not proof. Shorter musters evidence to trace the changes that have occurred in "sentiments" associated with courtship, the mother-child relationship, and the boundary line between the family and the surrounding community. That he has drawn an inference and expressed it in vivid language is to be noted as part of the evaluation of the historical research by the reader.

UTILIZATION OF HISTORICAL RESEARCH

The special character of historical research calls for widening the idea of utilization applicable to social science research. The perspective of Chapter 4, Utilization of Research, is nevertheless acceptable, and so are some of the specific questions, especially for social-scientific historical research. Our purpose in this section is to stimulate the reader to ask additional questions in considering how a piece of historical research can be useful to the social worker or other practitioner.

Conclusions of historical research are unlikely to be applicable to a specific practice or policy question in the same sense that a conclusion from behavioral research may be taken into account as a guide to action. There is an approach to this when historical research alters a prior view of the social worker about an intervention decision, the character of an institution, or a policy that might enter into a decision the social worker is about to take. For example, knowledge from historical research showing that deinstitutionalization has not decreased control over clientele may alter a recommendation a social worker may make. But this is not commonly the sort of knowledge historical research produces, and it would be a limited part of the basis for an informed decision.

Historical research may prove more useful because it clarifies understanding, sharpens insights, or provokes new ways of thinking about a problem or an aspect of practice. Such clarifications may seem to contribute more to the general educational level of the reader than to professional knowledge. But when the subject matter fits a current or potential area of responsibility, the research can have specific relevance. The reader might therefore ask of historical research: How close is the subject matter to areas of my practice and responsibility as a social worker?

Historical research on social work and social welfare institutions is likely to attract social work readers. Advancement of professional education is clearly gained by reading the history of intervention and treatment methods, or research on the development of theories about a social problem, or studies of the background of programs or institutions. In the same manner, potential value should be considered for social historical research on social groups, ethnic populations, the life conditions of families, the context of life in urban neighborhoods, employment settings, and the like.

What are some of the ways historical research may provide useful insights and understandings? We may suggest a number of features of history to consider: (1) the demythifying, corrective contribution, (2) the provision of a time dimension and of continuity in attempting to understand phenomena, (3) the usefulness of a comparative perspective, in both time and place, (4) the sense of humility and the encouragement of patience in the face of difficult professional tasks.

The correction of beliefs about the past by substitution of grounded evidence of the reality of an earlier period—demythifying—has been mentioned earlier as a characteristic result of social-scientific history. The correction of some views of an earlier time may be of only casual interest. Revision of the accepted view of the past may be more significant when that view has been important as part of an analysis leading to social policies. For example, the research of Gutman and others modifies a widespread belief that under slavery and during Reconstruction black families were primarily characterized by disorganization and instability. By demonstrating extensive stability and continuity, the unfounded belief on which social programs for urban black families has been based is challenged. In another field of interest, the demonstration of variability in family size, age of marriage, geographical mobility, and declines in fertility prior to industrialization has required reexamination of the theory of demographic transition and the social policies based on it for population control in less developed countries in the post–World War II period. A key question of utilization for the reader to ask is: Does the research change an important belief about the background of the phenomenon in question that has entered into theories and policies of the practice areas of interest? Often the historian will point out such connections for the reader. But it is advantageous for the social work reader to be alert to special ways in which such correctives bear on social work approaches to a problem. For example, whereas historical research mentioned earlier on relationships between employment of women and family life helps to modify a general theory of family change, it may stimulate immediate implications for programs today concerned with problems of families and children.

Is there a point at which demythifying becomes the chronicle of failure and hence constitutes only discouragement rather than enlightenment for the practitioner and policy maker? Many studies of reform of social welfare institutions—prisons, asylums, public schools, juvenile courts, clinical programs to mention some—seem to trace failures (see D. Rothman and Wheeler, 1981, p. 14). This is analogous to negative results of outcome studies in program evaluation, which are often disturbing to practitioners who, unlike social scientists and historians, cannot escape responsibility for continuing efforts to deal with the problems involved. Thoughtful readers should not be unduly discouraged by such studies any more than they should be unduly encouraged by studies with opposite results. The research reader should apply the same criteria to both. In addition to asking whether the conclusions are sound and based on valid evidence, the reader can seek in the research suggestions of where the sources of failure or success might lie and try thereby to make present efforts more effective.

Appreciation of the course of development of social institutions, views of social problems, programs and modes of intervention is a second aspect of historical research that the reader can look for when considering usefulness. Little attention is given to the time dimension in social work training, especially with respect to social and institutional change. The reader may find that research about some aspect of social welfare history bears on understanding institutions in which the social worker is involved.

Appreciation of the time dimension has potential value even when continuity is tenuous between the historical period and present-day social forms, as in the study of behavior in sixteenth-century English villages. The values of a comparative view of social behavior apply in time as well as geographical location and cultural diversity. The reader should consider how problems and processes of present concern have been defined and dealt with in other cultural settings. Differences are important not because they may be exotic. Comparative analysis, as Landes and Tilly (1971, p. 73) put it, involves "the systematic, standardized analysis of similar social processes of phenomena in different settings in order to develop and test general ideas of how these processes or phenomena work." This is where the value lies. The research reader should keep in mind this potential for historical research even if the researcher has not specifically addressed the subject of study in this manner.

An additional value to be looked for in historical research can be a heightening of humanistic sensitivities and broadening of the sense of appreciation for the varied ways of facing problems and trying to deal with the issues of living that characterize the human species. That a sense of humility, patience, and alternating visions of hope and despair are of use in the practice of the social worker may be more an act of faith than demonstrable. It is nevertheless appropriate to call to the attention of the reader of historical research that additional enlightenment and appreciation of humanistic values is a potential benefit to readers who, as do the authors of this book, believe social work to be a profession requiring such values.

To conclude the discussion of utilization of historical research that ends this chapter, we note what was learned when social historians and social policy makers were brought together in a conference to consider how history and policy might be related. We draw from the Introduction to *Social History and Social Policy* (D. Rothman and Wheeler, 1981) to summarize some of the issues. The questions they raise about the role of historical analysis in social policy may be adapted for readers assessing the usefulness of historical research.

1. "When is historical understanding rich or deep enough to be taken seriously by those developing social policy?" We call this question "evaluation" in this chapter. It asks the reader for a judgment of how adequate and sufficient the history reported may be as a basis for changing views previously held and accepting the report as a new and valid view. Usually it will take a series of replicating studies to revise the historical view but each research study can be assessed for its own contribution.

2. Is the historian promoting a view of the subject to support an end of social policy of his own, deliberately or unintentionally? Aware of such a risk, the reader can be wary of relying on a limited number of studies. The reader can also look for alternative interpretations from the evidence presented, alert to whether sufficient and inclusive evidence has been offered to permit a judgment about the researcher's bias.

3. Does the historical research as reported relate to a particular social policy or program, or to understanding of a broader general climate within which matters of policy and program are considered? Both of these possibilities are potentially useful but need to be distinguished. Each will yield a different utility in the practice and professional performance of the social worker.

4. Does the historical research reported contain directly or by implication recommendations that may express a "conservative," traditional, preserving orientation toward institutional forms (for example, the family) or a "muck-

raking," change-requiring orientation (for example, with respect to prisons)? Alert to such possibilities in the historian's hidden agenda, the reader may suspend judgment and seek additional knowledge on which to reach a conclusion.

5. What further historical research would appear desirable to add usefulness to that found in the report just read? Stimulation to visualize how additional knowledge from research might be helpful to the reader is itself a quality to be valued in historical research as in other research. This, too, represents one way historical research may be utilized for the enlightenment of the social worker.

Chapter 6

Assessing Program Evaluation Research

Program evaluation research is the use of social research strategies and methods for determining the extent to which programs are implemented, effective, and efficient. Regarded as applied social science, the terminology of program evaluation, although not standardized, has been evolving rapidly over the past decade (Posavac and Carey, 1980, pp. 2–16). New journals such as *Evaluation, Evaluation Quarterly, Evaluation and Program Planning,* and *Evaluation and the Helping Professions* have appeared, and professional societies such as Evaluation Research Society and Evaluation Network have emerged (Windle, 1979). Whereas Geismar (1972) reported on 13 evaluative studies in social work that reflected the state of the art in the 1960s, Reid (1979) located 97 studies of evaluation research in social work whose abstracts were published in *Social Work Research and Abstracts* from 1975 through 1978.

In the first edition of this book we subtyped *program evaluation studies* as a form of quantitative-descriptive research; however, it can be shown that all types of research strategies can be used for program evaluation. Indeed, it can be argued that varying research approaches such as case study, survey, and experimentation are applied differentially for evaluating social programs that are in different stages of development (Tripodi, Fellin, and Epstein, 1978). Moreover, Reid (1979) concluded from his recent review of evaluation research in social work that the methods employed in evaluations have become increasingly varied and sophisticated. This is further evident in the number of books on program evaluation that have been published; for example, *Handbook of Evaluation Research,* Volumes 1 and 2 (Struening and Guttentag, 1975), *Readings in Evaluation Research,* Second Edition (Caro, 1977), *Research Techniques for Program Planning, Monitoring and Evaluation* (Epstein and Tripodi, 1977), *Evaluation: A Systematic Approach* (Rossi, Freeman, and Wright, 1979), and *Program Evaluation: Methods and Case Studies* (Posavac and Carey, 1980).

Because there are a variety of research approaches used in program evaluation research, reported increasingly by social agencies as well as in professional publications, we have concluded that the assessment of program evaluation research merits a separate chapter in this second edition of *The Assessment of Social Research.* In addition, we eliminated the subtype of program evaluation studies from our classification system of research studies (see Chapter 2) because program evaluation research can include experimental, quantitative-descriptive, and exploratory approaches. Although the reader can use the evaluative questions we delineated in Chapter 3 for evaluating a program evaluation study, we believe that there are additional specific concepts related to programs and their evaluations that are critical for sound assessment. Accordingly, we have organized this chapter to include the following topics: process of program evaluation; description of social programs, program evaluation objectives, knowledge attainment, and empirical generality; and the utility of program evaluations.

PROCESS OF PROGRAM EVALUATION RESEARCH

Program evaluation research involves a series of interrelated tasks, which are discussed in detail in textbooks on program evaluation. Below we briefly describe ten steps in program evaluation research in order to provide a notion of its complexities. This list should serve as a context for the development of more specific evaluative questions in subsequent portions of the chapter:

1. Determining what is to be evaluated
2. Locating the appropriate consumers of the research
3. Soliciting the cooperation of program administration and staff
4. Specifying program objectives
5. Delineating evaluation objectives
6. Selecting variables
7. Devising a research design
8. Implementing the research

    9. Analyzing and interpreting the findings

   10. Reporting and implementing the results

The first step typically involves discussions among program administrators, sponsors, and evaluators. An administrator may be interested in hiring a researcher to evaluate a particular part of the program, for example, the extent to which social workers are effective in applying a particular intervention technique; or a sponsor may call for a comprehensive evaluation of all of the activities in a social program; or there may be organizational or personnel problems that administrators or sponsors hope can be solved by an evaluation; and so forth. The task at this point is to decide on the major focus of an evaluation and whether there are sufficient resources, time, and money to conduct the necessary research. Often the major focus for the evaluation does not emerge until there are discussions about the knowledge desired and the time and costs involved to pursue that knowledge.

Interrelated with whether or not a program evaluation is to be comprehensive or focused on partial aspects of a program is the location of the primary consumer of the evaluation. Consumers can be program sponsors, administrators, staff, clientele, or the general public. While the program sponsors may be interested in the overall costs of a program, clients may be more concerned about whether or not the program has met specific needs. Hence, different consumers are often interested in diverse types and amounts of information, and the evaluator, as much as possible, gears efforts to maximizing relevant information for the primary consumer.

Since program evaluation research is applied research that takes place in agencies and organizations within particular communities, it is important that evaluators solicit and secure the cooperation of key administrative and staff persons. Adequate cooperation can facilitate the collection and gathering of data, while a lack of cooperation can result in unreliable information, time delays, or no data at all.

The specification of program objectives is necessary if one is to measure the effectiveness of a program or its component parts. As Weiss (1972, p. 4) indicates, the purpose of evaluation is ". . . to measure the effects of a program against the goals it set out to accomplish as a means of contributing to subsequent decision making about the program and improving future programming." Program goals or objectives may be clearly written in formal documents required by a program sponsor, or they may be articulated in program policies and practices. Often, program objectives are vaguely stated and need further specification concerning the desired services and resultant changes that are expected for specific target populations. Discussions between the evaluator and program personnel may be profitable in deciding whether or not there are clear program objectives whose attainment can be evaluated. At this point in the process, program evaluations may or may not ensue. If there are no specific objectives, an evaluation may still be desired, especially by program sponsors, to determine the effects of program activities, whether they are beneficial, innocuous, or deleterious for specific client groups.

If program evaluation research is to proceed, it is important that the evaluation objectives be clarified. There are two main types of evaluative research: formative and summative (Scriven, 1967). Formative evaluation is mainly concerned with evaluating a specific program as it is developing and disseminating the results of the evaluation to program administration and staff, without regard to the generality of the results. Summative evaluation has the purpose of providing information that is supposed to be generalized to other comparable programs and situations (Epstein and Tripodi, 1977, p. 112). The evaluator and the evaluation consumer should decide on the major type of evaluative research; then they should decide on which types of evaluation objectives are to be pursued.

There are three major objectives in program evaluation research (Tripodi, Fellin, and Epstein, 1978, p. 39):

1. To provide descriptive information about the type and quantity of program activities or inputs (program effort).
2. To provide information about the achievement of the goals of the current stage of program development (program effectiveness).
3. To provide information about program effectiveness relative to program effort (program efficiency).

In addition to these objectives an evaluation can provide information on program effectiveness in relation to community need for the program's services and on the extent to which unintended effects (side effects) occur.

Once the evaluation objectives are specified, the evaluator selects variables that relate to those objectives. The variables should produce reliable and valid data, and they should be sufficiently sensitive to register change. Change variables are the dependent variables of the evaluation. For example, an objective of a community information service may be to provide knowledge of social services for a specific community. A test of knowledge may be devised so that the degree of knowledge ranges from 0 items to 50 items correct. Change is reflected in statistically significant increases in the number of correct items for two test administrations, prior to and subsequent to program intervention.

The selection of appropriate variables for program evaluations of social service agencies is a difficult task and requires a great deal of thought and effort. In many instances, it may be inappropriate to specify only one variable, for there may be many indicators pertinent to the extent to which program efforts result in change. Hence, Meyer, Borgatta, and Jones (1965) used a number of criteria to evaluate casework and group work services aimed at the prevention of difficulties in groups of girls at a vocational high school in New York City, and Jayaratne, Stuart, and Tripodi (1974, p. 168) concluded on the basis of three evaluative research efforts attempting to measure the effectiveness of a behavioral treatment program in dealing with the problems of adolescents in schools that "The evaluation of treatment outcome requires multiple measurement."

A research design is devised in relation to the knowledge level that is desired. Exploratory research designs are geared to the refinement of concepts and the formulation of hypotheses about program effectiveness and efficiency. Quantitative-descriptive approaches are focused on accurate, quantitative descriptions pertaining to programs, staffs, and needs assessments of their clientele. Quantitative-descriptive studies that are aimed at testing hypotheses can produce correlational knowledge, which shows the amount of empirical relationship between program intervention and one or more dependent variables (that is, change variables). And experimental studies are designed to produce knowledge that demonstrates causal relationships between program intervention and desirable program outcomes.

The implementation of research designs involves a great deal of planning, cooperation, and luck. Successful implementations involve the careful monitoring of research procedures, as well as the serious participation of clientele and program staff. An evaluator must be prepared to change design features in the context of the sociopolitical environment in which the program takes place. For example, it may not be possible to conduct a field experiment, but quasi-experimental designs such as an interrupted time-series design may serve as a useful approximation (Epstein and Tripodi, 1977, pp. 117–30).

The results of program evaluation research depend on sound data and effective research procedures for producing desired knowledge levels. Summative evaluations, moreover, require adequate sampling plans as well as the control of external validity factors as discussed by Campbell and Stanley (1966). Procedures for analyzing data should be rigorously employed with respect to the measurement scales on which variables are specified (nominal, ordinal, interval, or ratio levels of measurement) and the levels of desired knowledge (conceptual and hypothetical, descriptive, correlational, or cause-effect: Tripodi, 1974, pp. 43–73).

After the data are thoroughly analyzed, the evaluator may discuss the findings with program administration and staff to further interpret and validate them. When the study is complete, the evaluator will ideally have two sets of results: one set that is directly supportable by the data of the research; another set that pertains to hypotheses and ideas generated from the researcher's observations and speculations but are not based on empirical data. In this way the evaluation consumer can better focus on the soundness of knowledge that is produced. Furthermore, the evaluator ideally presents and clarifies the results to the program administration and staff. The information should then be used for the purpose of making further decisions related to program development, expansion, or contraction.

DESCRIPTION OF SOCIAL PROGRAMS

The reader of a program evaluation study should understand the nature of the program that is being evaluated. The program needs to be described sufficiently so that the independent variables of the research are clearly explicated. This allows for a careful scrutiny of the research with respect to issues about control and generality, and it makes it possible for evaluation consumers to replicate programs.

The term "social programs" covers the gamut of possible interventions and activities that can occur within and between human service organizations, and it behooves the evaluator to specify salient program parameters. In *Differential Social Program Evaluation* (Tripodi, Fellin, and Epstein, 1978, pp. 5–6) it was indicated that:

> Social programs are conceived broadly as having the goals of providing health, education, or welfare services for the advancement of individual or social change. Programs vary in dimensions such as the range and complexity of objectives, staff size and diversity, administrative structure, length of time in operation, operating expenditures, sources of support, and physical location. . . .
>
> . . . all of the following may be considered social programs: the total operations of a public welfare department; the activities of a welfare rights organization; an effort to deliver chest x-ray services to a rural poor group; inoculation programs for influenza; reading tutorials; and the entire activities of a public school system.

The following seven dimensions are provided as a frame of reference for posing questions that the reader should attempt to answer about a program or program component that is the object of evaluation research: setting, technology, target population, size, objectives, costs, and decisions. These are adapted and modified from the works of Sarri and Selo (1974), Suchman (1967), and Shortell and Richardson (1978). Within each of these dimensions we provide exemplary questions that the reader can use in assessing the evaluator's description of the program.

Setting

The setting of a program refers to its geographical, social, and political context. The current context of any program is influenced by its history of successes and failures, its relationship with other competing organizations and with social and political forces within the community in which it is located, and the extent to which it has been or is entangled in social and public controversies. Questions such as the following can be useful:

1. Where is the program located?
2. Are there any past or current controversies with which the program is involved?
3. For how long is the program funded?
4. What is the relationship between the program staff and other community programs?
5. What kind of public image does the program have in the community?
6. What community or organizational constraints impinge on the program's attainment of its objectives?

Technology

The technology of programs includes specific staff activities and their use of resources for providing services and/or administering planned interventions. Some programs (for example, those of community mental health centers) may offer a variety of services with many intervention techniques. Other programs may be focused on a specific intervention, for example, a ten-session clinic devoted to help clients lose weight based on a specific diet and behavior modification techniques. The entire content of technologies cannot be completely determined in advance; details are typically modified as a function of the social interactions between program staff and particular clientele. Specificity of programs also varies by purpose and is affected by characteristics of clientele. For example, a given set of instructions concerned with providing clients with knowledge about social agencies can be easily delineated. In contrast, the articulation of interventions involved in psychotherapy with disturbed borderline clients is much more difficult. Nevertheless, the report of an evaluation study can be relatively precise in describing what transpired in a program. The number and duration of program contacts can be indicated; summaries of the contents, obtained through tape recordings and process notes, of program contacts can be presented, in narrative form, or more systematically through content analysis (Tripodi and Epstein, 1980). The reader can ask these types of questions about a program's technology:

1. What are the specific contents of the technology? What does the staff do, and what resources do they use?
2. How often is the technology employed? Over what period of time?
3. Is there a specified minimum or maximum number of program contacts?

4. Is the technology uniformly administered from client to client?

5. Did the evaluator attempt to describe the technology so that it could be replicated?

6. Are there any procedures that the evaluator could have used to describe the technology more adequately?

Target Population

The target population is that group which a technology is intended to benefit. It is comprised of those clients and/or representatives of organizations who are eligible for program services and interventions. Programs may have eligibility requirements based on client characteristics such as ethnic status, age, fixed income levels, legal status, and so forth. A correctional program, for example, may be geared to adolescent males who are on probation within a certain geographical area; "hot-line" services from a suicide prevention clinic may be available to anyone who phones.

Social programs do not always reach the entire target population, especially when the need for the program's services is great and the program's resources are limited. Hence, it is important for the evaluator to indicate to what extent the target sample (those eligible for the program who received program services) is representative of the target population, and whether or not the program's resources are sufficient to provide services for the entire target population.

The reader of an evaluation study should focus on questions that pertain to a description of the target sample and the population from which it was drawn. Questions such as these can be raised:

1. What are the program's eligibility requirements?

2. How are clients selected and processed for the program? Are there any particular characteristics or processes that lead to client selection? For example, a drug abuse program may be formally open to all drug abusers within a geographical area but all of its clients may be those who are referred by the state's Department of Mental Health.

3. What personal, social, and psychological characteristics of the target sample were measured by the evaluation? What other characteristics should have been measured and why?

4. To what extent did the evaluator demonstrate that the target sample is representative of the target population?

5. Were there clients who did not receive full program services, or who dropped out of the program? If so, did the evaluator indicate the extent to which program dropouts were similar to or different from other clients?

6. Did the evaluator provide evidence with respect to whether or not the program services were uniformly received by clients of different gender, ethnic identification, and religion?

Size

Program size is used broadly to refer to the numbers and types of hired persons and volunteers, services and interventions, and objectives. It therefore includes program complexity, and it also refers to such dimensions as the length of time a program has been operative.

In referring to hired staff and volunteers, it is important to know who is administering the technology. The reader should also look for the evaluator's description of staff characteristics, considering such variables as experience in using the technology, pertinent education, gender, ethnic identity, and so forth. These descriptions may be suggestive of critical staff-client interactions; for example, there may be differences in program efforts, effectiveness, and efficiency as a function of similar or dissimilar matchings between clients' and staff's ethnic identities. The inclusion of volunteers is useful information when considering the cost-effectiveness of a social program.

Specification of the number and types of objectives, services, and interventions provides information about the complexity of a program. From those data a reader can infer whether the evaluator's objectives are appropriate. If an evaluator aims to provide a comprehensive evaluation, then all of the program's objectives should be considered. However, a partial evaluation focusing on a limited number of objectives may be sufficient, especially when the evaluator and the evaluation consumer have agreed on the purpose of the evaluation.

The following are illustrative questions that can be asked about a program's size:

1. How many persons are employed to administer and operate the program?

2. What are the personal, social, and psychological characteristics of program staff?

3. Are volunteers used by the program? If so, what are their roles and characteristics?

4. In the evaluation report did the evaluator discuss the complexity of the program in terms of the number and type of services, interventions, and objectives?

5. To what extent did the evaluator provide information about the similarities and differences between program staff and clientele?

6. Did the evaluator provide information relating to the extent to which the program has sufficient resources to provide services for the target population?

Objectives

As used here, objectives refer to program expectations. These expectations vary as programs advance through different stages of program development: initiation, contact, and implementation (Tripodi, Fellin, and Epstein, 1978, pp. 6–8). Objectives in an initiation stage are concerned with translating ideas about a program into a plan of action. Prior to delivering program services, it is necessary to procure material resources, hire staff, select appropriate technologies, and so on. These are immediate objectives and are the inputs of a program. Intermediate objectives are those that indicate the active engagement of a target sample with program staff. They occur in the contact stage of development in which program directors are concerned with the effective delivery of services, that is, the desired number of contacts with the target sample, for example, the number of completed interviews, the number of educational sessions, and so forth. In a sense, intermediate objectives are indicators of the implementation of program services or interventions; they can also be regarded as process variables which can be "... defined as the effects produced during the period of intervention" (Sarri and Selo, 1974, p. 263). When programs are fully implemented, objectives are focused on the attainment of the results of program implementation. These ultimate objectives are longer-range expectations of the results of program services and interventions, and they are the objectives that social researchers often focus on in their evaluations of social programs.

Program objectives should be clear and precise, including operational definitions of the dependent variables or change variables of the evaluation. Shortell and Richardson (1978, pp. 18–20) specify a number of dimensions for describing program objectives. Four salient characteristics are short-term versus long-term effects, magnitude of effect, stability of effect, and unintended consequences. Short-term effects are those that are expected to occur more quickly than long-term effects. Hence, a meals-on-wheels program may have an immediate expectation of providing sufficient food to avoid starvation and a longer-term effect of providing balanced diets for program recipients. Or a delinquency program may have the short-term objective of helping delinquents successfully follow the rules for probation and the longer-term objective of reducing the crime rates of delinquents after they are no longer on probation. The magnitude of effects is the amount of expected change; for example, it might be expected that 20 percent of the clients who receive a program of job training will secure employment. Stability of effect is the amount of time for which the expected effect will persist. Of those clients who obtain jobs, it might be expected that 80 percent will keep their jobs for six months or longer. Evaluators should think through, prior to their evaluation, possible "side effects" or unplanned consequences (by the program administration and staff). For example, clients who receive assertiveness training to help them increase the number of their interpersonal relationships may become "too assertive" (obnoxious), which may unexpectedly decrease their interpersonal relationships.

These are representative questions that can be formulated to focus on program objectives:

1. What are the primary objectives of the program?

2. What kind of objectives are the focus of the evaluation: immediate, intermediate, and/or ultimate?

3. For each objective, what is the expected magnitude of effect? When is that effect expected to occur? For what period of time will it last?

4. Has the evaluator specified objectives in collaboration with program administration and staff? If not, are the objectives sufficiently clear and operationally specific?

5. Did the evaluator obtain measures indicative of unintended consequences?

Costs

Program costs are the total amounts of monies needed to operate a program. Included in costs are such items as salary; rental of equipment, furniture, and space; office supplies; and so forth. Costs also contain voluntary contributions, donated space, equivalent salaries for the work done by volunteers, and so on; although these costs may not increase the cash outlay to a specific program, they are important items to consider when program replication is at issue in summative evaluation.

Many program evaluations do not include program costs, but it is a highly recommended procedure. It is especially necessary in times of budget restrictions and in view of competition for program funds. Costs of program inputs can be used for cost-effectiveness analyses for comparing the relative efficiency of social programs with similar ultimate objectives (Epstein and Tripodi, 1977, pp. 152–53; Rossi, Freeman, and Wright, 1979, pp. 241–82).

Illustrative questions pertaining to program costs are:

1. How much does it cost to operate the program for a designated time period, for example, three months or one year?

2. What is the equivalent amount of money that is contributed to the program through donations, contributions of volunteers, and so forth?

3. What are the average costs for each client within a specified period of program operation, such as a fiscal year?

4. What are the relationships between program costs and indicators of program effectiveness?

5. Has the evaluator included information about program costs, and has he attempted to determine the extent to which cost data are reliable and valid?

Decisions

Program sponsors, administrators, and other consumers of evaluation often use the results of evaluation research as inputs relative to program decisions. An administrator may wish to reduce or eliminate a program component that is relatively inefficient and ineffective; a sponsor may be in the process of deciding whether or not to fund similar programs in other areas; a staff worker may be choosing one of two alternative techniques; and so forth.

An important role of a program evaluator is to identify program decisions for which the evaluation consumer requires data from program evaluation. In formative evaluation program decisions pertain to the accomplishment of immediate and intermediate objectives: hiring staff, engaging clientele by making transportation available, and so on. Data from summative program evaluations provide generalizations about the attainment of ultimate objectives, which is informative to program sponsors as well as those involved in the development of programs and policies. Suggestive questions regarding program decisions are:

1. Has the evaluator identified decisions for which the program evaluation is relevant?
2. What is the basic nature of decisions facing the evaluation consumer?
3. If the evaluation consumer doesn't require evaluative data for program decisions, what is the consumer's purpose for the evaluation?
4. What key decisions do the program administration and staff have to make for the continuing development and operation of the program?

PROGRAM EVALUATION OBJECTIVES

The reader of a program evaluation research study can evaluate it by discerning the study's objectives and determining the extent to which the evaluator has accomplished those objectives. Basically evaluators seek to provide data that are relevant to the accomplishment of program objectives and to the identification of desirable results related to program activities and procedures. Since there are typically many program objectives for which data can be obtained, it is often necessary for the program evaluator to prioritize them, preferably in negotiations with the evaluation consumer. Considering the available resources for conducting a program evaluation and the time available for the study, the evaluator focuses his research so that it is manageable. He also makes basic decisions about the extent of the evaluation, that is, whether it is comprehensive or partial, and its type, that is, formative, summative, or a combination thereof.

To assist the reader in identifying evaluation objectives we offer three primary dimensions: evaluation criteria, knowledge level, and degree of generality. The evaluation objectives should be relatively clear if the criteria for evaluation are specified, the level of knowledge desired is at least implicit, and the desired degree of generality is indicated.

Evaluation Criteria

As previously indicated, major objectives are expressed in the three criteria: program *efforts, effectiveness,* and *efficiency* (Tripodi, Fellin, and Epstein, 1978, pp. 40–46). An evaluation of program efforts is an assessment of the amounts and kinds of program activities. It includes program inputs such as funds, space, and equipment as well as staff time and involvement. Quantitative and qualitative descriptions of program efforts are an indication of program activity. They do not indicate how well program tasks are carried out or whether program expectations are realized. However, although not sufficient, program efforts are necessary for the attainment of program objectives.

Program effectiveness refers to the extent to which a program's objectives are realized. It also includes unanticipated consequences—desirable and undesirable—that are the result of program activities and procedures. Furthermore, effectiveness can be considered in relation to community needs for the program, providing an index of a program's impact on a particular community. For example, effectiveness of a program that has the objective of reducing the consumption of alcohol by specified amounts might be evaluated in relation to the proportion of clients that have reduced their alcoholic consumption compared to nonclients or to an earlier consumption level of the clients. If there are no deleterious side effects traceable to the program and if clients "feel better" and are able to function more effectively on their jobs, the program can be regarded as successful. The program can also be considered successful at the community level if it can be demonstrated that community needs for a more steady work force are being partly met by the program.

Program efficiency is an index of the relative costs for achieving program objectives. It is the relationship between effectiveness and efforts, and may be considered as the ratio of effectiveness to costs. It is a useful criterion when one is interested in comparing two or more programs with respect to their relative degrees of cost-effectiveness, where efforts are specified in terms of cost. For example, one program may achieve its objectives at X costs, while another program may be twice as cost-effective, achieving the same objectives at $X/2$ costs.

The reader should raise questions such as these about a program evaluation study:

1. What evaluation criteria were used by the evaluator?
2. What additional evaluation criteria might the evaluator have used?
3. To what extent are the specifications of the evaluation criteria geared to the program's *objectives*?
4. Are the evaluation criteria relevant to the program's activities?

Examples of illustrative evaluation questions that evaluators can ask of programs that are fully implemented or operational can serve as stimuli for locating more specific evaluation questions that evaluators might attempt to answer in program evaluation research. Delineating evaluation objectives is one way in which evaluation objectives can be specified. The following questions related to the criteria of effort, effectiveness and efficiency are from *Differential Social Program Evaluation* (Tripodi, Fellin, and Epstein, 1978, pp. 54–55):

EFFORT

1. How much time and energy are devoted to a review of staff objectives and activities?
2. What staff efforts are involved in the respecification of goals and in the location of additional resources judged necessary to achieve program results?
3. How much effort is devoted to the specification of criteria for program termination and necessary follow-up activities?
4. How much time and activity are devoted to the procurement of follow-up information from program beneficiaries?
5. How much effort is devoted to the consideration and specification of policies for the reentry of dropouts?

EFFECTIVENESS

1. What results have been achieved that could be attributed to the program; are there discernible changes in the knowledge, attitudes, or skills of the program beneficiaries; are there changes in behavior on the part of individuals, groups, or organizations?
2. What results could have been obtained without the content of the program (would changes have taken place anyway)?
3. Are there any unplanned outcomes, either desirable or undesirable, that could be attributed to the program?
4. How effective is the program in relation to the need of the intended target population?

EFFICIENCY

1. What are the relative costs of different techniques used to achieve similar results?
2. What is the relation of costs of program effort to the benefits of results achieved?

3. What are the relative costs of the program in comparison with other programs with similar objectives?

4. Could the same results be achieved with a reduction in program efforts?

Knowledge Level

There are four basic knowledge levels that are sought in program evaluation research: hypothetical, descriptive, correlational, and cause-effect (Tripodi, 1974, pp. 47–59; Epstein and Tripodi, 1977, p. 32). Hypothetical knowledge refers to the formulation of concepts and hypotheses about program interventions, their delivery to designated target populations, and their results. The development of good ideas is vital, particularly when addressed to phenomena in which social programs have not appeared to be successful. For example, the objective of an evaluation may be to locate strategies and techniques that might increase the involvement of the parents of low-income youth in their education. As a result of exploratory studies of several programs focused on preschool education, it might be hypothesized that children of parents who receive a training program geared to facilitate the educational efforts of their children are more likely to have favorable attitudes toward education than are children of parents who do not receive the program. Such an hypothesis would be subject to refinement as it is implemented and tested by further programming and research.

Descriptive knowledge may focus on the program, staff, clientele, or their interactions. Essentially it is the compilation of descriptive facts. For example, program evaluation research may describe the parameters of services delivered such as qualitative descriptions of their contents and the number of hours of program contact with clientele; the characteristics of staff including their education, experience, age, gender, ethnicity, and social attitudes; and the distinguishing characteristics of clientele who drop out of social programs as compared to those who complete them.

Correlational knowledge for program evaluation is the extent of empirical relationships between program technologies and variables regarded as indicators of effectiveness and/or efficiency. It might be the objective of program evaluation, as an illustration, to discern whether or not male graduates of a job training program are more or less likely than female graduates to obtain jobs. In addition, such an evaluation may include a number of other variables such as type of job, previous employment experience, age, education, and so forth. Correlations of those variables with the criterion of job attainment are computed, and multiple regression techniques might be employed to determine the extent to which they explain or modify the relationship between gender and job attainment.

Cause-effect knowledge is the highest level of knowledge. Studies that aim to produce cause-effect knowledge treat program technologies as independent or causal variables and attempt to measure their impacts on the basis of changes in dependent or outcome variables. Both cause-effect and correlational knowledge are based on evidence of empirical relationships; however, studies that generate cause-effect relationships also demonstrate that independent variables precede dependent variables in time, and they rule out other possible explanations for observed changes in the dependent variables.

Program evaluation that is relatively comprehensive includes the study of more than one program objective, and it provides data regarding efforts, effectiveness, and efficiency, as well as their interrelationships. The evaluator may conduct several research studies, employing different research strategies. Consequently, it is possible that several levels of research knowledge are sought within one program evaluation. The reader should determine what the basic evaluation objectives are in terms of desired knowledge; this will provide a perspective regarding the evaluator's appropriate use of research techniques. These two basic questions about knowledge level can be raised about a program evaluation study:

1. What are the objectives of the research in terms of knowledge levels?
2. Were the levels of knowledge sought related to the research objectives, and were the basic research strategies employed appropriate?

Degree of Generality

The degree of generality is the extent to which the results of an evaluation study can be generalized. The essence of summative evaluation is generalizable knowledge. Generalizations can be made about specific technolo gies, staff personnel and clients. Particular technologies may be effective with only certain types of personnel and/or clients and, for summative evaluation, this type of knowledge is important.

The reader of program evaluation studies should discern whether or not the researchers intend to generalize their results. If so, the populations to which the results are to be generalized should be specified, for example, other clients, social workers with specified amounts of training, and so forth.

KNOWLEDGE ATTAINMENT AND EMPIRICAL GENERALITY

Knowledge attainment is the extent to which the objectives of program evaluation research have been achieved. Objectives are realized when the evaluator demonstrates that his methodology is sound and there is sufficient empirical evidence to achieve the specific levels of desired knowledge.

The reader can refer to Chapter 3 and use those questions for evaluating the methodology of evaluation research after classifying the research design into experimental, quantitative-descriptive, or exploratory studies. As previously noted, exploratory studies are used primarily to produce hypothetical and descriptive knowledge; quantitative-descriptive studies primarily for descriptive and correlational knowledge; and experimental studies for correlational and cause-effect knowledge. Another way the reader can evaluate the extent to which objectives are achieved is to follow these steps:

1. Identify the knowledge objectives of the study.
2. Specify the objectives into desired knowledge levels; hypothetical, descriptive, correlational, and cause-effect.
3. Determine whether or not the researcher's procedures and empirical evidence are sufficient to meet the criteria for the particular knowledge level desired.

Criteria for Assessing Knowledge Attainment

The criteria for hypothetical knowledge should indicate that the derived hypotheses are researchable and can be implemented by the program. The criteria include: clarity of the hypothesized relationship between program components and dependent variables, operational distinctness between the independent and dependent variables (that is, they are not defined in the same way), operational specificity of the variables, and feasibility, which refers to the possibility of program implementation and its evaluation, including the availability of costs and resources (Tripodi, 1974, pp. 62–64).

Quantitative descriptions are based on measures that are accurate, reliable, and valid. The measures should be obtained with relatively few mistakes in clerical processing. There should also be evidence regarding the consistency of measurement with repeated applications of the measuring instrument. For example, there should be correlations or percentage agreements of 70 percent or higher for interobserver reliability. And there should be data that bear on the content and/or predictive validity of the variables. Accurate, reliable, and valid measurements are necessary for the attainment of all levels of quantitative knowledge. Hence, correlational and cause-effect knowledge also require sound measurement procedures.

Correlational knowledge is also assessed by analyzing evidence for the relationship between program interventions and their outcomes. The reader should discern whether the evaluator has provided evidence of the strength, direction and predictability of relationships (Epstein and Tripodi, 1977, pp. 34–35). Strength of relationship may be shown by correlation coefficients, mean differences and percentage differences. Positive (direct) and negative (inverse) directional relationships are easily inferred from the tabular data on differences between means or percentages, or they are expressed directly by positive or negative signs for correlation coefficients such as r and rho. Predictability is the percentage of the variation on the dependent variable that can be explained by a program intervention variable. More technically, it is the amount of variance explained and can be determined by variance, covariance, correlational, or regression analyses. A rough procedure for determining predictability is to square a correlation coefficient and multiply it by 100. For example, if the correlation between participation in a nutritional program and improved dietary habits is 0.60, the predictability is 36 percent (0.60 × 100).

Cause-effect knowledge requires evidence of sound measurement, empirical relationship, temporal order, and control of internal validity factors. Temporal order signifies the occurrence of the program intervention variable prior to the observed changes in the dependent or effect variables, and internal validity factors are those variables other than the program intervention that might explain observed changes in the dependent variables. The control of temporal order and internal validity factors is the reason for the evaluator's use of experimental and quasi-experimental procedures. To appraise the extent to which these variables are controlled, refer to our discussion and criteria for evaluating experimental studies in Chapter 3. As indicated there, we use Campbell and Stanley's (1966) notions of internal validity factors: contemporary history, maturation, initial measurement effects, instrumentation, statistical regression, biased selection, subject mortality, and interactions. The more evidence there is for control of internal validity factors, the closer is the knowledge to cause-effect knowledge. Thus, an experiment that controls for all internal validity factors except interactions is more likely to produce cause-effect knowledge than an experiment that does not control for subject mortality and instrumentation.

Criteria for Assessing Empirical Generality

Empirical generality can be assessed by following these basic guidelines:

1. Determine whether or not the evaluator has indicated specific populations (for example, clientele intervenors, technologies) to which the results of the study are to be generalized.
2. Assess the procedures and evidence that were presented to support the evaluator's contentions of generality.

In general, five methods can be used to enhance generalizability: representative sampling, replications, experimental procedures, statistical comparisons of relevant variables, and the use of previous research. Representative sampling is the use of sampling procedures such as random sampling from the population of clients and from the population of available staff. Replications refer to the repeated implementations of program variables with different sets of clients, workers, and situations. The greater the number of replications with consistent results, the greater is the degree of generalizability. Experimental procedures can control for external validity factors, which are threats to inferences about generality (Campbell and Stanley, 1966). For example, placebo groups can be employed to control for the interactions of program intervention and faith in the authority and expertise of program staff, and the interaction between initial measurements and program intervention can be controlled by experiments that obtain measurements only on randomized populations after the program intervention is complete.

In addition, the reader can observe whether the evaluator provides data that show the comparability of the sample and the universe (that is, population) from which the sample is drawn. For example, the program staff may be comprised of social workers. The distributions of salient characteristics for those social workers such as gender, years of experience, and amount of education can be compared with the characteristics of the social work population, as observed in a directory of social workers. To the extent that there are no statistically significant differences between the sample and the population, it can be inferred that the sample is representative. The greater the number of variables for which there are no statistically significant differences, the greater is the degree of representativeness, assuming some relationship of the variables to characteristics of salience.

The evaluators might also resort to previous research that bears on the generalizability of the samples used in the program evaluation research. It is important for the reader to keep in mind which population is being discussed. The evaluator may have provided evidence that the sample of clients is representative of the potential population of clients the program could serve. However, that doesn't attest to the representativeness of program staff. For each relevant population, the reader should determine whether there are sufficient procedures and data that relate to the empirical generality of the sample in the program evaluation study. Of course, it should not be inferred that the samples are non-representative if there are insufficient procedures and data. The sample may or may not be representative; its actual degree of representativeness would be unknown. The reader can, however, assess the appropriateness of the conclusions and implications of the evaluator, who can distort the findings of his research by improper generalizations.

UTILITY OF PROGRAM EVALUATIONS

The principles and guidelines offered in Chapter 4, "Utilization of Research," are readily applicable to most reports of program evaluation research and can be followed by the research reader. If a place among those identified as evaluation consumers is assumed, the research reader can directly appreciate the usefulness of the report, after classifying the research (as in Chapter 2) and evaluating the research (as in Chapter 3). The reader need only decide how his or her own immediate or potential situation or interest resembles that of the evaluation consumers identified.

There are two basic types of knowledge that can result from evaluative research: substantive and methodological (Tripodi, 1974, pp. 75–76). Whereas substantive knowledge refers to the findings of studies in terms of the accomplishment of evaluation objectives and levels of knowledge, methodological knowledge is the use of research strategies and data-collection techniques for information processing. Both types of knowledge can be used in formative and summative evaluations. The results of research can inform decision makers of appropriate choices regarding program development and policies. Moreover, evaluative research can provide a conceptual frame of reference in which the program can be viewed in terms of relative effectiveness and efficiency of different interventions. Methodological knowledge is often an important by-product of program evaluation research. Instruments may be provided that facilitate the continual evaluation of a social program by program staff *per se*. Furthermore, efficient means of gathering and processing information may be used by policy makers, as well as by program administrators who are concerned with program development. To appraise the usefulness of knowledge from program evaluation research, the reader can use the following criteria: clarity of research communications, knowledge appraisal, relevancy, actual use, and potential utility.

Clarity of Research Communications

The results of research should be clearly communicated to appropriate evaluation consumers. Since the research is intended for use, it can not be used properly unless it is understood.

These questions can be posed by the reader of a program evaluation research report:

1. Is the report written so that it can be understood by evaluation consumers?

2. Did the evaluator provide any information that the findings were communicated to and understood by evaluation consumers?

3. Were the basic findings accurately summarized?

4. Was methodological procedure (e.g., use of tests and questionnaires) sufficiently described so that it could be understood by evaluation consumers?

Knowledge Appraisal

The reader should assess the evaluator's conclusions regarding the findings of the research. This can be done by examining the empirical evidence and procedures employed by the evaluator to accomplish objectives and determining the extent to which conclusions are consistent with the data provided in the report. It is paramount that the evidence for various levels of knowledge are satisfactorily realized and that the report of the evaluator is faithful to the evidence (or lack of evidence), not over- or underrepresenting attained knowledge levels. Furthermore, the reader should assess the extent to which the results are generalizable.

Methodological knowledge in the form of data-collection instruments should be appraised by their measurement accuracy, reliability, and validity. In addition, they should be assessed in relation to the knowledge they produce, as well as their feasibility (Tripodi and Epstein, 1980, pp. 37–47). Feasibility includes the direct costs for using an instrument, as well as the indirect costs of the time required for the instrument's proper administration. The reader should also assess the amount of training that is required to use the instrument. Questionnaires and some rating scales might be easily used with very little training whereas some projective tests, for example, may require much training, particularly for professional staff who are not psychologists.

Methodological knowledge concerning research design, information management, and statistical systems is assessed in relation to these factors' costs and successes in generating knowledge. Research designs that include measurements on selected variables before and after program intervention can easily be implemented in formative program evaluation; administrators and their staffs can produce correlational knowledge, showing the relationship of program intervention to effectiveness.

Relevancy

The contents of program evaluation are relevant when they provide information that is informative to the evaluation consumer. More specifically, the results and/or methods of program evaluation studies should be pertinent to decisions that are involved in program development or policy. For program development, administrators and staff should be provided with information bearing on the tasks of program operation, the nature of client systems, the social problems with which clients and staff are confronted, and the cost effectiveness of alternate procedures (Tripodi, 1974, pp. 89–92). To assist in the formulation and modification of policy, the findings from program evaluation research should be generalizable across clients, staff, and geographical areas; in addition, they should be comprehensive, as well as program specific, providing information related to the contraction and expansion of social programs (Windle and Bates, 1974).

The information should be provided before decisions are made by evaluation consumers. It might be argued that the results of evaluation might be used to justify decisions that have already been made, but that stance can lead to abuses of research, for consumers may pay attention only to those findings that justify actions already taken.

The results of an evaluation study should be geared to appropriate evaluation consumers if they are to be regarded as relevant. The evaluation consumers that are most critical are those who have the power or authority to make or influence decisions. An administrator and staff, for example, make decisions about the day-to-day operations of social programs, and they can implement the results of formative program evaluation.

Actual Use

The reader should assess the available evidence that bears on the actual use of program evaluation research. Information that relates to a specific program that is in the process of development can be used fairly quickly. Hence, new procedures may be implemented, data-gathering systems are installed, personnel changes can be made, and so forth. Data from summative evaluation that relate to policy decisions may not be forthcoming until a relatively long period of time after a program has been completed. Consequently, there may not be sufficient data contained in an evaluation report to appraise the ultimate impact of the evaluation. The reader can seek answers to questions such as these to estimate the extent of actual use of the results of a program evaluation study:

1. Were the results of the evaluation used by the evaluation consumer? If so, in what specific ways were they used?

2. Were any program operations modified as a result of the evaluation study?

3. Has the evaluation consumer's point of view about the social program changed as a result of the evaluation?

4. Were any decisions about program funding, its size, or its scope made as a result of the evaluation?

5. Did the evaluator provide any evidence regarding the actual use of substantive and/or methodological knowledge?

Potential Utility

Posavac and Carey (1980, pp. 299–304) indicate that the findings from program evaluation can be used if the evaluator assists in developing attitudes in program personnel that are receptive to program improvement. The role of the evaluator in implementing the results of evaluation is further underscored by Rossi, Freeman, and Wright (1979, p. 305), who say there are three important roles of evaluation in determining policy decisions: "deciding technical planning and management questions," providing "definitive information upon which decision makers" can act, and "changing the grounds of political argumentation."

The ultimate utility of evaluations depends on the evaluation consumer. Whether or not the results of a particular study are used is, in part, also influenced by political and organizational variables impinging on social programs. Hence, the potential use of knowledge is related to factors such as these: knowledge receptivity, value consonance, and capability for implementation (Tripodi, 1974, pp. 96–105).

Knowledge receptivity is the process in which the evaluation consumer is actively engaged in receiving communications about knowledge. After the evaluation consumer receives knowledge from the research, he is receptive to that knowledge if he seeks to understand and evaluate it, as well as considering ways in which it might be useful. For example, an administrator and staff that are receptive to knowledge would be sure that they thoroughly understand the results of the research. They, of course, would not seek to implement invalid knowledge. They might ask the evaluator to clarify the findings, and they might consider the relative advantages and disadvantages of this possible implementation.

Value consonance is the degree to which the findings from program evaluation research are compatible with the values of the evaluation consumer. Value systems of the key persons in an organization, the sponsors of the organization, and the organization's clientele can impede or facilitate the use of knowledge. If, for example, behavior modification techniques are regarded as unethical by the administration of a correctional agency, they will not be used, even if their application may be more cost-effective than techniques currently in use in that particular agency.

Capability for implementation is the extent to which the findings can actually be implemented. In addition to the decision-making power or influence of evaluation consumers, implementation depends on such factors as resources and organizational interest. Resources include necessary financial costs, manpower, time, equipment, and so forth. Organizational interest refers to the willingness of administration and staff to implement the results of evaluation. This involves discussion and selection of those results that the program staff wishes to implement, the coordination of efforts in program implementation, and the desire of program personnel to make recommended changes. In effect, the extent to which evaluation results can be implemented depends on personal and social organizational characteristics, as well as on other factors that could influence the adoption of an innovation or social change. It is clear that all the factors that could affect the implementation of the results of evaluation cannot be included in an evaluation report. Nevertheless, the reader can determine whether or not such factors have been considered by the evaluator. Moreover, the reader can estimate whether the findings are potentially useful by considering the answers to questions such as these:

1. Do the findings of the research appear to be relevant to evaluation consumers?

2. Are the findings valid?

3. Do the consumers identified by the evaluator have decision-making power or influence?

4. Are the potential users receptive to either substantive or methodological knowledge resulting from the program evaluation?

5. Are the values of the evaluation consumers consonant with the knowledge?

6. Is the knowledge timely?

7. Do the evaluation consumers have sufficient resources and manpower for implementing the knowledge?

8. Are key administrative and staff personnel interested in implementing the knowledge?

Chapter 7

Assessing Social Policy Research

Social policy research involves the use of methods of social research to generate knowledge that informs the formulation, implementation, and/or evaluation of social policies. As Mayer and Greenwood have noted, "It is the function of policy-oriented research to facilitate that process (policy making) by providing relevant technical information, without which an analysis of implications would be impaired" (Mayer and Greenwood, 1980, p. 5). Policy making has essential links to social programs, which leads Etzioni to define policy research as research "concerned with mapping alternative approaches and with specifying potential differences in the intention, effect, and cost of various programs" (Etzioni, 1971, p. 8). Our focus in this chapter is on the assessment and use of research in the process of policy making.

Social scientists, especially individuals from the academic disciplines of sociology, psychology, political science, and economics, have for some years participated in social policy research. Evidence of this involvement is found in policy studies published in academic and professional journals and in the participation of social scientists in the policy-making process as consultants, researchers, and policy analysts (Etzioni, 1971, pp. 8–21). The social work profession has an equally long history of concern about social policies, since these policies are so closely related to the alleviation of social problems and since human service organizations staffed by social workers implement social policies through social programs. In recent years social workers have become more involved than ever in policy making, especially through positions designed to provide input into policy and program decision making. In these positions, skills in assessing research reports for policy purposes are crucial. While our general guidelines for assessing social research in the early chapters of this book are useful for individuals in policy-related positions, the complexities of the policy process, including the development of social programs, suggest the need for special attention to the relationship of social research to social policy.

The art and practice of policy making is complex, as is the conduct and use of social research. In this chapter we view these processes from the viewpoint of a policy analyst, a person in an organization assigned to tasks which generate information for input into policy decision making. Social research enters the work of the policy analyst in the following way. The analyst seeks out and reviews research reports, selecting information about policy problems and issues. The analyst participates in the identification of needed information, may assist researchers in carrying out policy studies, or may actually serve as a researcher. The policy analyst rarely works alone and ordinarily must relate to a number of actors involved in the policy process, including other staff members, program administrators, and policy makers—both from inside and outside the organization.

A useful way of thinking about the relationship of social research to policy making is found in the work of Mayer and Greenwood, *The Design of Social Policy Research* (1980), and Freeman and Sherwood, *Social Research and Social Policy* (1970). These authors identify stages of policy making and suggest research designs that seem to provide the most appropriate fit for the particular stage of policy making. While their focus is on the design and conduct of research, their approach to matching policy phases to research designs gives us a framework for considering the utility of policy research.

An important feature of the utilization of social research is the organizational, social, and political context in which decision making takes place. In order to understand this context better, we examine some of the key characteristics of social policy and policy making. The writings of Tropman *et al., Strategic Perspectives on Social Policy* (1976); Gil, *Unravelling Social Policy* (1973); and Morris, *Social Policy of the American Welfare State* (1979) highlight the various phases of the policy process and enlighten us about internal and external influences on policy making.

Finally, the literature on the use of social science research in public policy making is particularly relevant to our concerns about utilization of research knowledge. Illustrative works include the writings of Weiss and Bucuvalas, *Social Science Research and Decision-Making* (1980); Rossi and Williams, *Evaluating Social Programs* (1972); and Weiss, *Using Social Research in Public Policy Making* (1977). This literature deals with questions such as: To what extent do policy makers use social science research? What obstacles stand in the way of use of research knowledge? What conditions facilitate the application of social research to policy decisions? What characteristics of decision makers suggest a likelihood that research will be used in the policy process? While the emphasis in these writings is on evaluative research and policy making, our interest is in utilization of knowledge from a variety of research designs.

THE NATURE OF SOCIAL POLICY

What is social policy? Social policy can be defined most easily in relation to governmental policies, although it is appropriate to refer to some nongovernmental policies of organizations as "social policies." Social policy, as government policy, is the collection of policies that emerges from governmental units and is designed to meet "social objectives." Such policies are said to be "organizing principles established to guide action," to bring about changes within the social system (Morris, 1979, p. 1). The boundaries of social policies remain unclear, especially vis-à-vis economic policies, but "In general social policies are identified as those through which government seeks to correct inequities, to improve the condition of the disadvantaged, and to provide assistance to the less powerful" (Morris, 1979, p. 1). Using this definition, most social welfare policies come under the umbrella of social policy.

Most policy critics agree that the United States has no single national social policy, that is, no integrated system of social policies. Boulding (1967), for example, notes that "in contrast with economic policy, social policy looks like a sticky conglomeration of the ad hoc" (Boulding, 1967, p. 4). When policies are considered in relation to the social needs or social problems of specific groups, such as family, children, or aged, again there is no evidence that a single unified policy exists in any of these areas. There is general recognition, however, that social policies developed at the federal level provide a major direction for social programs at all levels of government. Social policies at the national level are generated through the executive, judicial, and legislative branches of government and are under constant revision and reinterpretation by these governmental branches.

There are, of course, social policies that are established and implemented by state and local governmental units. In the case of social welfare policies, states vary in the goals of the policies and the kinds and amounts of resources that they devote to the implementation of the policies. Similar kinds of variations can be found in local governmental units. State governmental units often operate under a mix of federal and state policies, and local public service organizations generally relate to many social policies established at higher levels of government.

The organizational levels under which public social policies are estabished must be taken into account as we explore the role of research vis-à-vis social policy. The political process and the numbers and kinds of actors involved in policy making will differ at each level of government, as will the size and structure of the organization implementing the policies through social programs. These differences set some parameters in relation to the need for and use of technical information in relation to social policy.

All social policies are not governmental. There are numerous organizations in the private sector that establish social policies. Many voluntary organizations, including social welfare organizations, professional associations, industrial corporations, foundations, and labor unions operate at national, state, and local levels under the direction of social policies established by membership and by boards of directors. Some of these organizations have specialized goals and seek to improve conditions of the membership, while others have more general goals and objectives. While we recognize that there are differences between governmental and nongovernmental organizations, we expect that some basic aspects of policy making will apply to all human service organizations.

Because of the close association between social policies and social programs, it is useful to note distinctions between policy goals, objectives, and programs. Policies state goals, "the intention to attain some end state" (Mayer and Greenwood, 1980, p. 6) such as "to equalize educational opportunity . . . to provide decent housing. . . ." An example from the area of social welfare can be noted in Title XX of the Social Security Act (as amended in 1974), which established as a goal the provision of "social services to low-income individuals and families" (Title XX). An example of a social policy of a state government, as related to Title XX, is the policy "to meet the financial, social and health needs of those persons whose requirements are beyond their individual abilities to provide." Specific goals are directly related to the federal policy, "to provide for health and financial maintenance, protection from abuse, neglect, exploitation, reduction of inappropriate institutionalization, and to provide for self-sufficiency and self-support." An objective is a specific end to be attained by a specific plan or policy, for example, "to increase the number of American families living in standard housing by 20 percent by 1980" (Mayer and Greenwood, 1980). Federal and state social policies may be broad in nature, but once adopted, they will be carried out "by a series or set of programs which deal with a small part of the social system" (Tropman et al., 1976, p. xiii). Thus, according to Tropman, social programs are adopted to "achieve a certain set of limited objectives and goals" (Tropman et al., 1976, p. xiii). Examples of programs established under Title XX to meet social welfare goals include day care for children, protective services, family services, and delinquency services.

Social policy goals are expected to be achieved through social programs. It is therefore natural to think of evaluation of programs as the major means for evaluating social policy. However, we do not wish to limit the input of research knowledge to social program evaluation, important as it may be to the policy maker. We will consider the evaluation and utilization of empirical research with regard to policy goals, objectives, and social programs at all levels and phases of policy making. As we examine these phases, we must always be attuned to the fact that they overlap and that strict delineation between phases in actual policy making is unlikely. At the same time, this approach to policy making allows us a useful framework for describing social policy research.

POLICIES, POLITICS, AND VALUES

Before we examine the major phases of policy-making process, the impact of politics and values on the policy process should be highlighted. When governmental entities are used as our frame of reference, the political nature of policy making is apparent, as the policy makers are public officials and "social problems" are "political problems" (Teicher, 1980, p. 16). Social policies are inherently linked to social problems. As policy makers establish policy goals, they not only draw upon their own values but also relate to the values and/or norms of their constituencies. As Tropman notes, policy directs the allocation of resources, as action which is based on values. Thus, "the formulation of social policy and the choosing of goals involves us in making priority choices among values" (Tropman et al., 1976, p. 9).

A political atmosphere surrounds the making of public social policy. As a consequence, research knowledge is only one factor in a process in which politics and values may outweigh all other influences brought to bear upon the policy process. Research knowledge can provide an "information base" for the decision maker in the formulation of policy, but hardly ever will the information be sufficient or persuasive enough to determine the selection of policy goals. Research data provide us with a base for "technical rationality" and go along with "political rationality" in the making of social policy. Despite the kinds and nature of the information, experience has shown that the values of the individual decision makers will play a prominent role. Teicher maintains that "social policy has to be based on value judgments" (Teicher, 1980, p. 16). For example, he notes that in regard to welfare reform, despite extensive research and experiments concerned with income maintenance, there remain unanswered questions about the effects of various policies and "fundamental value conflicts" (Teicher,

1980, p. 16). Teicher contends that the basis of policy making always involves a mix of empirical information and the values of the decision makers. It is also important to recognize that the researchers who provide knowledge for policy making also have value commitments, and this must be taken into account as the input from scientific efforts is considered.

CHARACTERISTICS OF SOCIAL POLICY RESEARCH

The term "social policy research" covers a broad spectrum of types of research design and research knowledge that can contribute to social policy making. Almost any kind of social research that informs policy making can be included under the rubric of policy research, including such types as studies of social problems, descriptive studies of the characteristics of target populations, needs assessment, and social program evaluations. We do not wish to limit our definition of policy research to research carried out with the specific intent of obtaining findings for policy purposes. We also include studies and findings, including descriptive data from secondary sources, which relate to policy questions. Perhaps the type of policy research most often mentioned is social program evaluation, since policies lead to programs, and we expect research on programs to be useful for assessment of the initial policies. Because of the importance given to social program evaluation by policy makers and administrators, we have devoted Chapter 6 to this topic. Social program evaluations are not necessarily related to social policy, as some simply have the objective of determining how effective or efficient a particular program is in relation to its purposes. However, there is often an overlap of function in social program evaluations, serving to inform policy making and also impacting on program decision making.

Types of social policy research, varied as they are, still appear to have some common characteristics. Mayer and Greenwood (1980) note that policy research is goal-oriented, has a system perspective, is focused on action, involves manipulable variables, is comprehensive, and is multidisciplinary. These should be regarded not as existing and necessary characteristics, but rather as desirable characteristics. Research need not have all of these characteristics to be social policy research. Some relationship of the research to goals is essential, as policies are goal statements. Policy research can help in the definition of goals, the selection of goals, the assessment of goal attainment, and the reformulation of goals. The impact of policy research is likely to be enhanced when it is guided by a systems perspective. A system perspective takes into account all actors who will be affected by the policy, including the policy makers, administrators of social programs, target populations, vested interest groups, and others. Closely related to this characteristic is the idea that policy research should strive to be comprehensive. When looking at social programs, which are the implementation of policy, the research should deal with as many factors as possible, such as the organizational arrangements for interventions, the technology of interventions, the recipients of services, and the providers of service. When the policy research is focused on actual programs, it will be concerned with "action," the delivery of services, the use of interventions to bring about change. This action will involve factors (or variables) that are manipulated by program design.

Two major cautions should be considered in relation to policy research. First, there may be ethical implications of the research, both in the conduct of the research and in the use of its findings for policy making. Precautions for honoring the rights of participants in the conduct of research are dealt with in the literature on research methods. When policy research leads to social programs, ethical questions may arise in regard to who is helped and who is harmed by the policy. Secondly, "a characteristic of all forms of action-oriented research is uncertainty" (Mayer and Greenwood, 1980, p. 44). No single research effort or collection of studies will provide certainty with regard to prediction of expected policy options. We have noted that a variety of research methods can be used to inform policy making, and these methods lead to varied degrees of confidence in the findings. Even under the best of circumstances for producing research findings, we must recognize that action-oriented research will not eliminate all uncertainty. Cowhig (1971) emphasizes these conditions in stating: "Policy decisions always involve important ethical, budgetary, and political judgments. Research may help make clearer the probable consequences of alternative actions; it cannot eliminate the need to make decisions based on less than perfect information" (Cowhig, 1971, p. 66).

Another approach to defining social policy research comes from the work of Rein (1970). Rein describes three types of research that may contribute to the development of social policy: needs-resource studies, distributional research, and allocative research. Rein is critical of needs-resource research, typically found in social welfare organizations, because this research assumes current services are "good" and looks for gaps between need and resources to generate an argument for more resources. This type of research is unlikely to lead to reconsideration of social policy. The second type, distributional research, examines the use of resources within a program and looks at how reorganization and reallocation of resources, such as personnel, can take place. This research may then lead to new policy directions. The third type, allocative research, considers alternative programs designed to achieve policy goals. This research attempts to analyze a social problem or social program in order to influence policy choices. Rein considers both the distributional and allocative policy research models to be the most desirable, as they do not accept, but challenge "the premise on which policy and operating systems operate" (Rein, 1970, p. 467). Etzioni refers to this feature of policy research as "critical," in that it examines and reexamines the assumptions which underlie a policy (Etzioni, 1971, p. 9). The key idea for our consideration from Rein's work is that these different types of policy research are likely to lead to different policy recommendations. We also note that they are likely to be carried out at different points of the policy-making process.

POLICY MAKING

Our approach to assessing policy research is to focus on the contributions social research can make in the major phases of policy making. In the practice of policy making these phases overlap. Also, in any given situation the actual activity of policy makers may be quite different from our conceptualization of the process. Lindblom's (1959) classic description of policy making as the "science of muddling through" alerts us to the likelihood of a gap between academic conceptualizations and the actual practice of policy making. Nevertheless, we find that some attention to "stages" or "phases" of the policy process is helpful in assessing the contributions of policy research. The terms we have used for major phases of policy making are: (1) social policy formulation, (2) social program development, (3) social policy implementation through social programs, and (4) social policy evaluation. Evaluation may occur at all stages, but there is an emphasis given to social program evaluation during both the third and the fourth stages. Also, policy research may vary in relation to whether it relates to new social policy initiatives or to reformulation of existing social policies.

The first phase of policy making, *policy formulation,* is the initiation of social policy through "planning" and "analysis." The focus in this stage is on the choice and specification of policy goals and objectives. As the policy goals are established it is necessary to specify, through a statement of objectives, the targets of change. This step involves the identification of existing social conditions and the aspect of the social problem to be changed, the population to which a social program will be directed, and a time frame during which change in the condition of the population can be expected. In this planning process, the values of policy makers and the elements of resources and time available to carry out the objectives will be significant factors in the formulation of policy.

In the next stage of policy making, *program development,* there is a consideration of alternative approaches for reaching policy objectives. The policy analyst will look for any kinds of evidence about alternative programs that speak to the efficiency, effectiveness, feasibility, and ethics of programs. It is not uncommon to find that many existing programs have never been evaluated. In this phase, one or more social programs are designed in keeping with the policy statement.

Program implementation follows program design, with the social program(s) actually carried out. As noted in our earlier chapter on evaluation, some types of evaluation will take place while the program is in the implementation phase.

Most authors identify *policy evaluation* as the final phase of the policy process. The test of a social policy is seen in terms of the degree to which intended outcomes are achieved through social programs. The view of this activity of evaluation as a final phase in the policy process comes from the fact that some of the major evaluation designs require that at least some part of the program be completed before outcome evaluation results are possible.

As we have noted in our chapter on program evaluation, some designs for evaluation can provide ongoing information to the analyst and policy maker, such as monitoring activities during the implementation of a program. Program evaluations provide "feedback" to administrators and policy makers which can have a major influence on the continuation, modification, or termination of a social program. Such evaluations provide an input into the reformulation of social policy. Detailed attention to criteria for social program evaluations are found in Chapter 6.

At each of these stages the policy analyst relates to the research from the following perspective. First, the analyst seeks information that already exists and is available, and is relevant to the social policy goals, policy objectives, and social programs. When it is ascertained that sufficient information for decision making is lacking, and time permits, there may be an effort to initiate and conduct research activities, either with internal staff or through contracts with outside researchers, in order to obtain the input and benefits of social research.

RESEARCH FOR POLICY FORMULATION

The creation of social policy statements involves the formulation and selection of goals. Tropman refers to this initial stage as involving policy research and analysis, because data and information about existing social conditions must be assembled and analyzed (Tropman *et al.*, 1976, p. 90). Policy makers need information about a social problem in order to consider the problem in relation to perceived gaps between present and desired social conditions. This forms a basis for establishing goals, which are expressed in a policy statement. The task of the policy analyst at this stage is to "collect and synthesize available information . . . so that issues may be clarified, problems defined, needs assessed, all for the purpose of selecting alternatives and strategies" (Baumheier and Schorr, 1977, p. 1453).

The data needs for policy formulation will vary, depending on the type of unit establishing the policy, for example, a federal agency, such as the

Department of Health and Human Services, a state social services department, or a unit of local government. The kinds and number of actors involved will vary depending on the size of the policy-making organization, for example, a child care policy to be approved by a local county policy board or a state policy to be approved by a state legislature or a state department administration. The measures of existing social conditions will vary according to the nature of the problems, such as mental health, crime, housing, or education. For any given social problem area, there will be different sets of information available to the policy analyst. The most common and accessible data are descriptive, such as census data (Taeuber, 1971, p. 62). A large amount of data is available through data banks and from information retrieval systems. Most of the data will involve descriptive statistics, incidence and prevalence rates, and other summary information derived from secondary data sources. Examples are found in problem areas such as juvenile delinquency, family violence, crime, income maintenance, housing, unemployment and poverty, and health care. Needs assessments provide another source of data on social conditions. This is a popular approach to collecting data on social problems; that is, "the act of estimating, evaluating or appraising a condition in which something necessary or desirable is required or wanted" (Kimmel, 1977, p. 12). In a number of social areas, the federal government has required needs assessments as a condition for funding, and as a basis for planning, policy formulation, and program development. It is evident that needs assessment usually requires substantial resources, and some critics doubt that there is adequate payoff from such efforts.

There are a number of approaches to needs assessment, including the gathering of opinions and judgments from individuals, community forums, public hearings, and so on; the collection of service statistics; epidemiological studies; social indicators; surveys; and secondary analysis of data (Kimmel, 1977, p. 15). We would expect the policy analyst to be able to evaluate data from these sources in order to contribute to policy making. Based on some history of the availability of needs assessment in policy making, there is question as to the extent to which this approach really impacts on policy makers. Some critics say that the "primary impact of needs assessment is to lend credibility to or legitimize what is already known" (Kimmel, 1977, p. 25), and it is therefore seen as a bureaucratic and/or political tool. Needs assessments clearly have much to contribute to the making of social policy. However, before initiating new studies of needs, the analyst should engage in an analysis of existing data. Such analysis may contribute more, and in a more timely manner, to policy making than extensive data collection through needs-assessment methods (Kimmel, 1977, p. 66).

Another approach used to help establish policy goals by specifying the nature of social conditions is the use of "social indicators." This is a particularly useful way to relate to policy making, as indicators establish data at different points in time to show changes in behaviors, conditions, norms, values, relationships, and so on. This approach is not unlike the use of economic indicators by policy makers. Although there is some disagreement as to what should be labeled a social indicator, indicators are clearly quantitative measures, that is, social statistics in a time series. The policy analyst will need to assess the units of measurement to insure that they represent the phenomena being studied. There are also problems in determining the frequency in which observations are made in order to describe changes, as in crime reports, hospital admissions, or recipients of welfare payments. Despite some of the cautions that must be made with regard to the use of "social indicators," information of this type does provide "a system of early warning of growing imbalances, social disbenefits, dissatisfactions, and emerging social needs" (Freeman and Sheldon, 1977, pp. 1350–54). Social indicators information can be used to describe social conditions, show trends, and in some cases, allow for studies of social change and clues to future trends. However, Freeman and Sheldon warn that "when used for purposes of setting goals and priorities, indicators must be regarded as inputs into a complex political mosaic" (Freeman and Sheldon, 1979, p. 1353).

Freeman and Sherwood have noted the risks of bias that may accompany the use of descriptive data, particularly from the ways in which data are aggregated or disaggregated. For example, data on races and other special groups such as age groups may involve an undercount or "overcount" (Freeman and Sherwood, 1970). Several questions should be posed: Is the selection of data relevant to the policy problem? Can the data be misused? The key factor at this phase is the establishment of baseline data on social conditions in an effort to determine policy goals and objectives.

There are, of course, additional sources of knowledge about social problems from research. Thus, the analyst may seek out studies of the various types we have described in the early chapters of this book, such as quantitative-descriptive studies that demonstrate relationships between variables, exploratory studies that indicate possible explanations for conditions and include hypotheses about relationships of factors to each other, and social program evaluations. For understanding aspects of social problems, the analyst will look to the academic literature, to historical research related to the area, and to government-sponsored research reports to find studies on the particular problem for which the policy is addressed. This source of knowledge not only provides ideas and perspectives on setting goals, but is valuable as a foundation for the next steps in policy making, that of program development and implementation.

The policy analyst will need to make several decisions at this point in the policy-making process. Are the available data sufficient, or must new data be collected? Are there biases in the available data that reduce their reliability and validity? Is the research knowledge in a form which can be communicated to and understood by policy makers? What is known about the norms and attitudes of the interested parties, such as client groups, or political groups? It is important to recognize that while demographic data and social research findings are normally considered in the setting of policy, values and normative knowledge are also of significant import to goal setting.

Tropman (1976) emphasizes the need to develop alternative goals and objectives in order to maximize the quality of policy decisions (Tropman *et al.,* 1976, p. 90). Data are needed to deal with questions about policy preference: What do people want? Are there current programs that relate to the social policy goals? What are present costs for existing programs that seek to meet current policy goals? What are the projected costs for programs under a changed new policy? What are the benefits of the alternative policies? (Lyday, 1972, p. 385 ff.)

One approach to obtaining information about "policy preferences," which will enhance the analyst's fund of knowledge relevant to policy formulation, is content analysis of reports from the media. Gil (1968) suggests that content analysis of the political process provides one way of looking at social policy development. The media usually reveal the "struggles between competing social forces and interest groups that underlie the formulation of every social policy" (Gil, 1968, p. 17). Other approaches to obtaining knowledge about policy preferences include participant observation techniques particularly used with regard to "non"-political interest groups; the use of interviews of political figures, administrators, clients, and so on; examination of recorded proceedings of meetings of private and public groups, legislatures, and other organizations interested in the policy issue; analysis of the decisions of the courts, which may apply to the policy. These approaches allow the analyst to obtain information about value preferences that would not ordinarily be revealed through other data sets.

RESEARCH FOR PROGRAM DEVELOPMENT

Once a social policy has been created and adopted through legislation or executive order, there must be a translation of policy into a program or set of programs. Three sets of information are useful at this stage: data on the target population, findings from studies of the use of intervention strategies, and information on costs, staff needs, and other organizational and administrative factors related to program delivery. A specific target population must be identified, at least in terms of criteria for coverage of benefits or service under the policy. When the size of the population is unknown, estimates of the number to be served must be made in order to assemble personnel and other resources needed for a program. The program administrator needs valid and reliable data about the potential target population, its characteristics and needs. The data used in the formulation of a policy will be used as a framework for program development.

As Epstein and Tripodi (1977) have noted, "In choosing specific intervention strategies, patterns of service delivery, or therapeutic techniques, the administrator requires sound information about the comparative effectiveness and efficiency of different program strategies" (Epstein and Tripodi, 1977, p. 6). The administrator and/or the analyst will use knowledge available about the experiences of other programs that have implemented strategies of service in order to choose a program direction and strategy for a new program. Epstein and Tripodi refer to this phase as program planning, and they identify approaches, such as questionnaires and interviews, to securing information from potential clients and practicing professionals, and about existing programs and possible reactions to the new program services.

The principles for assessing research reports for program development specified by Epstein and Tripodi (1977) are useful for the policy analyst. The analyst is particularly concerned with assessing and using empirical findings in order to recommend intervention strategies, that is, "the techniques and procedures that might be employed by staff in social programs of various kinds" (Epstein and Tripodi, 1977, p. 30). In making this assessment, the analyst examines the research report on relevant intervention strategies from the following perspectives: (a) obtains an overview of the report—is the information relevant to the policy and program objectives? (b) identifies how the strategy is operationalized, (c) determines how effective and efficient the strategy is, (d) determines the level of knowledge presented in the report (descriptive, correlational, cause-effect), (e) evaluates the evidence of the accuracy, reliability, and validity of measures used in the study, (f) assesses the relationship between the intervention strategy and the desired outcome, (g) assesses the empirical generality of the findings, (h) assesses the adequacy of internal control procedure in the study, (i) assesses possibilities of implementation (Epstein and Tripodi, 1977, pp. 31–38).

As a result of the application of this kind of examination of relevant research, the analyst communicates with program administrators with regard to a plan of action, that is, a social program that can be expected to achieve the goals of a social policy. Before actually implementing a social program, planning and preparation goes into the procurement or selection of material resources, staff, technology, and clientele. The analyst uses whatever data are available to project the specific needs of the program in order to prepare for the initiation of the program. It is at this stage that the analyst must focus on the policy objectives, and assure that there is a logical relationship between them and the program design. It is also at this stage that evaluation designs must be identified so that the program can be assessed in terms of policy objectives.

Hopefully the information used by the analyst to identify the target population for a program will be useful as the program staff make contact with the clientele. Information from studies of social programs will be helpful in identifying any kinds of obstacles that might intrude upon the delivery of services, such as physical, psychological, social, and/or community factors.

RESEARCH FOR PROGRAM IMPLEMENTATION

Policy implementation is the actual conduct of social program activities oriented toward policy goals. It usually involves the application of some type of technology to reach clients, to provide services, and/or social or fiscal resources. Administrators and staff in operating bureaucracies have major roles at this stage—as Tropman points out, "the heart of policy is administration" (Tropman et al., 1976, p. 147). Research activities employed in this stage contribute to policy assessment and evaluation. Our chapter on social program evaluation has elaborated upon the evaluation strategies which can be employed in this stage: monitoring, cost-analytic strategics, and social research strategies. These strategies seek to provide systematic information about program efforts, effectiveness, and efficiency. This information from these evaluation strategies is essential for the policy assessment that occurs during the implementation of a program. Evaluation tasks are carried out to assess policy in terms of program activities and outcomes and to reshape, reformulate, or reinforce policy. Ideally, there is sufficient evaluation during this stage to inform administrators and policy makers of information which will assist the policy-making tasks. However, in many instances, decisions about policy continuance are made before all program evaluation results are reported. It must also be recognized that the policy research during this period may lend support to the policy, but not provide a definitive answer in terms of outcomes.

It is important during the operation of a program for the policy analyst to make use of all the data available from the evaluation strategies in informing policy makers about program activities and outcomes. However, there are limits to the effects this information will have on policy reformulation. We hope that the information will inform us as to whether or not the goals of the policy have been reached. To accomplish this, we need an appropriate research design and adequate resources for obtaining the information and analyzing it. The program must be operating a certain length of time before such assessments can be made, and a number of political and social factors may intervene during the administration of the program and intrude into the process of evaluation.

Rather than waiting for the final results of some aspects of program evaluation, we may need to utilize other mechanisms such as simulation, forecasting, and projecting. At the same time, social program evaluation along the lines in Chapter 6 provides a powerful tool for assessing social policy. When a social policy is carried out by a number of social programs, the set of evaluations will provide a substantial base of information for considering program and policy changes and alternatives. Since the types of designs and resources devoted to program evaluation will vary from organization to organization, the policy analyst will have to be alert to the questions in Chapter 6 regarding the assessment of program evaluations. These questions deal with an assessment of the soundness of the research, the levels of knowledge obtained, and the relevance of the evaluations to the guiding policies.

SOCIAL POLICY EVALUATION

As we have already noted, policies are frequently evaluated in terms of the outcomes of the program or programs designed to implement policies. Consequently, a major source of research input into policy evaluation is program evaluation studies. Chapter 6 on program evaluation provides guidelines for assessing these types of research. Policy makers are especially interested in information on the efforts, effectiveness, and efficiency of social programs as a basis for evaluating social policy which generates the programs. As we have noted, the knowledge level of program evaluations may be hypothetical, descriptive, correlational, and cause-effect. The nature of the knowledge produced in program evaluations will affect the acceptability and generalizability of the research findings for policy purposes. We expect program evaluations to provide information that will be useful to policy makers regarding choices for future policies. In Chapter 6 we have identified a number of questions to help the analyst appraise the usefulness of knowledge from program evaluation research, such as the clarity of research communications, knowledge appraisal, relevancy, actual use, and potential use. We now look at some additional features of utilization of all types of social policy research.

UTILIZATION OF SOCIAL POLICY RESEARCH

In our discussions of phases of policy making we have indicated that various kinds of research designs can be expected to produce information which will be useful in policy decision making. Our general guidelines developed in Chapter 4 to guide the professional social worker in knowledge utilization are appropriate for the use of social policy research. However, there are some features of knowledge utilization which need highlighting in relation to the area of social policy.

As we view utilization from the position of the policy analyst, we ask the following questions:

1. In what phase of policy making is the research knowledge relevant?
2. Is the subject matter of the research relevant to the social problem issue to which the social policy is addressed?
3. What are the time limits placed on the analyst to produce information, and for what decisions?
4. What are the competing sets of information or other forces, social, political, which bear upon the policy-making activity?

The literature on the use of social science research in decision making (Weiss and Bucuvalas, 1980) alerts us to some of the complications that the analyst may expect in relation to these questions. Thus, the fact is that policy making is an ongoing process and the phases we have identified are overlapping and at best crude indicators of a complex process. It is not likely that a single study or research report will provide an answer to a policy-making question. More common is the need to assemble information which has direct and indirect implications for the policy decision at hand. Our second guideline question alerts us to a significant feature of research related to policy making, that is, that our sense of utility cannot be restricted to data. There is no question that "facts" are the basic form of knowledge for utilization, but there is ample evidence that the "general perspectives" generated by social research are useful to policy makers. This point is best illustrated in examples of the use of social research by government officials and legislators in consideration of policies on mental health, crime and delinquency, child welfare, education, and other areas.

As we have noted previously, the use of research knowledge is carried out in the context of information from various sources, impressions, personal testimony, value preferences, political pressures, and interest groups. The argument that knowledge from social research makes decision making more rational seems not to be persuasive in policy-making circles. Weighing the evidence and making a decision is not the general pattern in policy making; it is only a part of the process. As Weiss (1977, p. 17) notes, there is a big leap in policy making from data to policy recommendations.

In thinking about the social work practitioner's utilization of research for policy making, we face a dilemma. There seems to be a renewal of emphasis on the use of research knowledge in policy making, as evidenced by the employment of information specialists, policy analysts, systems analysts, and others in government and private sectors. There is a recognition of the importance of program evaluation by funding of evaluations and the requirements of government that projects have monitoring and evaluation plans. At the same time, the social science literature continues to highlight the fact that social research is underutilized or ignored in relation to policy making. As a step toward rectifying this situation, it is useful to identify what appear to be obstacles to utility. Weiss (1977) provides a useful framework for dealing with issues around utilization of resources. The framework specifies three interlocking systems: the knowledge producing system, the policy setting system, and the linkage system.

First, the "inside" analyst must deal with the system that produces the knowledge. Some say utility will be enhanced when the research is done by "insiders," since it is most likely to speak directly to the policy question, in contrast to research produced by academic institutions and research institutes. Secondly, there is the policy-setting and administrative system that may use the knowledge: What is the relationship of the analyst to this system? Thirdly, there is the linkage system, with staff who carry out the roles of relating research needs to researchers and their research knowledge back to policy makers. The analyst is most frequently a part of the linkage system. Weiss (1977, p. 16) notes that obstacles to use of research knowledge exist in all three systems.

Guideline questions have been composed from the issues that Weiss identifies in regard to these systems. In relation to the research producing system, we have the following questions:

1. What kind of knowledge does the research offer, for example, substantive, conceptual, methodological?

2. Can the research knowledge be applied directly to the policy question, or does it have indirect implications?

3. Does the research point to feasible recommendations? Is there agreement between decision makers' definition of the problem and that of the researcher?

4. Are there conditions about the policy and/or social problem that the researcher ignores?

5. Is the research sufficiently broad to generalize from it to the policy/program area of decision making?

6. Are the data sources and methodologies sound and sufficient in relation to the policy question?

7. Is the report of the research clear and understandable?

8. Are there any variables in the study that can readily be controlled or manipulated?

9. Are the results of the research consistent with other studies?

10. If the results show that a program is not working, are there reasons that suggest corrective action?

11. Are the social conditions now and in the future similar to when the research was conducted?

The policy-setting and administrative system has obstacles to the use of the research. Individuals in administrative positions must relate to organizational constraints, to outside forces, such as legislatures, political actors, and the public. There are many actors involved in policy making. Actors change frequently, policy issues shift with public opinion, and research may lag behind these changes. The more experienced the policy maker, the less likely he will overly depend on the research knowledge. Actors not only want the best solution to the specific problem, but also need to relate to constituent groups. Therefore, they are prone to compromise, despite what limited facts may have to say. Guideline questions related to this system are as follows:

1. Do the findings and recommendations from the research conform to the values of the officials and policy makers who may use them?

2. What factors in the organization, for example, political forces, agency administration and structure, community group pressures, may limit the use of the research?

3. To what extent does the analyst have contact with the various actors which influence decision making, that is, officials, administrators, politicians, other agencies?

4. Is there sufficient stability in the employment of policy makers to allow for use of research knowledge?

5. Are the decision makers willing to wait for the analyst to get a report to them?

6. Are the recommendations in keeping with the resources of the agency?

Generally speaking, the social work policy analyst is a part of a linkage system with regard to the utilization of research knowledge. In order to be effective in a linkage role, the analyst must be politically astute, informed of who makes decisions and when, and in a position to provide timely information. The following questions assist us in considering the input through linkage into the policy making system.

1. Does the agency organization have a mechanism for disseminating research reports? What role does the analyst have?

2. Is the style of the presentation of the research information such that it facilitates communication, or does the analyst have to translate the information for utilization?

3. What are the "images" of the analyst's role in the minds of the policy makers? Do they facilitate utilization?

A good deal of concern about utilization of policy research has been focused on the relationships and communications between social researchers and policy makers. From our viewpoint, that of the role of the social worker as policy analyst, the analyst is part of a linkage system and stands in a significant position for enhancing policy research utilization. This individual must spend a lot of time not only assembling research information but also communicating to administrators and policy makers. The usual method of communication between researchers and others is through publication of research reports. The policy analyst goes beyond the use of this method by "policy analysis" statements and face-to-face interchanges with policy makers (Etzioni, 1971, p. 10).

The various roles and opportunities for utilization of policy research will be reflected in organizational structures related to policy making. There are a number of alternative structures for the conduct of policy research, such as research and evaluation units within an organization, specialized private policy research organizations, task forces, and others. Some research-producing structures that have the capacity of providing relevant and useful policy research, such as policy institutes or university research centers, will probably require linkage to policy makers. It is in this linkage role that the social worker as policy analyst can play a significant part in policy making.

SUMMARY

In this chapter we have presented a framework for understanding the basic elements of the practice of policy making and have identified some of the ways in which empirical research can inform the policy process. Our purpose has been to assist the reader in assessing and utilizing social research for policy purposes. Once the reader has completed this chapter, it will be helpful to review again the earlier chapters on classification, evaluation, and utilization of research. Of special note is the fact that our major types of research are all employed in studies directed at social policy questions. We should also recognize that "social policy research" not only includes policy-oriented studies, but also empirical findings that have been established for other purposes. This latter type of research knowledge, such as found in secondary sources, studies of social problems, and so forth, is particularly relevant to the early stages of policy formulation. As Etzioni (1971) has pointed out, there are obvious differences in basic, applied, and policy research, especially in terms of the research objectives. However, our interest in the utilization of research knowledge for policy making directs us to the potential uses of all types of research.

The volume of research knowledge potentially useful for policy making is extremely large. To enhance utilization, the policy analyst must be selective, and must keep in mind the advantages of knowledge which is relevant, practical, and accurate.

Finally, it bears repeating that the art and practice of policy making is a complex and essentially political process. Both the further study of social policy and policy making, and the actual practice of professional roles (such as policy analyst) will enhance the reader's capacity for using social research.

Bibliographic References

Achenbaum, W. Andrew, *Old Age in the New Land: The American Experience Since 1790* (Baltimore: Johns Hopkins University Press, 1978).

American Psychological Association, *Publication Manual* (Washington, D.C., 1967 Revision).

Anderson, John E., "Methods of Child Psychology," in *Manual of Child Psychology,* 2nd ed., Leonard Carmichael (New York: John Wiley and Sons, 1954), pp. 52–54.

Aries, Philippe, *Centuries of Childhood: A Social History of Family Life,* translated from the French by Robert Baldick (New York: Alfred A. Knopf, 1962).

Austin, Michael J., and Betten, Neil, "Intellectual Origins of Community Organizing: 1920–1939," *Social Service Review* 51 (March 1977): 155–70.

Ayllon, T., "Intensive Treatment of Psychotic Behaviour by Stimulus Satiation and Food Reinforcement," *Behaviour Research and Therapy,* 1 (May 1963): 53–61.

Bacon, Margaret K.; Child, Irvin L.; and Barry, Herbert, III, "A Cross-Cultural Study of Correlates of Crime," *Journal of Abnormal and Social Psychology,* 66 (April 1963): 291–300.

Bartlett, Harriett M.; Kadushin, Alfred; Thomas, Edwin J.; Maas, Henry S.; Gordon, William E.; and Murphy, Marjorie, *Building Social Work Knowledge* (New York: National Association of Social Workers, 1964).

Barzun, Jacques, *Clio and the Doctors: Psycho-History, Quanto-History and History* (Chicago: University of Chicago Press, 1974).

Baumheier, Edward C. and Schorr, Alvin, "Social Policy," *Social Work Encyclopedia* (Washington, D.C.: National Association of Social Workers, 1977), pp. 1453–62.

Bennis, Warren G.; Benne, Kenneth D.; and Chin, Robert, *The Planning of Change* (New York: Holt, Rinehart and Winston, 1961).

Beringer, R. E., *Historical Analysis: Contemporary Approaches to Clio's Craft* (New York: John Wiley and Sons, 1978).

Berlson, Bernard, "Content Analysis," in *Handbook of Social Psychology: Vol. 1, Theory and Method,* ed. G. Lindzey (Reading, Mass.: Addison-Wesley Publishing Company, 1954), pp. 488–522.

Bieri, James; Atkins, Alvin L.; Briar, Scott; Leaman, Robin Lobeck; Miller, Henry; and Tripodi, Tony, *Clinical and Social Judgment* (New York: John Wiley and Sons, 1966).

Billingsley, Andrew, "The Role of the Social Worker in a Child Protective Agency," *Child Welfare* 43 (November 1964): 473–79, 497.

Blalock, Hubert M., *Social Statistics* (New York: McGraw-Hill Book Company, 1960).

———, *Causal Inferences in Nonexperimental Research* (Chapel Hill, N.C.: The University of North Carolina Press, 1961).

Bonjean, Charles M., "Community Leadership: A Case Study and Conceptual Refinement," *American Journal of Sociology* 68 (May 1963): 672–81.

Boulding, Kenneth E., "The Boundaries of Social Policy," *Social Work* 12 (January 1967): 3–11.

Campbell, Donald T., and Stanley, Julian C., *Experimental and Quasi-Experimental Designs for Research* (Chicago: Rand McNally, 1966).

———, "Experimental and Quasi-Experimental Designs for Research on Teaching," in *Handbook of Research on Teaching,* ed. N. L. Gage (Chicago: Rand McNally, 1963), pp. 171–246.

Caplow, Theodore, "Official Reports and Proceedings," *American Sociological Review* 23 (December 1958): 704–11.

Caro, Francis G., ed., *Readings in Evaluation Research,* 2nd ed. (New York: Russell Sage, 1977).

Chein, Isidor, "An Introduction to Sampling," in *Research Methods in Social Relations,* rev. ed., ed. Claire Selltiz, Marie Jahoda, Morton Deutsch, and Stuart W. Cook (New York: Henry Holt and Company, 1959).

Clement, Priscilla F., "Family and Foster Care: Philadelphia in the Late 19th Century," *Social Service Review* 53 (September 1979): 406–20.

Council on Social Work Education, *Manual of Accrediting Standards for Graduate Professional Schools of Social Work* (New York: Council on Social Work Education, 1971), pp. 57–58.

Cowhig, James, "Federal Grant-Supported Social Research and 'Relevance': Some Reservations," *The American Sociologist* 6 (1971): 65–69.

Dawley, Allen, *Class and Community: The Industrial Revolution in Lynn* (Cambridge, Mass.: Harvard University Press, 1976).

Day, Robert C., and Hamblin, Robert L., "Some Effects of Close and Punitive Styles of Supervision," *American Journal of Sociology* 69 (March 1964): 499–510.

Demos, John, "History and the Formation of Social Policy Toward Children: A Case Study," in *Social History and Social Policy*, ed. David J. Rothman and Stanton Wheeler (New York: Academic Press, 1981), pp. 301–24.

Eaton, Joseph W., "Science, 'Art,' and Uncertainty," *Social Work* 3 (July 1958): 3–10.

Edwards, Allen L., *Experimental Design in Psychological Research*, rev. ed. (New York: Holt, Rinehart and Winston, 1960).

_____, *Statistical Methods for the Behavioral Sciences* (New York: Holt, Rinehart and Winston, 1961).

Epstein, Irwin, and Tripodi, Tony, *Research Techniques for Program Planning, Monitoring, and Evaluation* (New York: Columbia University Press, 1977).

Etzioni, Amitai, "Policy Research," *The American Sociologist* 6 (June 1971): 8–12.

Fanshel, David, "Research in Child Welfare: A Critical Analysis," *Child Welfare* 41 (December 1962a): 484–507.

_____, ed., *Research in Social Welfare Administration: Its Contributions and Problems* (New York: National Association of Social Workers, 1962b).

Faunce, William A., and Clelland, Donald A., "Professionalization and Stratification Patterns in an Industrial Community," *American Journal of Sociology* 72 (January 1967): 341–50.

Fellin, Phillip; Tripodi, Tony; and Meyer, Henry J., eds., *Exemplars of Social Research* (Itasca, Ill.: F. E. Peacock Publishers, 1969).

Festinger, Leon, "Laboratory Experiments," in *Research Methods in the Behavioral Sciences*, ed. Leon Festinger and Daniel Katz (New York: The Dryden Press, 1953), pp. 136–72.

_____, and Katz, Daniel, eds., *Research Methods in the Behavioral Sciences* (New York: The Dryden Press, 1953).

Field, Martha Heineman, "Social Casework Practice during the 'Psychiatric Deluge'," *Social Service Review* 54 (December 1980): 482–507.

Finestone, Samuel, "The Critical Review of a Research Monograph: A Teaching Unit in a Social Work Research Course," in *Selected Papers in Methods of Teaching Research in the Social Work Curriculum* (New York: Council on Social Work Education, 1959), pp. 33–37.

Fischer, David H., *Growing Old in America* (New York: Oxford University Press, 1977).

Flanagan, John C., "The Critical Incident Technique," *Psychological Bulletin* 51 (July 1954): 327–28.

Fogelson, Robert M., "The Morass: An Essay on the Public Employee Pension Problem," in *Social History and Social Policy*, ed. David J. Rothman and Stanton Wheeler (New York: Academic Press, 1981), pp. 145–73.

Francel, Edward W.; Crane, John A.; Fanshel, David; Jahn, Julius A.; MacDonald, Mary E.; and O'Reilly, Charles, "Task Force Report on Research on M.S.W. Curriculum," *Social Work Education Reporter* (March 1968): 13, 20–21.

Franks, Virginia L., "Usefulness of Research," Letter to the Editor, *Social Work* 13 (April 1968): 142–43.

Freeman, Howard, and Sheldon, Eleanor, "Social Indicators," *Encyclopedia of Social Work* (New York: National Association of Social Workers, 1977).

Freeman, Howard, and Sherwood, Clarence C., *Social Research and Social Policy* (Englewood Cliffs, N.J.: Prentice-Hall, 1970).

French, John R. P., Jr., "Experiments in Field Settings," in *Research Methods in the Behavioral Sciences,* ed. Leon Festinger and Daniel Katz (New York: The Dryden Press, 1953), pp. 98–135.

Gamson, William A., "Reputation and Resources in Community Politics," *American Journal of Sociology* 71 (September, 1966): 121–31.

Geismar, Ludwig L., "Thirteen Evaluative Studies," in *Evaluation of Social Intervention,* ed. Edward J. Mullen, James R. Dumpson and Associates (San Francisco: Jossey-Bass, 1972), pp. 15–38.

Gil, David, *Unravelling Social Policy* (Cambridge, Mass.: Schenkman Publishing Co., 1973).

_____, "Research: A Basic Ingredient in the Study of Social Policy and Social Services," *Journal of Education for Social Work* 4 (Spring 1968): 14–20.

Gillis, John R., *Youth and History: Tradition and Change in European Age Relations, 1770–Present* (New York: Academic Press, 1974).

Glaser, Barney G., and Strauss, Anselm L., *The Discovery of Grounded Theory: Strategies for Qualitative Research* (Chicago: Aldine Publishing Company, 1967).

Goldstein, Harris K., "Criteria for Evaluating Research," *Social Casework* 43 (November 1962): 474–77.

_____, *Research Standards and Methods for Social Workers* (New Orleans, La.: The Hauser Press, 1963), pp. 303–19.

_____, *Identifying and Maximizing Research Learning Potential for Social Work Students* (New Orleans, La.: School of Social Work, Tulane Studies in Social Welfare, Tulane University, 1967).

Goode, William J., and Hatt, Paul K., *Methods in Social Research* (New York: McGraw-Hill Book Company, 1952).

Goodman, L. A., "Ecological Regression and Behavior of Individuals," *American Sociological Review* 18 (December 1953): 663–64.

Goodrich, D. Wells, and Boomer, Donald S., "Some Concepts about Therapeutic Interventions with Hyperaggressive Children: Part I," *Social Casework* 39 (April, 1958a): 207–13.

_____, "Some Concepts about Therapeutic Interventions with Hyperaggressive Children: Part II," *Social Casework* 39 (May, 1958b): 286–92.

Gordon, Michael, ed., *The American Family in Social-Historical Perspective* (New York: St. Martin's Press, 1973).

Gouldner, Alvin W., "Explorations in Applied Social Science," *Social Problems* 3 (January 1956): 169–81.

_____, "Theoretical Requirements of the Applied Social Sciences," *American Sociological Review* 22 (February 1957): 92–102.

_____, "Explorations in Applied Social Science," in *Applied Sociology: Opportunities and Problems,* ed. Alvin W. Gouldner and S. M. Miller (New York: The Free Press, 1965), pp. 5–22.

_____, and Miller, S. M., eds., *Applied Sociology: Opportunities and Problems* (New York: The Free Press, 1965).

Greenwood, Ernest, "Social Science and Social Work: A Theory of Their Relationships," *Social Service Review* 29 (March 1955): 20–33.

―――, "Social Work Research: A Decade of Reappraisal," *Social Service Review* 31 (September 1957): 311–20.

―――, *Lectures in Research Methodology for Social Welfare Students,* University of California Syllabus Series No. 388 (Berkeley, Calif.: University of California, 1960).

―――, "The Practice of Science and the Science of Practice," in *The Planning of Change,* ed. Warren G. Bennis, *et al.* (New York: Holt, Rinehart and Winston, 1961), pp. 73–82.

Greven, Philip J., "Family Structure in Seventeenth-Century Andover, Massachusetts," in *The American Family in Social-Historical Perspective,* ed. Michael Gordon (New York: St. Martin's Press, 1973).

Grinnell, Richard M., *Social Work Research and Evaluation* (Itasca, Ill.: F. E. Peacock Publishers, 1981).

Gutman, Herbert G., *The Black Family in Slavery and Freedom, 1750–1925* (New York: Random House, 1975).

Guttentag, Marcia, and Struening, Elmer L., eds., *Handbook of Evaluation Research, Volume 2* (Beverly Hills, Calif.: Sage, 1975).

Haynes, John E., "The Rank and File Movement in Private Social Work," *Labor History* 16 (Winter 1975): 78–79.

Herzog, Elizabeth, *Some Guidelines for Evaluative Research: Assessing Psychosocial Change in Individuals* (Washington, D.C.: U.S. Department of Health, Education, and Welfare, Social Security Administration, Children's Bureau, 1959).

―――, *About the Poor* (Washington, D.C.: Children's Bureau, 1967).

Hirschi, Travis, and Selvin, Hanan, *Delinquency Research: An Appraisal of Analytic Methods* (New York: The Free Press, 1967).

Hollingshead, August B., and Redlich, Frederick C., *Social Class and Mental Illness* (New York: John Wiley and Sons, 1958).

Hyman, Herbert, *Survey Design and Analysis* (Glencoe, Ill.: The Free Press, 1955).

Jackson, P., "Black Charity in Progressive Era Chicago," *Social Service Review* 52 (1978): 400–17.

Jansyn, Leon R., Jr., "Solidarity and Delinquency in a Street Corner Group," *American Sociological Review* 31 (October 1966): 600–14.

Jayaratne, Srinika; Stuart, Richard B.; and Tripodi, Tony, "Methodological Issues and Problems in Evaluating Treatment Outcomes in the Family and School Consultation Project, 1970–1973," in *Evaluation of Behavioral Programs in Community, Residential and School Settings,* ed. Park O. Davidson, Frank W. Clark, and Leo A. Hamerlynck (Chicago: Research Press, 1974), pp. 141–74.

Kadushin, Alfred, "Assembling Social Work Knowledge," in *Building Social Work Knowledge* (New York: National Association of Social Workers, 1964), pp. 16–37.

Kahn, Alfred J., ed., *Issues in American Social Work* (New York: Columbia University Press, 1959).

————, "The Design of Research," in *Social Work Research,* ed. Norman A. Polansky (Chicago: The University of Chicago Press, 1960), pp. 48–73.

Kaplan, G. J., "Reformers and Charity: The Abolition of Public Outdoor Relief in New York City, 1870–1899," *Social Service Review* 52 (June 1978): 202–14.

Katz, Daniel, "Field Studies," in *Research Methods in the Behavioral Sciences,* ed. Leon Festinger and Daniel Katz (New York: The Dryden Press, Inc., 1953), pp. 56–97.

Katz, Michael B., "Education and Inequality: A Historical Perspective," in *Social History and Social Policy,* ed. David J. Rothman and Stanton Wheeler (New York: Academic Press, 1981), pp. 57–101.

Kendall, Patricia L., and Lazarsfeld, Paul F., "Problems of Survey Analysis," in *Continuities in Social Research: Studies in the Scope and Method of "The American Soldier,"* ed. Robert K. Merton and Paul F. Lazarsfeld (Glencoe, Illinois: The Free Press, 1959).

Kerlinger, Fred N., *Foundations of Behavioral Research: Educational and Psychological Inquiry* (New York: Holt, Rinehart and Winston, 1967).

Kett, Joseph F., "Adolescence and Youth in Nineteenth-Century America," in *The Family in History: Interdisciplinary Essays,* ed. Theodore K. Rabb and Robert I. Rotberg (New York: Harper and Row, 1973).

Kimmel, Wayne A., *Needs Assessment: A Critical Perspective* (Washington, D.C.: Department of Health, Education and Welfare, Office of Program Systems, Office of the Assistant Secretary for Planning and Evaluation, December 1977).

Knop, Edward, "Suggestions to Aid the Student in Systematic Interpretation and Analysis of Empirical Sociological Journal Presentations," *The American Sociologist* 2 (May 1967): 90–92.

Kogan, Leonard S., ed., *Social Science Theory and Social Work Research* (New York: National Association of Social Workers, 1960a).

————, "Principles of Measurement," in *Social Work Research,* ed. Norman Polansky (Chicago: The University of Chicago Press, 1960b), pp. 87–105.

Krasner, Leonard, and Ulmann, Leonard P., eds., *Research in Behavior Modification* (New York: Holt, Rinehart and Winston, 1965).

Landes, D. S., and Tilly, Charles, eds., *History in Social Science* (Englewood Cliffs, N.J.: Prentice-Hall, 1971).

Laslett, Peter, "Age at Menarche in Europe Since the Eighteenth Century," in *The Family in History: Interdisciplinary Essays,* ed. Theodore K. Rabb and Robert I. Rotberg (New York: Harper and Row, 1973).

Laslett, Peter (with R. Woll, eds.), *Household and Family in Past Time* (Cambridge, Mass.: Harvard University Press, 1972).

Laslett, Peter; Oosterveen, Karla; and Smith, Richard M., eds., *Bastardy and Its Comparative History: Studies in the History of Illegitimacy and Marital Non-Conformism in Britain, France, Germany, Sweden, North America, Jamaica and Japan* (Cambridge, Mass.: Harvard University Press, 1980).

Lazarsfeld, Paul F., and Rosenberg, Morris, eds., *The Language of Social Research* (Glencoe, Ill: The Free Press, 1955).

Lazarsfeld, Paul F.; Sewell, William H.; and Wilensky, Harold L., eds., *The Uses of Sociology* (New York: Basic Books, 1967).

Leiby, James, *A History of Social Welfare and Social Work in the United States* (New York: Columbia University Press, 1978).

Levinger, George, "Continuance in Casework and Other Helping Relationships: A Review of Current Research," *Social Work* 5 (July 1960): 40–51.

Lewin, Kurt; Lippitt, Ronald; and White, R. K., "Patterns of Aggressive Behavior in Experimentally Created Social Climates," *Journal of Social Psychology* 10 (May 1939): 271–99.

Lewis, Oscar, *The Children of Sanchez* (New York: Random House, 1961).

Likert, Rensis, and Lippitt, Ronald, "The Utilization of Social Science," in *Research Methods in the Behavioral Sciences,* ed. Leon Festinger and Daniel Katz (New York: The Dryden Press, 1953).

Lindblom, Charles E., "The Science of Muddling Through," *Public Administration Review* (1959).

Lubove, Roy, *The Professional Altruist: The Emergence of Social Work as a Career, 1880–1930* (Cambridge, Mass.: Harvard University Press, 1965).

Lundberg, G., *Social Research* (New York: Longmans, Green and Company, 1942).

Lyday, J., "An Advocate's Process Outline for Policy Analysis: The Case of Welfare Reform," *Urban Affairs Quarterly* 7 (June 1972): 385–402.

Maas, Henry A., "The Young Adult Adjustment of Twenty Wartime Residential Nursery Children," *Child Welfare* (February 1963): 57–72.

———, ed., *Five Fields of Social Service: Reviews of Research* (New York: National Association of Social Workers, 1966).

———, ed., *Research in the Social Services* (New York: National Association of Social Workers, 1971).

———, ed., *Social Service Research* (New York: National Association of Social Workers, 1978).

MacDonald, Mary E., "Methods of Teaching Research in the Social Work Curriculum" in *Selected Papers in Methods of Teaching Research in the Social Work Curriculum* (New York: Council on Social Work Education, 1959), pp. 5–9.

———, "Social Work Research: A Perspective," in *Social Work Research,* ed. Norman A. Polansky (Chicago: The University of Chicago Press, 1960).

———, "Reunion at Vocational High: An Analysis of Girls at Vocational High: An Experiment in Social Work Intervention," *Social Service Review* 40 (June 1966): 175–89.

Main, Marjorie W., and MacDonald, Mary E., "Professional Functions and Opinions of Social Group Workers," *Social Service Review* 36 (December 1962): 421–32.

Malinowski, Bronislaw, *Crime and Custom in Savage Society* (New York: Harcourt, Brace and World, 1926).

Mandelbaum, Seymour J., "Urban Pasts and Urban Policies," in *Social History and Social Policy,* ed. David J. Rothman and Stanton Wheeler (New York: Academic Press, 1981), pp. 275–300.

Marks, Rachel, "Research Reporting," in *Social Work Research,* ed. Norman A. Polansky (Chicago: The University of Chicago Press, 1960), pp. 187–200.

Mayer, Robert, and Greenwood, Ernest, *The Design of Social Policy Research* (Englewood Cliffs, N.J.: Prentice-Hall, 1980).

McLaughlin, Virginia Y., "Patterns of Work and Family Organization: Buffalo's Italians," in *The Family in History: Interdisciplinary Essays,* ed. Theodore K. Rabb and Robert I. Rotberg (New York: Harper and Row, 1973), pp. 111–26.

Merton, Robert K.; Broom, Leonard; and Cottrell, Leonard S., Jr., *Sociology Today: Problems and Prospects* (New York: Basic Books, Inc., 1959).

Meyer, Henry J.; Borgatta, Edgar F.; Jones, Wyatt C., "An Experiment in Prevention Through Social Work Intervention," in *Behavioral Science for Social Workers,* ed. Edwin J. Thomas (New York: The Free Press, 1967).

Meyer, Henry J.; Borgatta, Edgar F.; Jones, Wyatt C., *Girls at Vocational High: An Experiment in Social Work Intervention* (New York: Russell Sage Foundation, 1965).

Meyer, Henry J.; Jones, Wyatt; and Borgatta, Edgar F., "The Decision by Unmarried Mothers to Keep or Surrender Their Babies," *Social Work* 1 (April, 1956): 103–09.

Meyer, Henry J., "Social Work," *International Encyclopedia of the Social Sciences* (New York. Macmillan Co. & Free Press, 1968).

Meyer, Henry J.; Litwak, Eugene; Thomas, Edwin J.; and Vinter, Robert D., "Social Work and Social Welfare," in *The Uses of Sociology,* ed. Paul F. Lazarsfeld, William H. Sewell, and Harold L. Wilensky (New York: Basic Books, 1967), pp. 156–90.

Miller, Roger R., "An Experimental Study of the Observational Process in Casework," *Social Work* 3 (April 1958): 96–102.

Morgan, Margaret; Goodglass, Harold; Folsom, Angela; and Quadfasel, Fred A., "Epilepsy and Social Ajustment," *Social Work* 12 (April 1967): 70–76.

Morris, Robert, *Social Policy of the American Welfare State* (New York: Harper and Row, 1979).

Moser, C. A., *Survey Methods in Social Investigation* (London: Heinemann Educational Books, 1958).

Nagel, Ernest, ed., *John Stuart Mill's Philosophy of Scientific Method* (New York: Hafner Publishing Company, 1950).

Nagel, Stuart, ed., *Improving Policy Analysis* (Beverly Hills, Calif.: Sage Publications, 1980).

Norris, Miriam, and Wallace, Barbara, eds., *The Known and Unknown in Child Welfare Research* (New York: National Association of Social Workers, 1965).

Northcutt, Travis J., Jr.; Landsman, Theodore; Neill, John S.; and Gorman, Joanna F., "Rehabilitation of Former Mental Patients: An Evaluation of a Coordinated Community Aftercare Program," *American Journal of Public Health* 55 (April 1965): 570–77.

Orcutt, Ben A., "A Study of Anchoring Effects in Clinical Judgment," *Social Service Review* 38 (December 1964): 408–17.

Parnicky, Joseph J., and Brown, Leonard N., "Introducing Institutionalized Retardates to the Community," *Social Work* 9 (January 1964): 79–85.

Paul, Gordon L., *Insight vs. Desensitization in Psychotherapy: An Experiment in Anxiety Reduction* (Stanford, Calif.: Stanford University Press, 1966).

_____, "Insight versus Desensitization in Psychotherapy Two Years after Termination," *Journal of Consulting Psychology* 31 (August 1967): 333–48.

Pflanczer, Steven, and Kinney, Thomas, *Social Policy and Services: A Process-Oriented Reader* (Albany, N.Y.: State University of New York at Albany, 1979).

Platt, Anthony, *The Child Savers: The Invention of Delinquency* (Chicago: The Universty of Chicago Press, 1969).

Polansky, Norman A., ed., *Social Work Research* (Chicago: The University of Chicago Press, 1960).

———, *Social Work Research,* rev. ed. (Chicago: The University of Chicago Press, 1975).

Pollak, Otto, "Worker Assignment in Casework with Marriage Partners," *Social Service Review* 37 (March 1963): 41–53.

Posavac, Emil J., and Carey, Raymond G., *Program Evaluation: Methods and Case Studies* (Englewood Cliffs, N.J.: Prentice-Hall, 1980).

Poser, Ernest G., "The Effect of Therapists' Training on Group Therapeutic Outcome," *Journal of Consulting Psychology* 30 (August 1966): 283–89.

Quaife, G. R., *Wanton Wenches and Wayward Wives: Peasants and Illicit Sex in Early 17th Century England* (London: Croom Helm, 1979).

Rabb, Theodore K., and Rotberg, Robert I., eds., *The Family in History: Interdisciplinary Essays* (New York: Harper and Row, 1973).

Reid, William J., "Evaluation Research in Social Work," *Evaluation and Program Planning* 2 (1979): 209–18.

Reik, Theodor, *Listening with the Third Ear* (New York: Farrar, Straus and Cudahy, 1948).

Rein, Martin, *Social Policy* (New York: Random House, 1970).

Riley, Matilda White, *Sociological Research* (New York: Harcourt, Brace and World, 1963).

Ripple, Lilian, "Motivation, Capacity, and Opportunity as Related to the Use of Casework Service: Theoretical Base and Plan of Study," *Social Service Review* 29 (June 1955): 172–93.

Ripple, Lilian, and Alexander, Ernestina, "Motivation, Capacity, and Opportunity as Related to the Use of Casework Service: Nature of the Client's Problem," *Social Service Review* 30 (March 1956): 38–54.

Roberts, Albert R., "Police Social Workers: A History," *Social Work* 21 (1976): 294–99.

Robinson, W. S., "Ecological Correlations and the Behavior of Individuals," *American Sociological Review* 15 (June 1950): 351–57.

Roethlisberger, F. J., and Dickson, W. J., *Management and the Worker* (Cambridge, Mass.: Harvard University Press, 1939).

Rosenberg, Charles E., ed., *The Family in History* (Philadelphia: University of Pennsylvania Press, 1975).

———, "And Heal the Sick: The Hospital and the Patient in 19th Century America," *Journal of Social History* 10 (June 1977): 425–47.

———, "Inward Vision and Outward Glance: The Shaping of the American Hospital, 1880–1914," in *Social History and Social Policy,* ed. David J. Rothman and Stanton Wheeler (New York: Academic Press, 1981), pp. 19–55.

Rosenblatt, Aaron, "The Practitioner's Use and Evaluation of Research," *Social Work* 13 (January 1968): 53–59.

Rossi, Peter H.; Freeman, Howard E.; and Wright, Sonia R., *Evaluation: A Systematic Approach* (Beverly Hills, Calif.: Sage, 1979).

Rossi, Peter H., and Williams, Walter, eds., *Evaluating Social Programs* (New York: Seminar Press, 1972).

Rothman, David J., *The Discovery of the Asylum: Social Order and Disorder in the New Republic* (Boston: Little, Brown, 1971).

———, *Conscience and Convenience: The Asylum and Its Alternatives in Progressive America* (Boston: Little, Brown, 1980).

———, "The Diary of an Institution: The Fate of Progressive Reform at the Norfolk Penitentiary," in *Social History and Social Policy,* ed. David J. Rothman and Stanton Wheeler (New York: Academic Press, 1981), pp. 103–41.

———, and Wheeler, Stanton, eds., *Social History and Social Policy* (New York: Academic Press, 1981).

Rothman, Sheila, "Women's Clinics or Doctor's Offices: The Sheppard-Towner Act and the Promotion of Preventive Health Care," in *Social History and Social Policy,* ed. David J. Rothman and Stanton Wheeler (New York: Academic Press, 1981), pp. 175–201.

Sarri, Rosemary C., and Selo, Elaine, "Evaluation Process and Outcome in Juvenile Corrections: Musings on a Grim Tale," in *Evaluation of Behavioral Programs in Community, Residential and School Settings,* ed. Park O. Davidson, Frank W. Clark, and Leo A. Hamerlynck (Chicago: Research Press, 1974), pp. 253–302.

Sarri, Rosemary C., and Vinter, Robert C., "Organizational Requisites for a Socio-Behavioral Technology," in *The Socio-Behavioral Approach and Applications to Social Work,* ed. Edwin J. Thomas (New York: Council on Social Work Education, 1967), pp. 87–99.

Schwartz, Edward E., ed., *Manpower in Social Welfare* (New York: National Association of Social Workers, 1966).

Scott, Joan W., and Tilly, Louise, "Women's Work and the Family in Nineteenth-Century Europe," in *The Family in History,* ed. Charles E. Rosenberg (Philadelphia: University of Pennsylvania Press, 1975), pp. 145–78.

Scott, W. Richard, "Reactions to Supervision in a Heteronomous Professional Organization," *Administrative Science Quarterly* 10 (June 1965): 65–81.

Scriven, Michael, "The Methodology of Evaluation," in *Perspectives of Curriculum Evaluation,* ed. R. W. Tyler, R. M. Gagne, and M. Scriven, AERA Monograph Series on Curriculum Evaluation, No. 1 (Chicago: Rand McNally, 1967), pp. 39–83.

Selltiz, Claire; Jahoda, Marie; Deutsch, Morton, and Cook, Stuart W., *Research Methods in Social Relations,* rev. ed. (New York: Holt, Rinehart and Winston, 1959).

Shortell, Stephen M., and Richardson, William C., *Health Program Evaluation* (St. Louis, Mo.: the C. V. Mosby Company, 1978).

Shorter, Edward, "Illegitimacy, Sexual Revolution and Social Change in Modern Europe," in *The Family in History: Interdisciplinary Essays,* ed. Theodore K. Rabb and Robert I. Rotberg (New York: Harper and Row, 1973), pp. 48–84.

———, *The Making of the Modern Family* (New York: Basic Books, 1975).

Shulman, Lawrence, "Scapegoats, Group Workers, and Preemptive Intervention," *Social Work* 12 (April 1967): 37–43.

Shyne, Ann, "Casework Research: Past and Present," *Social Casework* 43 (November 1962): 467–73.

———, "Social Work Research," in *Encyclopedia of Social Work,* ed. Harry L. Lurie (New York: National Association of Social Workers, 1965).

Silverman, Marvin, "Knowledge in Social Group Work: A Review of the Literature," *Social Work* 11 (July 1966): 56–62.

Smith, Daniel S., and Hindus, Michael S., "Premarital Pregnancy in America, 1640–1971: An Overview and Interpretation," *Journal of Interdisciplinary History* 5 (Spring 1975): 537–70.

Social Science Research Council, *The Social Sciences in Historical Study* (New York: Social Science Research Council, 1954).

Specht, Harry, "Casework Practice and Social Policy Formulation," *Social Work* 13 (January 1968): 42–52.

Stein, Herman D., and Cloward, Richard A., *Social Perspectives on Behavior* (Glencoe, Ill.: The Free Press, 1958).

Stollak, Gary E.; Guerney, Bernard G.; and Rothberg, Meyer, eds., *Psychotherapy Research* (Chicago: Rand McNally, 1966).

Stone, Lawrence, *The Family, Sex and Marriage in England, 1500–1800* (New York: Harper and Row, 1977).

———, "Family History in the 1980's," *Journal of Interdisciplinary History* 12 (1981): 51–87.

Struening, Elmer L., and Guttentag, Marcia, eds., *Handbook of Evaluation Research, Volume 1* (Beverly Hills, Calif.: Sage, 1975).

Stuart, Paul, "Historical Research," in *Social Work Research and Evaluation,* ed. Richard M. Grinnell (Itasca, Ill.: F. E. Peacock Publishers, 1981), pp. 316–32.

Suchman, Edward A., *Evaluative Research: Principles and Practice in Public Service and Social Action Programs* (New York: Russell Sage Foundation, 1967), pp. 51–73.

———, "The 'Hang-Loose' Ethic and the Spirit of Drug Use," *Journal of Health and Social Behavior* 9 (June 1968): 146–55.

Sussman, Marvin, "Experimental Research," in *Handbook of Marriage and the Family,* ed. Harold T. Christensen (Chicago: Rand McNally, 1964).

Taeuber, Conrad, "Providing Relevant Data," *The American Sociologist* 6 (1971): 62–65.

Teicher, Morton, "Social Policy and Social Science," *Journal of Applied Social Sciences* 5 (1980): 14–18.

Thomas, Edwin J., "Field Experiments and Demonstrations," in *Social Work Research,* ed. Norman Polansky (Chicago: The University of Chicago Press, 1960), pp. 87–105.

———, "Selecting Knowledge from Behavioral Science," in *Building Social Work Knowledge* (New York: National Association of Social Workers, 1964), pp. 38–48.

———, ed., *Behavioral Science for Social Workers* (New York: The Free Press, 1967a).

———, ed., *The Socio-Behavioral Approach and Applications to Social Work* (New York: Council on Social Work Education, 1967b).

————, and McLeod, Donna B., *In-Service Training and Reduced Workloads: Experiments in a State Department of Welfare* (New York: Russell Sage Foundation, 1960).

Tilly, Louise, and Scott, Joan W., *Women, Work and Family* (New York: Holt, Rinehart and Winston, 1978).

Townsend, Peter, "Strategies in Meeting Poverty." Paper presented at the International Conference on Family Poverty and Social Policy, Manchester, England, September 1969.

Tripodi, Tony, *Uses and Abuses of Social Research in Social Work* (New York: Columbia University Press, 1974).

Tripodi, Tony, and Epstein, Irwin, *Research Techniques for Clinical Social Workers* (New York: Columbia University Press, 1980).

Tripodi, Tony; Fellin, Phillip; and Epstein, Irwin, *Differential Social Program Evaluation* (Itasca, Ill.: F. E. Peacock Publishers, 1978).

Tripodi, Tony, and Miller, Henry, "The Clinical Judgment Process: A Review of the Literature," *Social Work* 2 (July 1966): 63–69.

Tropman, J. E.; Dluhy, M.; Lind, R.; Vasey, W.; and Croxton, T., *Strategic Perspectives on Social Policy* (New York: Pergamon Press, 1976).

Trumbach, Randolph, "London's Sodomites: Homosexual Behavior and Western Culture in the 18th Century," *Journal of Social History* 11 (Fall 1977): 1–33.

Use of Judgments as Data in Social Work Research (New York: National Association of Social Workers, 1959).

Webb, Eugene J.; Campbell, Donald T.; Schwartz, Richard D.; and Sechrest, Lee, *Unobtrusive Measures: Nonreactive Research in the Social Sciences* (Chicago: Rand McNally, 1966).

Weinberger, Roslyn, and Tripodi, Tony, "Trends in Types of Research Reported in Selected Social Work Journals: 1956–1965," University of Michigan School of Social Work, mimeographed (May 1968).

Weiss, Carol H., *Evaluation Research: Methods for Assessing Program Effectiveness* (Englewood Cliffs, N.J.: Prentice-Hall, 1972).

————, *Using Social Research in Public Policy Making* (Lexington, Mass.: Lexington Books, 1977).

———— (with Michael Bucuvalas), *Social Science Research and Decision-Making* (New York: Columbia University Press, 1980).

Wells, Robert V., "Demographic Change and the Life Cycle of American Families," in *The Family in History: Interdisciplinary Essays*, ed. Theodore K. Rabb and Robert I. Rotberg (New York: Harper and Row, 1973).

Whyte, William Foote, *Street Corner Society: The Social Structure of an Italian Slum* (Chicago: The University of Chicago Press, 1943).

Windle, Charles, "Developmental Trends in Program Evaluation," *Evaluation and Program Planning* 2 (1979): 193–96.

————, and Bates, Peter, "Evaluating Program Evaluation: A Suggested Approach," in *Evaluation of Behavioral Programs in Community, Residential and School Settings*, ed. Park O. Davidson, Frank W. Clark, and Leo A. Hamerlynck (Chicago: Research Press, 1974), pp. 253–302.

Zald, Mayer N., ed., *Social Welfare Institutions* (New York: John Wiley and Sons, 1965).

Zander, Alvin, and Newcomb, Theodore, Jr., "Group Levels of Aspiration in United Fund Campaigns," *Journal of Personality and Social Psychology* 5 (June 1967): 157–62.

Zetterberg, Hans I., *On Theory and Verification in Sociology* (New York: The Tressler Press, 1954).

———, *Social Theory and Social Practice* (New York: Bedminister Press, 1962).

Name Index

Subject Index

THE BOOK MANUFACTURE

The Assessment of Social Research, Second Edition was typeset by Compositors, Cedar Rapids, Iowa. Printing and binding was by Edwards Brothers of Ann Arbor, Michigan. Cover design was by Mead Design. Internal design was by F.E. Peacock Publishers art department. The type is Times Roman with Futura display.